THE
STAR-SPANGLED HERESY:
AMERICANISM

Solange Hertz

Cover art work by Larry Fisher, Los Angeles, California

Set in Palatin type by MediPrint, Medical Lake, Washington

ISBN 1-883511-01-1

First Printing, September, 1992
Second Printing, June, 1993

Published by:
Veritas Press
P.O. Box 1704
Santa Monica, California 90406

Printed and bound in the United States of America

CONTENTS

God revealed to us that misfortunes otherwise inexplicable are the work of the author of
evil : *"An enemy has done this ! "* (*Matt. 13:28*).

CAVEAT LECTOR...

CAVEAT LECTOR. . .

In his undergraduate days the humorist Robert Benchley was assigned a paper on the great Fisheries Dispute, to be written from the standpoint of one of the interested parties. Everyone knows that history is no mere chronicling of unvarnished facts. Any scribe can record events, but interpreting them requires a particular point of view. Benchley chose the fish. His professor may or may not have been amused, but certainly the fish provided a valid slant, albeit one not usually encountered.

To illuminate the scenario as it unrolls, some principle exterior to the events but present to the historian — if not always to his readers — must shed its light. Julius Caesar, if one is to judge by his *Gallic Wars,* might have admitted flatfootedly that history is a record kept with a special purpose in mind. His own seems to have been nothing more complicated than self-promotion. Henry Ford said history is bunk. Napoleon called it "a collection of lies statesmen have agreed upon."

After the execution of the French king, Hébert told the French revolutionary assembly, " History will have to be re-written for the people, " and it was. In those days it was generally assumed that whoever rules the world will write the history books. Now it appears that whoever writes the history books will rule the world. Modern history has become little more than propaganda, a highly developed kind of fiction which entered the world scene with another form of fiction known as "scientific truth." Neither is concerned with substantial reality, but only with what is useful or politically correct at the moment.

With sophisticated technology at his disposal, the father of lies can revise history with every turn of events. Knowing it is not revolutions, nor the Rights of Man, but truth alone which sets men free, he has raised " disinformation" to high art. Today true history cries to be written, not only with the poor fish in mind, but especially with the devil in mind, if it is to make any sense. As seemingly unrelated conflicts of interest moil and roil before our eyes and explode in our faces, only faith can discern the mortal battle between right and wrong that is going on among nations as among individuals.

The root causes of mankind's incomprehensible turmoil will never be uncovered in the public schools or the media. As Hilaire Belloc put it in *Europe and the Faith* : "*In proportion as an historical matter is of import to mankind, in that proportion does it spring not from apparent — let alone material — causes, but from some hidden revolution in the human spirit. . . The greater the affair, the more directly does it proceed from unseen sources which the theologian may catalog, the poet see in vision, the philosopher explain, but with which positive external history cannot deal, and which the mere historian cannot handle.*"

God revealed to us that misfortunes otherwise inexplicable are the work of the author of evil : "*An enemy has done this !* " (*Matt. 13:28*). Whoever does not believe in the oft-ridiculed "conspiracy theory" of history quite simply does not believe in the existence of the devil, who moves both men and events. Great numbers of his dupes labor to promote satanic causes without necessarily being aware of the source of their inspiration. This is the essence of conspiracy, literally a "co-inspiration." Harnessing masses of witless sinners by appealing to their vices and appetites, fallen angelic intelligences do indeed influence the course of history. The less their victims know the better.

There will have to be historians of the eleventh hour who can tell it like it is. These are not the days of Herodotus or Julius Caesar, when history could be written on a purely natural level. Since then the Son of God has entered history as man and proclaimed himself Christ the King. He has endowed human events with a completely new dimension. Not to take into account their metaphysical mainsprings in our day is to slip into unreality, into a miasma of unrelated "facts" lending themselves to any kind of manipulation. Faith alone can assess them properly, through the gift of knowledge imparted by the Holy Ghost. It is simple truth to say that only a Christian can know what really goes on in the world.

So far only one modern historian has exposed the devil in history. It is the Mother of God, who pointed out at Fatima the true direction events were taking. Many years before, she dictated her autobiography to the humble Spanish nun Venerable Maria de Agreda, who described at her behest the great councils in hell, where Satan and his angels develop the strategy best suited to the destruction of Christ's kingdom. Whoever thinks history "just happens," needs to read *The Mystical City of God* for proper perspective. At best it will be seen "in a glass, darkly," for good history, like good biography, must begin at the end, and the universal judgment is not yet .

"*It will be only then that human history will begin,*" wrote Fr. Arminjon, whose work *The End of the Present World* was so esteemed by the Little Flower and her family : " *In the brightness of God's light will be seen clearly and in detail all crimes public and secret which were perpetrated in every place and at all times. The life of each human subject will be completely unfolded. No circumstance will be omitted; there will be not one action, one word, not one desire which will not be made known. . . . The judgment will untangle and pull out all the twisting threads of those cleverly woven intrigues. It will show in their true light those base retractions and cowardly connivances which men invested with public power sought to justify, either by invoking the specious excuse of reasons of state or by covering them with the mask of piety or disinterest.*"

Till then, only occasional glimpses of this other side of history can be caught. With very few minor changes in the text, the glimpses which follow are selected from the *Big Rock Papers* which were published in Leesburg, Virginia in the decade after 1973. They are frankly biased, and partisan to Christ the King. They lay no more claim to great scholarship than they do to impartiality. Although all deal with the universal revolution, the selections in this little volume focus on some American manifestations of it. Hopefully, they will provide something to ponder until the real historian arrives. Their author gratefully attributes the grace of their publication to the intercession of St. Philomena and Ven. Pauline Jaricot , with invaluable help from Christy Matt.

— Solange Hertz
Big Rock, Leesburg, Virginia
Feast of St. Philomena
July 5, 1992

THE OCCULT FRANKLIN

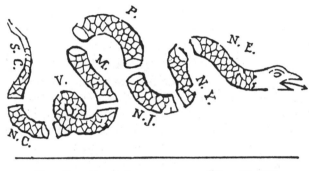

J O I N, or D I E.

The fractured rattlesnake pictured above is easily recognized by students of American history. It was designed by Benjamin Franklin at the time of the Albany Congress (the issue then at stake being joint action against the Indians rather than the British), and first appeared in Franklin's *Pennsylvania Gazette* on May 9, 1754. As the Revolution got under way, the reptile proliferated everywhere in various popular forms, landing even on an early naval flag, and others. The rattlesnake was a Franklin favorite as a political emblem, and by 1774 it had evolved into a symbol of American unity, for its fragmented sections had then not only joined, but its tail had got in its mouth.

That the serpent came to represent a land originally discovered and colonized in the name of Christ the King by Christendom's Catholics — some of them canonized saints — proves the struggle on this continent has never been one of flesh and blood, but against the powers of darkness in the very highest places. Evidently, when the

Immaculate Virgin of Guadalupe appeared to the Indian Juan Diego in the Spanish west in 1531 and promised to destroy the cult of the serpent there, the ancient dragon had nowhere to go but east, where he found more hospitable quarters among usurpers and heretics. Settling incognito in spots like his famous Green Dragon Tavern in Boston, he was free to get on with his Revolution with the help of Ben Franklin and his cronies, and did so.

He was incognito, of course, only to the ignorant, for by the time his tail reached his mouth he was quickly recognized by those in the know as the age-old *Ouroboros*, Alchemy's symbol of eternal perfection. There is an alchemical figure in the Leyden Papyrus dating from 250 A.D., called "Cleopatra's Gold-Making" which features him prominently, circling the Greek motto " 'εν τό πᾶν," "One is All," to which Americans may easily trace their well-known *E Pluribus Unum*, super-catchword of the man-made unity imposed on them in 1776.

From the beginning this old serpent was rightly named Lucifer, the "Light-Bearer," for he is the source of the "false light" which the Blessed Virgin told us at La Salette would soon "illumine the world," causing "extraordinary wonders every place because the true faith will be extinguished." Has not every spiritual master since St. Paul warned that the devil is most to be feared when he transforms himself into an "angel of light ?" (2 Cor. 11:14). In what other guise can he hope to supplant Him who declared, "I am the light of the world!" (John 8:12).

The light the serpent offers can only be the light of his own tremendous *natural knowledge*, for he is forever cut off from the supernatural world of grace and the light of the Holy Ghost; but this knowledge which he retains in his fallen state is incomparably beyond what the most learned human scientist can acquire by his own efforts, and it can be spiritually transmitted — with God's permission. It comprises a cosmic understanding of natural forces and how they operate, together with detailed angelic grasp of the most hidden properties and constituents of all forms of matter and/or energy. The Book of Job tells how the devil has "gone round about the earth and walked through it" (1:7), and the Gospels confirm the power God allows him over nature.

Satanic natural knowledge is the primordial *Gnosis* the serpent offered Eve, when he persuaded her that by its light alone gods can be made here below without help from above. This makes Satan not only father of lies, but father of all so-called Illuminati or "enlightened ones" peddling freedom and salvation through science rather than through the Redeemer who tells us, "Without Me, you can do *nothing!*" (John 15:5). Knowing our weakness, God so far has restrained the serpent from putting his full intellectual arsenal into our hands, but at La Salette our Lady warned that because of man's sins, in 1864 "Lucifer, together with a great number of devils" would be loosed from hell and "little by little will abolish the faith." She prefaced this statement by saying that the Pope must "beware of miracle workers, for the time has come for the most astonishing wonders to take place on the earth and in the air."

It would be foolish to look for miracles in the Catholic sense. The wonders our Lady speaks of can only be marvels of the natural order. They will be *scientific*, in the deepest and truest meaning of the word. Didn't the great Bossuet say, "The very things God has revealed happen in ways we could never have foreseen?"

• • •

It was to this end that Lucifer taught men Alchemy as part of witchcraft, as the Fathers of the Church declare, for despite all attempts to present these as contraries, *there remains an intrinsic relation between science and occultism.* Albert Pike, high priest of the Luciferians, knew whereof he spoke when he said, "At the bottom of magic. . . was *science* !"

The occult liturgist Aleister Crowley was on solid ground when he "resolved that my Ritual should celebrate the sublimity of the operation of natural forces without introducing disputable metaphysical theories. I would neither make nor imply any statement about nature which would not be endorsed by the most materialistic man of science. On the surface this may sound difficult; but in practice I found it perfectly simple to combine the most rigidly natural conceptions of phenomena with the most exalted and enthusiastic celebration of their sublimity." Thus may a "God of creation" — the prince of this world — be exalted without reference to the Creator of this same creation!

The psychic researcher Sir Oliver Lodge furthermore saw back in 1913 when addressing the British Association: "I am one of those who think that the methods of science are not so limited in their scope as has been thought; that they can be applied much more widely, and that the psychic region can be studied and be brought under law, too." And Sax Rohmer comments, "Certainly we are better equipped today, in some respects, for exploration, than were the ancients.

Could we but establish links between the exact sciences thus far rendered exact — and those at present termed occult, great progress would shortly be recorded." He would no doubt be gratified at the number of such research projects now carried on with public funds. Hasn't the Church ever warned us that the devil uses the same natural means to confect false apparitions and other spiritism that science uses to produce its wonders on the material level? Although requiring divine permission, even diabolical possession is a merely natural phenomenon.

Schoolchildren are therefore rightly taught that modern sciences sprang from Alchemy and the occult arts, yet they are led to believe the association between them dissolved long ago, and that science inherited only a strange collection of flasks and retorts, or at most some primitive laboratory techniques. They are not told that the underlying philosophy remains unchanged. Nor are they told what the Great Work, the *Magnum Opus* secretly carried on by alchemists boiling and bubbling their brews and powders, actually was: *the total regeneration of mankind by purely natural means,* without reference to God or His supernatural economy. In negative terms it is *the destruction of the Church.* Yet, if modern science inherited anything at all from Alchemy, it is precisely the Great Work, no longer pursued secretly in dark corners, but now engaged in openly with unparalleled fervor by neo-alchemists all over the earth. As our Lady said, "Little by little they will abolish the faith," simply by shifting attention slowly but surely from the eternal things which are not seen to those temporal ones which are not only seen, but are now measured, manipulated and channeled into unheard of uses for pleasure and profit to the exclusion of God.

Like science today, Alchemy had its innocent side, taken seriously even by devout churchmen, intent primarily on a better understanding of God's creation or bettering the lot of their fellows. At least it was accepted as a fact of life by the Church. A treatise on the subject is attributed to Pope John XXII, who nevertheless issued the Decretal *Spondent quas non exhibent* against its illegal practice. Rooted in philosophy, Alchemy's declared purpose was compatible with orthodoxy, for by seeking to perfect matter and its relation to the spiritual world, it could be directed to a right ordering of reality. Pope John's consistorial advocate considered Alchemy a true art, holding that alchemists do not sin as long as they attribute their power to God, an opinion approved by many later canonists.

This view was held as late as 1949 by Dr. F. Sherwood Taylor in *The Alchemists, Founders of Modern Chemistry:* " Its philosophy aimed at the unification of all nature in a single scheme, the author of which was avowed to be God. The attitude of the alchemist was a religious one. His view was hierarchical: he ranged the substances of which the world was composed in grades of worthiness. The angels were worthier than man; man, than the animals; animals, than plants; plants, than the elements; the fifth element was worthier than the others; fire, than air; air, than water; water, than gold; gold, than the other metals. The changes in nature were thought of as exaltations or degradations of that scale."

• • •

Unfortunately Alchemy had its darker side, whose findings were never put into the hands of the mob like some products of its modern labs. From time immemorial it remained open to inspirations inconsistent with faith. Its very name *al-chemia* or "the black earth" was a synonym for the "Egyptian art," *Khem* being the ancient name for Egypt. It was, in other words, the Hermetic philosophy in practice. It could be called *experimental gnosticism*, the implementation under controlled conditions of the Secret Doctrine inherited from Cain and passed on to the Cathars and Albigensians of every age by the Hebrew kabbalists. Revealed only to carefully chosen adepts, it was habitually veiled in elaborate symbolism to escape the lawful authorities. By the 14th century many ecclesiastics were tried for practicing alchemy, often combined with charges of heresy. In 1323 all Dominicans not renouncing the art and burning their books within eight days were declared excommunicate. Thereafter Alchemy had a bad name, but its progress was not checked.

The "*Khem*" of Alchemy carried overtones of the Greek word Xumeia, which referred to the casting of metals. This fitted the popular conception of an alchemist as some harmless old wizard who spent his days trying to make gold from the hypothetical "philosopher's stone," or longing to re-capture his lost youth by concocting the "elixir of life." Such illusions were encouraged by the craft, inasmuch as they provided ready pretexts for cozening countless Christian monarchs and nobility into subsidizing research. The Holy Roman Emperor Rudolf of Hapsburg supported whole stables of alchemists and dabbled himself, abetted by his unsavory Jesuit confessor Fr. "Zani" Damiano, handed over for execution by the Inquisition in 1616 for heresy and occultism. There were also many quacks, like the notorious Dr. John Dee and Sir Edward Kelly who took in Queen Elizabeth. Still, even the great St. Thomas Aquinas had addressed himself to the problem of whether gold produced by alchemy could be sold as real gold, and he had concluded it could, provided it really possessed the properties of gold. Today his conclusion remains valid for any artificial or synthetic product.

Needless to say, the "gold" alchemists were really after was not the metal we know, but the perfect substance, Prime Matter in solid form, whose liquid form was the celebrated "Elixir." Its symbol was the sun, Ormuzd, the god of Mithraism, of Gnosticism — and of Freemasonry. Thus "was created the jargon of alchemy," writes Grand Commander Pike in *Morals and Dogma of Freemasonry,* "a continual deception for the vulgar herd, greedy of gold, and a living language for the true disciples of Hermes alone!"

This living language, largely derived from the Kabbala, thrives now as the sacred tongue of speculative Masonry, into which Alchemy injected itself via the Rosicrucians, "true disciples of Hermes" who comprised the Society of Alchemists formed by Christian Rosenkreutz at the Hague in 1459. Under orders to maintain secrecy for 200 years, they nevertheless acquired powerful affiliates, particularly in Germany, and eventually the art spread to England, where even the scientist Robert Boyle, a professing Christian and father of "Boyle's Law," established an alchemical society at Oxford. The archeologist Elias Ashmole and the celebrated Isaac Newton assisted in the project, for which a Rosicrucian from Strasburg came to lecture, with John Locke and Christopher Wren enrolled as pupils. Ashmole, whose "Astrological and Hermetical Association" permeated Europe and reached its zenith in 1675, had become a Mason in 1646, with Newton very probably doing likewise in due time.

It was Newton, says Bernard Fay in *Freemasonry and Revolution,* who made possible the great Masonic crusade of the 18th century now know as "the Enlightenment," which produced not only our American Revolution, but all the others, especially the Industrial one. By proposing his cosmic theory, which became a veritable cult among the intelligentsia, Newton united scientific astrology, pantheism and deism all under the same banner. As "science" they have marched together ever since.

Fay, who disclaims knowing whether or not the Jew Albert Einstein, the "new Newton," was ever a Mason, nevertheless points out that whole pages of his personal credo as enunciated in his *Religion and Science* are in perfect accord not only with Judaism, but especially with the Rosicrucian founders of modern Masonry, who saw religion as a kind of enthusiasm for the wonders of nature. Others allege that Einstein's space/time continuum lay concealed for centuries in the obscure language of the eighth of the Emerald Tablets of Hermes Trismegistus, legendary founder of Alchemy, where it can be deciphered today by the initiate.

• • •

The foundation of the Grand Lodge of England, whereby Free and Accepted Masons officially merged with the Alchemical Society of the Rosicrucians, took place in London on June 24, 1717. The seven founders, all prominent alchemists, were the naturalist Jean-Theophile Desaguliers, a close friend of Newton's, who had been named Chaplain to the Prince of Wales by George II; the libertine Scotch clergyman James Anderson, Oxford graduate and preacher to the king; plus George Payne, James King, a certain Calvert, Lumden-Madden and Elliott. According to an Italian Masonic document which came to light in 1945, these men offered Masonry the advantages of their widespread wealth and influence, in return for which they were able to shelter their alchemical researches behind the respectable facade of the Fraternity.

It was a congenial alliance. "Freemasonry and alchemy have sought the same results," says Mackey in his *Encyclopedia of Freemasonry,* "and they have both sought it by the same method of symbolism. It is not, therefore, strange that in the eighteenth century, and perhaps before, we find an incorporation of much of the science of alchemy into that of Freemasonry."

Indeed not. The aforementioned Fr. Damiano wrote in his memoirs that once while listening to the Emperor voice his aspirations concerning the Great Work in the imperial apartments, "Without thinking, I heard myself murmur, '*So mote it be!*' The Emperor looked at me in astonishment, realizing that I had spoken the magical formula adepts use when invoking the higher powers." He would have been even more astonished had he been able to hear a future Pope of the Roman Catholic Church, Paul VI, use this now well-known Masonic phrase not once, but twice in the course of a speech he delivered before the assembled body of the United Nations of the World on October 4, 1965 A.D.

In the Great Work, of course, gold-making was the merest preparatory maneuver. As Pike explains, "The Great Work is, above all things, *the creation of man by himself;* that is to say, the full and entire conquest which he effects of his faculties and his future. It is, above all, the perfect emancipation of his will, which assures him the universal empire of Azoth, and the domain of magnetism, that is, complete power over the universal Magical agent. This Magical agent, which the Ancient Hermetic philosophers disguised under the name of 'Prima Materia,' determines the forms of the modifiable Substance; and the Alchemists said by means of it they could attain the transmutation of metals and the universal medicine."

Although "occult," the Great Work is in no sense unnatural in the means it employs. On the contrary, it demands man's total descent into the natural. Alchemy has never pretended to create anything out of nothing. It will not admit that even God can do that, for God must "evolve" like the rest of the universe. Pike quotes Bl. Raymond Lulle, who postulates that even to make gold, one must start with some gold, for "Nothing is made out of nothing." The regeneration of man Alchemy seeks through the perfection of matter is a glorification of matter, in complete accord with classical Marxism and the false theory of evolution on which Communism depends.

"Magic," writes Masonry's mystical theologian J.D. Buck, "contemplates that all-around development which, liberating the intellect from the dominion of the senses and illuminating the spiritual perceptions, places the individual on the lines of least resistance with the inflexible laws of nature, and he becomes nature's co-worker or hand-maid. To all such, Nature makes obeisance, and delegates her powers, and they become Masters."

Rather, they become God, for Buck blasphemously contends, "In the Early Church, as in the Secret Doctrine, there was not one Christ for the whole world, but a *potential Christ* in every man. Theologians first made a fetish of the Impersonal, Omnipresent Divinity, and then tore the *Christos* from the hearts of all humanity in order to deify Jesus. . . The hand of Providence is always a human hand. Humanity is both the vehicle and the agent of what man has called the providence of God. Humanity *in toto*, then, is the only Personal God; and Christos is the realization, or perfection of this Divine Persona, in Individual conscious experience. . . It is far more important that men should strive to become Christs than that they should believe that Jesus was Christ, etc., etc." This is easily recognized as New Age religion.

Buck proves himself a true alchemist when he states, "Man's knowledge and power are no longer confined to, or circumscribed by, the lower plane, or the physical body: but, by transcending these by Regeneration and becoming perfect in Humanity, man attains Divinity. In other words, he becomes CHRISTOS. This is the meaning, aim and consummation of Human Evolution; and this Philosophy defines the one-only process by which it may be attained. The

Perfect Man is Christ: and Christ is God."

Thus spoke the Serpent to Eve, explaining how she could become God through her own natural efforts. That such highly heretical doctrine is now heard even from Catholic pulpits in the United States shows how thoroughly the Ouroboros sponsored by Benjamin Franklin has anchored his Great Work in American minds. Swallowing his tail at an ever faster rate, he is bent on making us believe that this is the way to transform ourselves into an ever higher form of something already inherent within us. He says the Great Work works.

• • •

"If you would study the secrets of Alchemy," nevertheless warns Albert Pike, "you must study the works of the Masters with patience and assiduity. Every word is often an enigma; and to him who reads in haste, the whole will seem absurd. Even when they seem to teach that the Great Work is the purification of the Soul, and so to deal only with morals, they must conceal their meaning, and deceive all but the Initiates."

There has hardly been a more devoted student of Alchemy than Franklin, who was well aware that the real aim of the Great Work was also social and political. A leaflet distributed by the Christophers in March, 1975 featured the following Prayer composed by him: "God grant, that not only the love of liberty, but a thorough knowledge of the rights of man, may pervade all the nations of the earth, so that a philosopher may set his foot anywhere on its surface and say, 'This is my country'." And this is followed by a truly singular rendition of the first verse of Psalm 126: "If the Lord does not build the house, in vain the masons (!) toil." Let him who reads understand where and by whom the dream of a man-made world government is nourished.

Franklin's religion does not have to be conjectured. Not only do we know he assisted David Williams in his *Apology for Professing the Religion of Nature* (complete with liturgy!), but he also left in writing his own "Articles of Belief," a document conveniently overlooked by those who would like to regard him as a Christian. Stirred by Newton's novel theories of the universe, he espoused the cosmic spiritualism of Alchemy based on hierarchies, much as described by Dr. Taylor.

He says furthermore, "I cannot conceive otherwise than that the *Infinite Father* expects or requires no Worship or Praise from us, but that he is even infinitely above it. But, since there is in Men something like a natural principle, which inclines them to DEVO-TION, or to worship of some unseen Power; and since Men are endued with Reason superior to all other Animals, that we are in our World acquainted with: Therefore I think it seems required of me, and my Duty as a Man, to pay Regards to SOMETHING.

"I conceive then, that the INFINITE has created many beings of Gods, vastly superior to Man, who can better conceive his Perfections than we, and return him a more rational and glorious Praise. . . It may be that these created Gods are immortal; or it may be that after many Ages, they are changed, and others supply their Places. . . It is that particular Wise and good God who is the author and owner of our system, that I propose for the object of my praise and adoration. For I conceive that he has in himself some of those Passions he has planted in us," and Franklin concludes from this that his God might like some praise after all. "Let me then not fail to praise my God continually, for it is his Due, and it is all I can return for his many Favours and great Goodness to me.

Clearly this created God with human passions, one among many, who made man merely one of the animals, is not the God of the Christians, but only Franklin's. Bernard Fay notes, "It is difficult to affirm that Franklin's credo was the Freemason's credo; but it is clear that it was a Masonic creed," corresponding "more exactly than any other to the tendencies of Freemasonry and to the phraseology which Desaguliers and Anderson utilized in their 'Constitutions of the Free-Masons.'" And we might add, corresponding to the tendencies of the dawning space-age: "This Masonic religiosity, as found in Desaguliers and Franklin, did not intervene as a conservative element in society, but as a ferment of transformation," precisely the stuff of the Great Work, now carried on in the New World as in the old.

Like all sophisticated Gnostics of any age, Franklin publicly supported the prevalent religion. Using the handy, ambiguous language of Masonry, his utterances are often accepted as orthodox Christianity by believers or half-believers, but interpreted correctly enough by the initiated. Franklin was a member in good standing of the Presbyterian Church and never missed a sermon of the young liberal Rev. Hemphill, who seldom mentioned God. When despite Franklin's defense Hemphill was evicted by his frustrated congregation, Franklin joined the Anglican Church.

He seldom attended its services, but when the famous preacher George Whitefield brought the "Great Awakening" to America,

Franklin became one of his most ardent supporters. This led many to believe he had suffered a conversion, but Fay remarks wryly, "The support given by Franklin was only a Masonic support conforming with Masonic doctrines and the spirit of Desaguliers," — indeed an early form of Marxist dialectics in action, for, "It is true Whitefield converted the crowds, but wherever he preached the parishes became detached from their pastors; wherever he passed, the life of the Church was disorganized" and the work of revolution furthered. As for Franklin, he said he saw "a positive advantage in the existence of many different churches, for that created competition, and after all, competition was good for every kind of trade."

He seems to have believed in some sort of immortality, if we are to credit the famous Epitaph he wrote for his tombstone: "The body of Benjamin Franklin, Printer, like the cover of an old book, its contents torn out and stript of its lettering and gilding, lies here food for worms. Yet the work itself shall not be lost, for it will, as he believed, appear once more in a new and beautiful edition, corrected and amended by the Author." This is no Christian Resurrection of the body, glorified through the Son of God. The immortality he expects would be only natural, a re-incarnation into another body of some kind. The 'work itself," as Franklin calls himself, is subject only to alchemical transmutation according to the alchemical maxim known to every neophyte: "No generation without corruption."

That Franklin recognized no extra-natural forces is easily proved by a celebrated anecdote. At a party at Lord Shelburne's in England, Fay relates, "There were a number of scholars from both the continent and England, some able ministers who succeeded in purifying God, such as Priestley and Price; other churchmen who were expert in avoiding God, like the Abbé Morellet of France who ministered to courtesans and atheists." Franklin and the Abbé were conversing, "about the Bible and Christ, and Franklin, half-smiling, said that the Biblical miracles no longer seemed like miracles to him, that he could calm the waters quite as easily as Jesus Christ. The Abbé was too polite to contradict him but too educated to believe the statement. . .

"Franklin sensed what was going on in his mind, and calling the company together, they went to the pond. A slight breeze was ruffling its surface with a thousand tiny ripples, and Franklin slowly encircled it while the party waited in a curious silence. Then, raising his staff abruptly, Franklin whirled it three times above the water and inscribed some magic hieroglyph in the air. With a wave of his hand, Franklin then turned to the company and showed that the water was calming down.

"In a few moments the pond was as glassy as a mirror and a vague light glimmered over the immobile watery surface. The spectators stared at each other without knowing what to think. Then they surrounded the doctor, overwhelming him with compliments and adulation, but he escaped from them and disappeared down a shady walk, still conversing with Morellet. He leaned on his cane heavily and laughed softly. The Abbé was frankly mystified, so Franklin then showed him that his staff was hollow and that he had filled it with oil. It was this oil, spread over the water, which had stilled it. A hedge fortunately hid them from the others, for the Abbé burst into a clear peal of laughter which was joined by Franklin's.

"They laughed all the more when they saw through the twigs that the party was still standing by the pond, fearfully exclaiming over the event. Franklin's miracles were the delight of the crowd, and deeply appreciated by the philosophers and Masons, for they enlightened humanity and made for progress. All the lodges of France and England sang the praises of their illustrious brother."

Disbelief in the miraculous explains Franklin's presence at the opening of the first Unitarian Chapel founded in England by Theophilus Lindsay, which became the meeting place for liberal reformers hoping to replace "outworn" Christianity by scientific truth, and where the aforementioned Joseph Priestley, discoverer of oxygen, was one of the clergy. Another companion of Franklin's at this event was his close friend Francis Dashwood, Lord Le Despencer, who had asked his help in revising the Church of England's Book of Common Prayer. Franklin himself tells us of the happy days he spent at the estate of this notorious libertine and student of the occult, who all the while supporting the village curate, was said to celebrate black Masses amid the ruins of an old abbey where he officiated as "Prior" to a community known as "the mad monks of Medmenham." His Lordship's American friend says of him, however, "But a pleasanter thing is the kind countenance, the facetious and very intelligent conversation of mine host, who having been for many years engaged in public affairs, seen all parts of Europe, and kept the best company in the world, is himself the best existing!"

He and Franklin "decided that the prayer-book was entirely too long," writes Sydney George Fisher in *The True Benjamin Franklin*. "Its prolixity kept people from going to church. The aged and infirm did not like to sit so long in cold churches in winter, and even the young and sinful might attend more willingly if the service were shorter. . . . All references to the sacraments and to the divinity of the

Saviour were, of course, stricken out and short work made of the Athanasian and the Apostles' Creed. Even the commandments in the catechism had the pen drawn through them, which was rather inconsistent with the importance Franklin attached to morals as against dogma. But both editors, no doubt, had painful recollections on this subject; and as Franklin would have been somewhat embarrassed by the seventh (the Sixth Commandment in Catholic catechisms), he settled the question by disposing of them all." The *Te Deum* and the *Venite* were both deleted. "The beautiful canticle 'All ye works of the Lord'... was entirely marked out. As this canticle is the nearest approach in the prayer-book to anything like the religion of nature, it is strange that it should have suffered."

Strange, too, that the only phrase Franklin asked Le Despencer to omit from his first Preface was the description of the Old Testament as "a Jewish book very curious, perhaps more fit for the perusal of the learned than suited to the capacities of the general illiterate part of mankind." His reasons for this, who knows? Although eventually he wrote only the final Preface, in America the work — purged of all references to king and parliament — became known far and wide as "Franklin's Prayer Book," doing much to strengthen his public image as a believer.

● ● ●

The popular scientific writer Roger Burlingame coined the phrase, "America was discovered; the United States was invented." He meant only to make a distinction between a principle and its application, but the eyes of faith see deeper than that: America is the creation of Almighty God and can indeed only be discovered, whereas the United States, being merely a political contrivance, can qualify only as a human invention. Mistaking one for the other has disastrous consequences, for contrivances may fall apart without warning, as the United States nearly did during its so-called Civil War and may do now by internal collapse.

Catholics who mistake the United States for God's America may furthermore easily fall into the heresy formally defined by Pope Leo XIII as Americanism. Basically, it is naturalism in American dress, and it accommodates itself to all the ideals of the Enlightenment. French radicals of the last century expected it then to produce a major schism in the Church under the able leadership of Catholic bishops in the United States, some of whom even dared preach Americanism to Europe. It was a threat, apparently, which drove

Leo XIII to approve of democracy in practice, if not in principle, rather than antagonize the enemy.

"But over there in America," wrote Emile Zola, "what fertile virgin soil for a triumphant heresy! How easy to see a Bishop Ireland one fine day lift the banner of revolt and become the apostle of the new religion, A RELIGION RELEASED FROM DOGMAS, MORE HUMAN, THE RELIGION WE DEMOCRATS ARE WAITING FOR!"

The United States had been only too well prepared for such regrettable leadership. Like Franklin, most of its Founding Fathers were not Christians. Although they often made references to the Deity, the God they invoked was their God, the alchemical God of nature in Christian dress. In fact the most influential among them were not so much deists as thoroughgoing pantheists, for, being avowed rationalists, they looked for divinity *only* in nature. Themselves products of the Enlightenment, they could hardly have been anything else.

In Alchemy, a Green Dragon signifies the Great Work in its beginnings, and it cannot have been coincidence that the Revolution was planned and carried out by men who met regularly in a Boston tavern of that very name. So diligently did they promote the serpent's cause that America today finds herself immersed in a sea of neo-Gnosticism so pervading and controlling her moral, intellectual and political life that, by comparison, the Albigensian heresy which once ravaged the whole of Christendom now looks like a harmless childhood disease. God preserve us from the Red Dragon, alchemical sign for the Great Work in its completion!

PART II: *Our State Religion*

Any citizen doubting that the Old Religion of the alchemists is the state religion of the U.S. need only make a pilgrimage to the nation's capital, beginning with the Prayer Room established in the Capitol by joint resolution of Congress in 1954. He will find there for his devotion a small central altar flanked by two seven-branched candelabra, above which rises a stained glass window showing George Washington kneeling. Below the Father of his country is the Great Seal of the United States. Above him is the truncated pyramid surmounted by the eye of Horus which constitutes the seal of Masonry and the Illuminati.

A Masonic Service Association pamphlet informs us that the capital's three most important monuments — the Capitol, the White House and the Washington Monument — were "all three begun under Masonic auspices; all three had cornerstones laid by Masonic hands; all three have Masonic associations which are a part of history, and the first of its forty cornerstones marking the boundaries of the District of Columbia... was also Masonically laid." The famous James Hoban, architect of the White House, also happened to be the first Master of Federal No. 1, Grand Lodge of the District of Columbia. A second cornerstone was laid at the Capitol on July 4, 1851, when construction began on the Senate and House wings. We are told, "Deposited in the cornerstone was a composition handwritten by Daniel Webster; in it he stated that the stone was laid by the President of the United States and the Grand Master of Masons." The third cornerstone was likewise Masonically laid on Sept. 18, 1932 beneath the east steps, and contained a copper box filled with Masonic relics and records.

Lest Catholics think they had no part in these rituals, we must note that the Archbishop of Baltimore's Masonic brother Daniel Carroll was present at such occasions in an official capacity. His cousin, Charles Carroll of Carrollton, quite gratuitously in his nineties took part in the Masonic ceremony inaugurating the nation's first railroad, the Baltimore and Ohio, on July 4, 1828, by turning over the first bit of earth with a silver spade. He remarked on the occasion, "I consider this among the most important acts of my life, second only to my signing of the Declaration of Independence, if second even to that!" — so clearly did he see how indispensable scientific progress was to the great work of democracy.

"Throughout the Colonies," says another Masonic pamphlet, "Masonry was everywhere active, indirectly as an Order, but directly through its members, in behalf of a nation 'conceived in liberty and dedicated to the proposition that all men are created equal'; which is one of the basic truths. It was not an accident that so many Masons signed the Declaration of Independence, or that Washington and most of his generals were members of the Craft. Nor was it by mere chance that our first President was a Mason, sworn into office on a Bible taken from a Masonic Altar, by the Grand Master of New York. Such facts are symbols of deeper facts, showing the place and power of Masonry in the making of the nation. Along the Atlantic coast, among the Great Lakes, in the wilderness of the Middle West, in the far South and the far West, everywhere, in centers of population and in little Upper Rooms on the frontier, the Lodge stood alongside the Home, the School and the Church."

As the "Old Charges" of Masonry declare, the only religion recognized by Masonry is "that natural religion in which all men agree." One of their "Short Talk Bulletins" points out that the signers of the Declaration believed in God, but, "He is no sectarian God; He is the Father of all men; He is *the energizing and controlling force of the universe.*" This is clearly not the Creator, yet, "It was that concept of Deity which Masonry adopted as early as 1723 in Anderson's *Constitutions.*" Regarding the U.S. Constitution we read: "That 31 Masons of 55 Deputies had the fundamental teachings of the Fraternity in mind when they labored to produce a fundamental law to act as a cement never to give way, between peoples and States of greatly varying size, power, wealth, industry, climate, ideas and ideals, is not only understandable — it was inevitable." Thus were all souls in God's America forced to "meet upon the level and part upon the square" of defined Masonry, whether they realized it or not.

The new state religion depended vitally on the Bill of Rights to keep its footing among a population still militantly Christian, especially on the first, fourth and fifth amendments. These guaranteed free exercise of any religion, including the necessary freedom of speech and press and the right to assemble, in order that falsehood might be propagated along with truth; no searching without proper warrants; and indictments for capital crimes only by a Grand jury. Our informant says that without such curbs, "An agent of a government not restrained from interfering with free speech could visit our Lodges, accuse any of us of prohibited speech, and arrest and punishment would follow," whereas, sheltered by the Bill, "In nearly 16,000 Lodges in the U.S., Freemasons peaceably assemble as often as they desire," and, "No civil authority may arrest a Freemason, throw him in jail, punish him in any manner, for being a Freemason," as was still possible in Christian Europe until fairly recently.

• • •

We are told, "Freemasonry is not, *per se*, a religion. It is *religion* in the abstract." It nevertheless manifested all the characteristics of "a" religion very early, even a trinitarian one, for curiously enough its theological virtues are three: Liberty, Equality and Fraternity. And these are ordered in turn to three human goals: life, liberty and the pursuit of happiness. We cannot help but wonder whether Masonry is not the mirror-image of something else.

In America Masonry produced its own trinity of persons quickly enough: George Washington, Benjamin Franklin and Thomas Jefferson, who stand today at the apex of an elaborate secular mythology. Washington, popularly known as "Father of his country," was apparently designated to fill the role of a Jovian God the Father. This is a bit of a joke in Virginia, which was closer to some of his personal activities than other parts of the country. In any case it is as Father that Brumidi blasphemously depicted him on the dome of the U.S. Capitol where he swirls in majesty among the splendors of the new heavens, lording it over an assembled revolutionary iconography where Franklin figures prominently, deep in conversation with Minerva.

Even on earth the atmosphere surrounding Washington was ultra-Masonic, as Masons themselves avow. All the staff officers he trusted were Masons, as were the leading generals. We have Lafayette's word that, "After I was made a Mason, General Washington seemed to have received a new light. I never from that moment had any cause to doubt his entire confidence. It was not long before I had a separate command of great importance." Anyone tempted to minimize Washington's serious connection with the Craft need only read J.F. Sachse's *Washington's Masonic Correspondence*, based on letters in the Library of Congress.

The young, dynamic Thomas Jefferson falls easily into the role of the "Holy Spirit" of America's new age. Although records of his initiation have not been found, he too is claimed quite rightly by Masonry. In close contact with the most radical intellectuals of the Enlightenment abroad, even the most disreputable, he breathed life visibly into the democratic scriptures then being penned, tracing with his own august finger the words of the Declaration of Independence — not to mention a vast personal correspondence. Jefferson was a kind of super-Mason, said to have been a high-ranking member of the Illuminati who directed the Great Work from above, and who formed his intimate acquaintance. Not only propagating their doctrine by writing, he contrived to have their insignia engraved secretly on the reverse of the Great Seal of the United States. By 1933 the Work had progressed to the point where Franklin Roosevelt, his spiritual descendant in the Presidency, could commemorate the New Deal by having the insignia printed on the one-dollar bill in plain sight without the slightest opposition. As we saw, twenty years later it was occupying the place of honor in the Capitol Chapel.

Although by far the oldest of the trio, to Benjamin Franklin must be accorded the place of "Son." Not only was he in the United States "in the beginning," but in a very real sense the United States was made through him. Certainly without him was made little or nothing that was made. In him the Great Work took on flesh, as it were, and became readily visible to all for the first time. Where the personally ambitious and money-loving Washington tended to be pedestrian and sanctimonious, and Jefferson preoccupied with words, ideas and sketches, Franklin concentrated on action. As we shall see, he fulfilled for Democracy a function very like the one Lenin performed for Communism. He put the Great Work to work, and to as many as received him, Franklin gave the power of becoming sons of *his* God.

• • •

It would be difficult to overrate the natural genius of this extraordinary man. In his Epitaph he calls himself a printer. And so he was, printing playing much the same role in his life that gold-making played in Alchemy. By its means he put together the first controlled press in America, his *Pennsylvania Gazette* soon heading a whole network of subsidiaries throughout the Colonies like the *New York Journal*, the *Boston Gazette*, and myriad lesser breed.

These constituted a Masonic press, staunchly anti-Papist and preaching its own doctrine indefatigably in political dress. Franklin was a master propagandist. It is well known how he maintained European indignation at fever pitch against the British and loyalist Americans by atrocity stories which could not get by at home, but which he circulated via his fake newspaper the *Boston Independent Chronicle,* regular "reprints" of which were distributed abroad from Holland. Bernard Fay concludes it was such papers, in conjunction with taverns, the Lodges and the cooperation of certain preachers and merchants which actually fabricated the American Revolution.

No informed historian will deny that Franklin was the most unwavering and orthodox of believers in eighteenth century Masonry. His conversion was entire and sincere, his passionate adherence to its tenets having occurred long before he ever joined a Lodge. As a matter of fact, he had to use certain unethical means to get accepted, for the Philadelphia establishment comprising the Lodge of St. John of Jerusalem was openly disdainful of the popular, witty little printer, who furthermore had had the audacity to form a debating society called the Junto, in some ways a rival organization composed of small artisans and proletariat. To make a long story short, he blackmailed the Lodge into admitting him, by printing in his *Gazette* on December 8, 1730 a report supposedly from London claiming to expose the Masonic mysteries. "Their Great Secret," it read, "is THAT THEY HAVE NO SECRET AT ALL!"

A few weeks later Franklin was invited to join, and thereafter the *Gazette* published only flattering allusions to the Brothers. In 1734 he put out an American edition of Anderson's *Constitutions*, the first Masonic book printed in America, and in 1752 planned the new Lodge building. Fay calls him "the soul of this Philadelphia Lodge, and the strongest link between all American Masons." A gifted linguist and tireless traveler, everywhere he went here and abroad, even in Holland and Germany, he seemed to leave behind him a veritable Franklin cult which canonized his jokes as it did his ideas. He served twice as Provincial Grand Master of Pennsylvania and later for two years as Worshipful Master of the famous French revolutionary Lodge of the Nine Muses, to which he introduced Voltaire. He also became a member of the French Order of St. John of Jerusalem, as well as Honorary Venerable of the Lodges of the Temple at Carcassonne and other provincial cities.

Fay believes, "Franklin's spiritual dictatorship in France would not have varied much from other French eighteenth century fads had he not been the champion of Masonry and its living symbol." There, "Through the Masons he had access to the newspapers which were officially controlled by the Government, but which were really written by the Masons and the philosophers, such as Morellet, Suard and De la Dixmerie, who were all Franklin's friends. Practically all of the French newspapers published outside of France were in the hands of the Masons also. Franklin had his writings accepted without any trouble" by these. He excelled as a diplomat, but with this battery behind him, it is easy to see how he was able almost singlehandedly to force the reluctant Louis XVI into the fateful Franco-American Alliance against the British which must have done violence to this pious king's deepest Catholic principles, and which turned the tide for the Revolution.

Franklin's links with English Masonry had been even closer, for entwined with his Masonic activities and his publishing enterprises was a flourishing official life. Even under English rule he had risen to the position of Deputy Postmaster General of the English Post Office in America, besides representing several of the Colonies to both Crown and Parliament before the Revolution. As member of the General Assembly of Pennsylvania delegated to the Albany Convention, he submitted a plan for colonial union illustrated, as we have seen, by the first formal effigy of the Ouroboros in America. As a first consequence, he was charged with raising troops and forts against the Indians in the wilderness. For Franklin and his fellows, Indians were not souls to convert, as they had been for Columbus and the Catholic explorers, but enemies to be driven back or exterminated.

While a delegate to the second Continental Congress, he corrected the first draft of the Declaration written by Jefferson, and later was named a member of the Constitutional Convention. With the Carrolls he formed part of the Commission to Canada which hoped to spread the revolt there, and eventually was chosen by Congress as one of three to discuss final peace terms with General Howe. From 1776 to 1785 he served as Ambassador to France, from whence John Adams wrote of him, "Franklin's reputation was more universal than that of Leibnitz or Newton, Frederick or Voltaire; and his character more esteemed and beloved than all of them."

Sheer lack of space forbids dwelling on all his other activities. He formed the first real police force in the Colonies, not to mention the fire department, a public library and an academy destined to become the University of Pennsylvania, besides laboring to improve street paving and lighting and hospital services. He even took time to campaign for paper currency and to invent his celebrated "Franklin stove" and countless lesser useful devices. As we shall see, however, he was no capricious dilettante. His most widely divergent interests were but so many scattered building stones for the greater Work to which he was dedicated. "Under cover of Masonry," Fay points out, "the Philadelphia sage elaborated his philosophical system, launched his ideas, and launched himself " in truly ouroboric style. Although blessed with little formal education, Franklin was honored by the freedom of the city of Edinburgh and made a Doctor of Laws by the University of St Andrews. Already a Master of Arts of Harvard, Yale and William and Mary at home, he was also made Doctor of Civil Law at Oxford, where he had so many intimate friends engaged like him in the Great Work.

• • •

The organ par excellence suited to his purpose was the American Philosophical Society, founded by him thirty years before the Revolution. Riding the crest of the vogue for science unleashed by Newton's theories, the Society was designed to assemble the sharpest minds in the Colonies for the promotion of scientific discovery and useful invention. Knowing America's pathetic craving for her vanished aristocracy, Franklin determined to supply her with one of the mind, drawn entirely from herself and free of allegiances to the ancient Christendom of which the United States never formed a part.

In the aura of the Philosophical Society, Franklin the Sage becomes Franklin the Mage, foremost alchemist of the secular age. Following in the footsteps of Desaguliers and Newton, he would capture the Universal Magical Agent and expose the secret of the universe!

Pike spoke of it in the authoritative *Morals and Dogma:* "There is in nature one most potent force, by means whereof a single man, who could possess himself of it, and should know how to direct it, could revolutionize and change the face of the world. . . this agent. . . is precisely what the Adepts of the middle ages called the elementary matter of the Great Work. The Gnostics held that it composed the igneous body of the Holy Spirit; and it was adored in the secret rites of the Sabbat or the Temple, under the hieroglyphic figure of Baphomet or the hermaphrodite goat of Mendes."

If we are to believe Pike and the alchemists, the Holy Ghost, God himself, is nothing but a supreme natural force, which men have persisted in investing with divinity. For them, penetrating the divine secrets is merely a matter of understanding the workings of nature. The venerated *Emerald Tablets of Hermes* lay down as principle that, "What is below is like what is above, and what is above is like what is below, to perpetrate the miracles of one thing." This is a direct contradiction of the revelation of the Son of God, Jesus Christ, who said, "He that cometh from above is above all. He that is of the earth, of the earth he speaketh" (John 3:31). Of what else can the Serpent speak, to whom God said, "Thou art cursed. . . and earth shalt thou eat all the days of thy life?" (Gen. 3:14).

But, objects Pike, "There is a Life-Principle of the world, a universal agent, wherein are two natures and a double current, of love and wrath. This ambient fluid penetrates everything. It is a ray detached from the glory of the Sun, and fixed by the weight of the atmosphere and the central attraction. It is the body of the Holy Spirit, the universal Agent, *the serpent devouring his own tail.* With this electromagnetic ether, this vital and luminous caloric, the ancients and the alchemists were familiar."

Seen in this context, Franklin's famous experiment with a kite and a key in a thunderstorm, known to every schoolchild, takes on wholly new and portentous meaning. Now we know what he was after: the "electromagnetic ether" of the alchemists, call it electricity, magnetism, life-force, serpent-power or what we will.

We have only Joseph Priestley's word that Franklin personally performed this risky feat, and if he did, the wonder is that he was not electrocuted, as happened to others. All we have from Franklin's pen is a detailed description of how to go about it, found in a letter to the London scientist Collinson dated Oct. 19, 1752, where he says that the suggestion he had made in France for drawing lightning from the clouds by means of an elevated rod had been successfully acted on, but that he thinks this kite idea is better. It was well known, as Fisher says, that he had "a rod erected on his house to draw down into it the mystical fire of any passing clouds, with bells arranged to warn him when his apparatus was working." The bells were in his study and caused his wife considerable uneasiness. Once he was struck senseless trying to electrocute a turkey - a bird he later proposed for our national emblem in lieu of the eagle.

He was only one of many such experimenters in his day, for "magnetism" was not only a craze among the revolutionary elite. It was the major sideshow attraction offered by wandering magicians and charlatans of all kinds on the village greens. As a matter of fact, it was one of these, a Dr. Spencer, who first acquainted Franklin with electricity in his youth. Everyone wanted to feel a shock. In Madrid Franklin's bitter rival and correspondent, the French priest-scientist Abbé Nollet, managed to electrify a whole regiment at once, and in Italy it was used as a cure for paralysis.

Franklin never wrote a book on science, but Collinson kept his letters, and when he published them in 1751 as *New Experiments and Observations in Electricity Made at Philadelphia in America,* their writer immediately became world famous. After Priestley put out *The History and Present State of Electricity* in 1767, Franklin actually displaced Newton as first sage of the universe in the popular mind. (Long the declared enemy of establishments political and religious, Priestley had deemed it healthier after the French Revolution to leave England for Pennsylvania, where he declined the chair of chemistry at the University of Pennsylvania in order to devote himself to Unitarianism.)

Franklin's fame justly rested on his resolution of the burning question of the day: Were lightning and electricity the same thing? In less than four years he demonstrated that they were, simply by showing that their characteristics were identical. He even proved this scientifically, eliminating in the process all the learned jargon concerning the "two kinds" of electricity which a century later Pike was still referring to esoterically as "two natures and a double current, of love and wrath." He called one positive and the other negative, and designated them by ordinary plus and minus signs.

• • •

The final triumph of Alchemy seemed imminent. Fay writes, "Lightning had become a plaything for men, and Jupiter, empty-handed, had nothing to do but return to Olympus and make love with Juno. He could no longer frighten human beings." When Franklin wrote "How to Secure Houses &c. from Lightning," with lightning-rods springing up all over the Colonies, America entered visibly into the Great Work of perfecting her matter and creating the Perfect State.

"Science had invented something practical and exciting for the first time; it had made progress which all could see, appreciate and utilize. By this brilliant invention Science had reduced the realms of religion and annexed those provinces which had hitherto belonged to Faith and Prayer. In all countries and in all religions, but especially in America, where man appeared so weak before the overwhelming forces of Nature, earthquakes and electrical storms seemed to be direct and wrathful manifestations of God. The doctrines of the New England clergymen were clear on this point. . . The most liberal of them admitted that there might be secondary causes, but that thunder had only the primary cause of God and His wrath. . . The lightning rod. . . became an object of attack for many churchmen."

No Catholic priests seem to have been among them. The liberal Fr. John Carroll, later a good friend of Franklin and first Bishop in America, would hardly have countenanced such sentimental resistance. So strongly sympathetic was he to the aims and ideals of the revolutionaries that he refused to take his oath of office until Rome agreed to delete from it the episcopal obligation "to extirpate heretics." As it is, the ministerial attacks draw only smiles today, when even lightning rods are smiled at; but these churchmen knew instinctively, if for the wrong reasons, that the Enemy was at work here, and they said so.

The promethean character of Franklin's apostolate was not lost on them. The French finance minister Turgot had in fact openly acclaimed Franklin as the new Prometheus, the ancient Gnostic hero of pagan mythology canonized by Aeschylus, who defiantly stole fire from heaven and gave it to man in order to release him from the tyranny of Zeus. The Great Work had just taken a giant stride, whereby modern man was soon to be released forever from his dependence on the Christian God. By means of electricity, Alchemy would achieve its age-old double objective: complete control of the forces of nature, and the indefinite prolongation of life. Soon, at last, man would create himself.

Over a century ago Pike predicted, "*It is a universal agent, whose supreme law is equilibrium; and whereby, if science can but learn to control it,* it will be possible to change the order of the Seasons, to produce in night the phenomena of day, to send a thought in an instant round the world, to heal or slay at a distance, to give our words universal success, and make them reverberate everywhere." To what degree all this has already come to pass, and how closely it has kept pace with the great Apostasy, is ominous.

Soon after these words were written, transmutation of matter was accomplished in very fact by Pierre and Marie Curie, and by now the electronic power locked within the atom has been ours for some time. Eugenics, exploring the secrets of human genes, is expecting to transmute mankind itself into a whole new species, for the New Age must have a New Man. Alchemy has dreamed for centuries of the *homunculus,* the artificial man spontaneously generated from the test tube, from which may issue legions of parentless progeny all enjoying the same bestial "equality" — if only to be destroyed *en masse* later by some nuclear blast.

THE TRIUMPH OF THE GREEN DRAGON

And they adored the DRAGON . . . and it was given unto him to make war with the saints, and to overcome them. And power was given him over every tribe, and people, and nation.

(Apoc. 13:4-9)

PART I: *The New U.S. Catholic Church*

The American Catholic Church (as distinct from the Catholic Church in America) can be said to have received its official charter from the New World's first revolutionary government in 1798, when Judge Addison, President of the Court of Common Pleas of the Fifth Circuit of Pennsylvania, decided a lawsuit between the first U.S. Catholic Bishop, John Carroll, and a recalcitrant German Franciscan priest called Fromm: "The Bishop of Baltimore has the sole episcopal authority over the Catholic Church of the United States. Every Catholic congregation within the United States is subject to his inspection; and without authority from him no Catholic priest can exercise any pastoral function over any congregation within the United States."

This extraordinary decision, hardly remembered today, injected the virus of the Revolution into the veins of Catholicism in America long before Vatican II did the same for the Church universal, for it recognized in principle a democratically selected, state-approved prelate as sole ruler of any Catholics residing in the U.S. Hailed by many as evidence of the new Constitution's sterling sense of religious propriety, it is actually a flagrant example of arbitration by secular authority in a purely ecclesiastical matter reserved to the Holy See. Its key words are certainly "The Catholic Church of the U.S.," for this is exactly what is here discerned and objectivized. Judge Addison saw the issue clearly.

And so did the recently consecrated John Carroll, only Bishop in the U.S. at the time, who availed himself of the decision. He knew whereof he spoke when he said, "In the U.S. our religious system has undergone a revolution, if possible, more extraordinary than our political one." As the American Revolution provided the dress rehearsal for the French Revolution and all subsequent revolts against

Christendom, thus did the American Church first show Catholics the world over how to set their pace to the new politics.

Unfortunately there was little difficulty in setting the precedent, for the Fr. Fromm in question who disputed the episcopal authority was unhappily one of many renegade clergy who had sought to escape just censures at home by taking refuge in the colonies. Priests were scarce in America. Many were accepted into hierarchical ranks who normally would have been excluded. Fr. Fromm, who died outside the Faith, and who had apparently desired to set up his own German-speaking, laity-owned parish for less than pure motives, succeeded in throwing the whole question of lay trusteeship and ethnic parishes into a bad light, making it appear that whoever supported such programs were persons rebellious to Church authority and right government.

That this was true in some cases cannot be denied, but the problem was in fact more complicated, more visceral, and fraught with the direst consequences to the Faith on these shores. This can be seen more clearly in the so-called "Reuter's Schism" which took place in Baltimore the very next year: Fr. Cesarius Reuter, armed with letters of authorization from the Holy See, had proceeded to construct a church for German-speaking Catholics which was to be independent of Carroll's strictly American jurisdiction. Such has always been Mother Church's way, profoundly respecting the nationalities and cultures God Himself had created, and in which He saw fit to embed the Faith.

As citizens in a wholly artificial nation suddenly put together from scratch by English Masonry, the non-English speaking faithful especially found their plight unbearable. Finding themselves being indiscriminately boiled down in the democratic melting-pot ably stirred by their English-speaking Bishop, and torn from all the natural supports true nationality gives the Faith and which were theirs by divine ordinance, they fell prey to justified misgivings. Reuter and his congregation fought hard, begging Rome to place them under a German Bishop, but despite Rome's help in the beginning, they were ultimately forced to submit to the one American Bishop sanctioned by the revolutionary government in the Fromm precedent, one who furthermore had lost no time in excommunicating Reuter.

Protesting to the Holy See, representing the German pastor as a serious disturber of the peace, Bishop Carroll wrote, "We live among non-Catholic sects, and there is no hope of the civil magistracy or the secular powers putting these stubborn men in their place." [Strange words in view of the Fromm decision so recently handed down!] "Therefore, it seems to me that it is of grave importance to strengthen the episcopal jurisdiction rather than to lessen it by exemptions; for, if the power of the Bishop fails, then all hope of regulating the moral conduct of the clergy and the laity perishes."

In the face of the dilemma, deeming it best to keep the Church under one head during its precarious American infancy, Rome backed down, but lifted the censure placed on Reuter by Carroll, having initially warned the latter that excommunication was much too severe a punishment under the circumstances. The scandal nevertheless continued for four years. That Reuter was not motivated by schismatic motives is clear from the fact that he asked the Bishop in 1801 to be restored to his priestly functions. He was accepted, but under the ironclad condition that he recognize the See of Baltimore as absolute, and that if a German church should in fact ever be permitted, it "shall not be entitled to the rights of a parochial church, but only as a chapel of ease to St. Peter's Church" — the Baltimore Cathedral. Devoted as he was to the ideals of '76, the Bishop had no intention of extending democratic privileges to "foreigners". Reading the records today one is struck by his insensitivity to the spiritual anguish of the uprooted recalcitrants, and his apparent lack of concern for their salvation in the face of the implacable demands of authority, so inconsistent with his liberal tendencies. Not that the situation didn't require a strong hand, but one is strangely reminded of the blind "obedience" demanded from traditionalists by intolerant ecclesiastical liberals two centuries later.

The controversy was waged hotly on both sides not only in Baltimore, but in Philadelphia by Frs. Goetz and Elling, and in other localities well into the nineteenth century and later. Whenever the Roman Curia moved to accede to the just complaints of the nationals, it would be met with reports such as the one submitted in 1834 by the Curia's own Cardinal Weld (altar boy at John Carroll's consecration and friend of the Carroll family) in which were set forth the "special conditions" existing in America which Rome was presumably incapable of understanding. Summarizing points made by the radical Bishop of Charleston, John England, (who habitually preached in Episcopalian and Presbyterian churches), the report reads in part: "The Americans are extremely patriotic; and are not inclined to be hospitable to foreigners who may be placed over them. Some of the priests in the United States not only do not become citizens but also declare their preference for foreign institutional methods. Nothing convinces the American people more quickly of the alleged incompatibility of Catholicism with the American Republic. . . "

In a letter to Propaganda from Baltimore on April 19, 1799, Fr. Reuter had accused Bishop Carroll of forcible attempts to Americanize the Germans. It would be useless to deny the truth of the accusation, for Carroll's support of the Revolution and all its principles — separation of Church and state, sovereignty of the people, freedom of conscience, universal equality, etc. — is well documented. In the English colonies the juridical Church had no past as in Europe, and Carroll's ilk felt free to innovate in conformity with the new order. Closely following the civil policy of the Founding Fathers, he sought to transform as quickly as possible all existing Catholic nationalities into the perfect "American Catholic" with no pre-existing cultural ties, in a spirit more than faintly smacking of the "new man" of Rousseau and Mao.

A case in point was his desire to introduce the vernacular into public worship. Be it noted, however, that the only vernacular in question was English, which in Anglo-Saxon Protestant America was to become the new sacred language, and for the foreign-born, far more incomprehensible than Latin ever was. Could he have been conscious of the unspeakable irony when he wrote in 1787: "Can there be anything more preposterous than an unknown tongue? And in this country, either for want of books or inability to read, the great part of our congregations must be utterly ignorant of the meaning and sense of the publick office of the Church." He was especially concerned about "the poor people and Negroes" who could not read. "To continue the practice of the Latin liturgy in the present state of things must be owing either to the chimerical fears of innovation or to indolence and inattention in the first pastors of the national Churches in not joining to solicit or indeed ordain this necessary alteration." (He sounds much like George Washington, who speaks of the Germans in his Diary as "so ignorant they can speak only Dutch!")

Later as Archbishop, in the Agreement signed in 1810 by him and his newly appointed suffragan bishops, he stipulated that the Sacraments be administered in the vernacular, except for the essential formulas. "Thus the first liturgical regulations in the U.S.," writes Fr. Andrew Greeley in *The American Catholic Experience*, conceded to American clergy the same privileges which were to be won again only with great difficulty in the *collectio rituum* of the

1950's and then to be taken away again until after the Vatican Council." America is indeed a land of pioneers.

God knows how many souls were lost to the Church by these first attempts to strip Catholics of their natural means of spiritual communication with one another and their Holy Mother in Europe. Despite the losses, however, the influx of Catholic immigrants became so great that statistics actually showed a steady "growth" of the Church here, slyly attributed to democratic freedom of conscience. Total population of the Colonies was about 3,000,000. The English Bishop Challoner, in his "Account of the Condition of the Catholic Religion in the English Colonies of America" in 1763, estimated there were some 16,000 in Maryland, about half of whom approached the Sacraments, and six or seven thousand in Pennsylvania, almost all Germans. Numbers elsewhere were unascertainable due to the harsh laws against them. So successful, however, was the Americanization policy that in due time the entire Church was affected.

In 1946 Fr. Philip Hughes would say in his *Popular History of the Catholic Church* that in 1789 the English population of the universal Church was "utterly negligible", and that "it is doubtful if there were so many as half a million English-speaking Catholics, and of these not 50,000 were of English blood." And although "English Catholics are still not a numerous body, . . . Catholics who speak the English language must, today, number close on 50 millions, one-sixth of the total Church." And these, it must be added, almost all indoctrinated from the cradle in the false principles of modern democracy, which they do not even think to question! If Vatican II did not actually originate in America, she certainly provided the first proving-ground for its reforms.

• • •

There were three men, all Carrolls and all Catholics, on whom the architects of the American Revolution depended to draw the Catholic colonials, and especially the Tory Maryland colony, into its ranks: John Carroll, his brother Daniel, and their cousin Charles. The first, spoken of thus far, was a Jesuit priest; the second a politician; and the third a financier. They constituted a powerful triumvirate without whose leadership it is difficult to understand the paradox of the "Catholic revolutionary", a contradiction in terms.

Catholics of the period found themselves between the devil and the deep blue sea, for although they had little enthusiasm for

England's terrible penal laws, their religion did not condone defiance of legitimate authority. Nor could they be expected to join forces with the Dissenters and Nonconformists who largely made up the revolutionary rabble, and whose fanatical anti-popery was if anything worse than the Church of England's. As Charles Evans pointed out in *American Bibliography*, "the struggle for civil liberty in the American colonies assumes something of the nature of religious warfare, in which the dissenting churches are opposed to the Established Church of England." It is being increasingly admitted that the Revolution was actually an anti-Catholic movement, at least in its origin.

Martin Griffin, in *Catholics and the American Revolution*, says mere oppressive taxes and restrictions on popular rights could hardly "have moved the body of the people to acts of resistance had not Religion been a moving force upon the minds of the people. The active malcontents or leaders of the Revolt sought to impress upon the people that Protestantism had been assailed and might in America be overthrown." One would have expected that George III constituted the lesser threat to Catholics, if only because he was across the sea, whereas the rabid dissenters were next door. Among the Germans in Pennsylvania, where Catholics were free to practice their Faith, almost all remained loyal to the Crown.

Writers of the period like de Tocqueville attest that Catholicism was then universally recognized as "the natural enemy of democracy." He is at some pains to explain how Catholics in the Colonies "faithful to the observances of their religion. . . fervent and zealous in the belief of their doctrines," nevertheless came to "constitute the most republican and most democratic class in the United States." He produces some tortuous reasoning, but the only real explanation is the Carrolls.

Descendants of the Charles Carroll who had settled in the Catholic colony of Maryland in 1688 and who was Lord Baltimore's friend and attorney general, they had been steeped in the spirit of the directives originally laid down by the first Proprietor in 1633: "that they suffer no scandal nor offence to be given to any of the protestants, whereby any just complaint may hereafter be made by them in Virginia or in England, and that for that end, they cause all acts of the Roman Catholique Religion to be done as privately as may be, and that they instruct all the Roman Catholiques *to be silent upon all occasions of discourse concerning matters of Religion. . .* " From this atmosphere of compromise the Carrolls carried the seeds of the Americanism later condemned by Leo XIII, to germination in the

American Revolution.

By that time Baltimore's ecumenical colony had long since fallen to its Protestant components, who not only proscribed the Faith, but even disbarred Catholic lawyers like Charles and Daniel from practice. Still convinced that "toleration" was the answer, however, John Carroll would declare publicly as Prefect Apostolic of the American missions that "America may come to exhibit a proof to the world that general and equal toleration, by giving a free circulation to fair argument, is the most effectual method to bring all denominations of Christians to a unity of faith."

This fond illusion had apparently been fed at the celebrated St. Omer's, the English college in French Flanders where the three Carrolls had all been sent to study in their youth, and where John later taught as a Jesuit. Founded by the Society of Jesus in 1592 for the education of English laymen denied Catholic education in England, this school might be expected to have been especially orthodox. Such was hardly the case by the 18th century, for it seems to have fallen very early under the direction of Jesuits like the equivocal Thomas Copley whose democratizing influence had become so powerful in the early days of the already liberal Maryland colony.

Thomas Lloyd, a Catholic Revolutionary War veteran who was in 1789 the official reporter of the House of Representatives, had studied seven years at St. Omer. He stated in his later years that there he had "been trained not only in religious and secular knowledge, but *in republican principles.*" These words take on added weight when we learn that two of his professors, John Carroll and Leonard Neale, became Archbishops of Baltimore, and that it was on the advice of the latter that Lloyd settled in the colonies in the first place, in St. Mary's County, Maryland.

• • •

Like most of the revolutionaries, the Carrolls were therefore not so much American as English products. They brought there in Catholic dress the same democratic ideas imported by the handful of English Masons who hatched the rebellion against the English monarchy in the Green Dragon Tavern in Boston.

Called by Daniel Webster the "Headquarters of the Revolution", this English pub with its occult, diabolic sign — Anglo-Saxon counterpart of the Feathered Serpent confronting the Faith on the other side of the continent in Spanish Mexico — was the seat of the

Massachusetts Provincial Grand Lodge, organized there back in 1719, and known as the Lodge of St. Andrew. It was from the Green Dragon that the Freemasons Paul Revere, Samuel Adams, John Hancock and other "Sons of Liberty" unleashed their long planned rebellion on the unsuspecting loyal majority in the colonies.

According to Masonic tradition it was also from there that a group of patriots disguised as Mohawk Indians issued on Dec. 16, 1773 to board the English ships in Boston harbor and destroy 342 chests of tea valued at $90,000. The Masonic Association Publication entitled *One if by Land and Two if by Sea* states: "Freemasons of the Colony undoubtedly had a large part in the destruction of the tea cargoes. The records of St. Andrew's Lodge, of which Paul Revere is a member, show that on the night of Nov. 30, 1773" — Feast of St. Andrew — "the night of the annual election of officers — only seven members were present. No election was held, and the presence of only seven members given as the reason according to the entries in the lodge minutes." The missing members had been busy since the 28th calling mass meetings and placing guards dockside to prevent unloading the tea. "Another meeting was called on the 30th, at which officers of two additional ships which had arrived in the meantime were made to promise that they would leave the harbor without unloading their tea cargoes."

Not generally disclosed is that one of the faults most held against the good king "Farmer George" was his uncompromising intolerance of Masonry in England. Balked in its conspiracy at home, Masonry brought it to the colonies, with the success we all know. The Masonic role in the Revolution is a secret now officially revealed: The beautiful full color Bicentennial booklet *We, the People*, offered to the public by the U.S. Capitol Historical Society in cooperation with the National Geographic Society in 1974, features photographs of building stones chiseled with Masonic symbols found under the Old House wing. Referring to the dedication of the Capitol, the text reads, "The day's program involved elaborate Masonic ceremonies, a common practice then, with roots going back to the link between medieval stone masons and the order," followed by a brief description of the service.

That the Carrolls collaborated with the Masonic framers of the Constitution is not hard to prove. To John Carroll is attributed, at least in part, Article Six Section 3, which declares that "no religious test shall ever be required as a qualification to any office or public trust under the United States," and also the First Amendment stating, "Congress shall make no law respecting an establishment of religion, or prohibiting the free exercise thereof."

When King George granted newly conquered French Canada free practice of its faith by the Quebec Act, the revolutionary propagandists didn't neglect exploiting this to the full, accusing him of being "a Roman Catholic tyrant" who had broken his Coronation Oath by establishing the "popish religion" in an English colony, and darkly predicting that this would soon become the rule in all the others. They hoped thus to rally all anti-Catholic sentiment, whether dissenters or adherents of the Church of England, to the revolutionary cause.

The Carrolls, astute politicians all three, were not dismayed by this ploy. They knew the Masons had no intention of stopping with a mere Declaration of Independence which would leave thirteen sovereign states with all their rights, but would proceed to unification under a Constitution where these would be severely limited. In a land where sects of all kinds abounded, it was a foregone conclusion that complete toleration and plurality would have to be enjoined by law. Aware of the advantages to Catholics under such a system — actually the same envisioned by Lord Baltimore a century before in the Maryland colony — they not only threw themselves publicly behind the Revolution, but drew thousands of Catholics after them.

• • •

Charles Carroll, born in Annapolis in 1737, had become very active politically on completing his education abroad. He served 23 years in the Maryland legislature as well as in the U.S. Senate until it became illegal to hold both offices simultaneously. At the time of the Revolution he was probably the richest man in America, owning some 80,000 acres in Maryland alone. Enjoying a reputation as a somewhat eccentric, but affable money-grubber, he was invaluable in managing the finances of the Continental Army. It has been pointed out that he stood most to lose should the Revolution fail: "There go a few millions!" exclaimed an onlooker who watched him sign the Declaration of Independence. But this was to lose sight of the fact that he also stood most to gain if the Revolution succeeded and English taxes thereby abolished. His gamble paid off gloriously.

He was the only Catholic to sign the Declaration, whose language a true son of the Church would have held under the deepest suspicion. Although he never denied the Faith and was sober and disciplined in his personal habits, he was not noted for any outbursts of piety. His birth may have been illegitimate, inasmuch as his parents' marriage document bears a date some twenty years after he was born. His wife died young, a victim of opiates, and he never re-married. All his children died out of the Church, his only son Charles of Homewood renouncing the Faith, taking to drink and never holding any position worth mentioning.

The Masonic builders of liberty had the utmost confidence in Charles Carroll. He not only helped win Maryland to the Articles of Confederation and later to the hotly resisted Constitution, but through his connections abroad, smoothed Franklin's path in Paris to seal the French Alliance whereby France threw her weight against the English king. In February 1776 the Continental Congress resolved "that a committee of three — two of whom to be members of Congress — be appointed to repair to Canada, there to pursue such instructions as shall be given them by that body." Those named were the dean of American Masonry, Benjamin Franklin, together with the Maryland Protestant Samuel Chase — and Charles Carroll. This despite the fact that he was only an observer at the Congress, Catholics being barred from serving as delegates.

More interesting was a special resolution requesting Charles Carroll "to prevail on Mr. John Carroll to accompany the Committee to Canada to assist them in such matters as they shall think useful." This idea seems to have originated in a letter written to Hancock by Charles Lee, who said, "I should think that if some Jesuit or religious of any other order (but he must be a man of liberal sentiments, large in mind and a manifest friend of civil liberty) could be found out and sent to Canada he would be worth battalions to us. This thought struck me some time ago and I am pleased to find from the conversation with Mr. Price and his fellow travellers that the thought was far from a wild me. Mr. Carroll has a relative who exactly follows the decription." And both Carrolls spoke French fluently.

William Harper Bennet, in *Catholic Footsteps in Old New York*, says, "John Carroll, a Marylander by birth and a Jesuit by vocation, was an American patriot in every fiber of his body, and his cousin Charles Carroll had no difficulty in prevailing on him to respond to the call of his country. 'No greater power of combined wealth, intellect and enthusiasm existed anywhere in America,' says a writer, 'than the union of the Carrolls and the Jesuits in Maryland in the person of John Carroll.'"

Echoing this opinion, Fr. Greeley says of the latter: "His years in the Jesuits and traveling through the European countries might have been presumed to dispose him toward assuming if not a conservative at least a Royalist position. But apparently it did not take him long after he returned to Maryland to size up the politics of the conflict between England and the colonies, and to make up his mind on which side he belonged. In fact, one of the reasons for settling at his mother's home in Rock Creek near the future capital, rather than at an established parish was that Carroll was extremely reluctant to accept the authority of Father John Lewis, superior of the Maryland mission, and the Vicar-General of the Bishop of London. Carroll was of no mind to associate himself publicly with ecclesiastical authority that resided in England. Thus when the peculiar request came from the Continental Congress for him to go on the ill-conceived mission to Quebec, there was no doubt in anyone's mind that Carroll was a man that could be trusted."

The object of the mission was simple: to win Catholic Canada to the Revolution as "the 14th state." Although vested with almost absolute powers, even military, the committee failed miserably, due largely to the alertness and open hostility of the French Bishop of Quebec, Jean Olivier Briand, who "by exhortation, admonitions, public penances, excommunications and suspensions," writes Bennet, "drew his clergy back from rebellion and held them loyal to Great Britain." He forbade his priests to hold any communication with Fr. Carroll. Fr. Pierre René Floquet, the only Jesuit in Montreal, was suspended for extending him hospitality. "There were 150,000 Catholics and 360 protestants in the province of Quebec, the Church had spoken in no uncertain terms, and her children had yielded obedience."

The good Bishop certainly could have had little love for his new British overlords, but he saw revolution — even now brewing ominously in France — as far the greater evil. Nor did he have any illusions about what the Founding Fathers down south really thought of the Faith. In his diary Charles Pinckney would quote Franklin, head of the mission as saying later, "I fully agree with General Washington that we must safeguard this young nation," and the reference included the "menace" of Roman Catholicism. John Adams, who sometimes attended services at "Romish chapels" to while away his Sunday boredom, described his impressions in a letter to his wife Abigail in 1774. He speaks of "the poor wretches fingering their beads, chanting Latin, not a word of which they understood; their pater nosters and ave Marias; their holy water;

their crossing themselves perpetually; their bowing to the name of Jesus, whenever they hear it; their bowings, kneelings and genuflections before the altar, etc." And he concludes, "I wonder how Luther ever broke the spell. Adieu."

• • •

De Courcy and Shea remark in their *History of the Catholic Church in America*, " In the extraordinary history of the Society of Jesus, the case of this Jesuit (John Carroll), ambassador from a Congress of Republican Protestants, is not the least remarkable episode; and while the democrats of every clime reproach the children of St. Ignatius with being the tools of despotic power, they can offer Father John Carroll as a sincere patriot, a zealous partisan of liberty and *one of the real founders of American independence.*" Thus two different currents were already at work in the Society as in the Church.

On the Canada mission was cemented a firm friendship between Fr. Carroll and the aging Franklin which later bore abundant fruit. On the trip Franklin wrote, "I find I grow daily more feeble, and I think I could hardly have got so far but for Mr. Carroll's friendly assistance and care of me." Years later he confides to his Diary for July 1, 1784, "The Pope's Nuncio called and acquainted me that the Pope had, *on my recommendation,* appointed Mr. John Carroll superior of the Catholic clergy in America, with many powers of bishop; and that, probably, he would be made bishop *in partibus* before the end of the year."

In the official letter to Carroll, Cardinal Antonelli confirms that he was chosen because "it is known that your appointment will please and gratify many members of that republic, and especially Mr. Franklin, the eminent individual who represents that republic at the court of the Most Christian King." Accepting the appointment, Carroll urged the Cardinal to find some method whereby in future it would not appear that the American Church was receiving its authority from a foreign power! He had petitioned the Pope not to leave American Catholics under the jurisdiction of their prelate in England, alleging this could not be done "without open offense of this supreme magistracy and political government."

Franklin had at first favored putting the Catholics under a French prelate in Europe. After the French Alliance brought Catholic France to the aid of the American Revolution and King Louis XVI ordered a *Te Deum* sung in thanksgiving for the victory at Yorktown,

Franklin knew what occult forces had gained control of the tottering French monarchy, itself now on the eve of the French Revolution. But John Carroll was even better. As a member of the Carroll clan, an American prelate was a positive asset to be cultivated.

The revolutionaries played a good game with the Catholics. It's of record that members of the Continental Congress actually attended Mass officially on four occasions — one offered in celebration of the Fourth of July in 1779, another for the Yorktown thanksgiving in 1781, and two Requiems, one for General de Coudray in 1777 and for the private Spanish agent Don Juan de Miralles in 1780. The Congress even bore the expense of Coudray's funeral. Needless to say, these items were not reported in the patriot press, which continued the anti-popery propaganda.

Soon John Carroll began pressuring Rome for an American bishop selected, if not actually appointed, by democratic process. "As for the method of nominating a bishop," he wrote the Cardinal, "I will say no more for the present than this — that we are imploring God in His wisdom and mercy to guide the judgment of the Holy See, that if He does not deem it proper to allow the priests who have labored for so many years in this vineyard of the Lord to propose to the Holy See the one they deem most fit, that some method will be adopted by which bad feeling may not be excited among the people of this country, Catholics and Protestants."

Be it noted that Carroll's nomination by his establishment was a foregone conclusion involving no risk on his part, for the only other possible candidate, John Lewis, was then too old for so strenuous an office. Rome took five years to accede to Carroll's wishes, and eventually revoked the unprecedented privilege, but by that time the democratic virus had been established, and it continued spreading silently until full eruption with Vatican II.

In 1785 Carroll wrote, "We desire that the Faith in its integrity, due obedience to the Apostolic See and perfect union should flourish; and at the same time that whatever can with safety to religion be granted shall be conceded to American Catholics in ecclesiastical affairs. In this way, we hope the distrust of Protestants now full of suspicion will be diminished and that our affairs can be solidly established." Alas, today the "distrust of Protestants" should be near the vanishing point in the face of Catholic compromising. John Carroll himself now occupies a prominent place in the stained glass window of a "Maryland Bay" in the ecumenical Protestant Washington National Cathedral in the nation's capital.

When George Washington died, Shea tells us, Bishop Carroll

"issued a circular to his clergy in regard to the celebration of the 22nd of February as a day of mourning, giving directions for such action as would be in conformity with the spirit of the Church, while attesting to the country the sorrow and regret experienced by Catholics at the great national loss." Carroll may therefore perhaps be credited with actually initiating the new sanctoral cycle of secular "saints" whose feast days now occur regularly in the national liturgy. Invited by a unanimous resolution of Congress in conjunction with the clergy of all denominations, he preached the first President's panegyric in Baltimore Cathedral — a truly ecumenical triumph for a Catholic prelate in those days.

Libraries are searched in vain for spiritual books written by our first Catholic Bishop, his famous "Prayer for Civil Authorities" apparently marking the summit of his spiritual development. He was the prototype of the Bishop-Administrator who came to dominate the American scene, who habitually left purely spiritual matters to technicians with less weighty civic responsibilities. His last public act was to decline, because of ill health, the honor of taking part in laying the Masonic cornerstone of the Washington Monument in 1815. He died in December.

• • •

In his Catholic empire-building Bishop Carroll had had not only the decisive help of his cousin Charles, but also that of his older brother Daniel, third member of the triumvirate, and a shining example of what heights a Catholic could scale who knew how to cooperate in the new order of 1776:

On Thursday, March 1, 1781, "According to the order of the day, the hon'ble John Hanson and Daniel Carroll... did, in behalf of the State of Maryland, sign and ratify the said Articles, by which act the Confederation of the United States of America was completed, each and every of the Thirteen United States... having adopted and confirmed, and by their delegates in Congress ratified the same." This was no mean achievement, largely engineered by the said Daniel, considering that in 1775 the Maryland Convention had formally instructed its delegates to the Continental Congress "to disavow in the most solemn manner, all design in the colonies for independence."

These Articles were the law of the land until the Federal Constitution was railroaded through in 1787. Daniel Carroll signed this too, having been one of the Catholic members of the Convention which framed it, the other being Thomas Fitz-Simons of Pennsylvania. Together with his cousin Charles he had, here too, been instrumental in bringing Maryland around, in opposition to the anti-Federalist faction of Samuel Chase, who had been one of the Canada mission. In a public letter to his balky constituents, who saw very well that with the adoption of the Constitution, "all the offices of government. . . which are transferred from the individual to the aggregate sovereignty of the States, will necessarily turn the stream of influence and emolument into a new channel," he categorically declared, "I am bold to assert that it is the best form of government which has ever been offered to the world!" — an astounding statement for an educated man to make, let alone a Catholic.

Taking it upon themselves to speak for all the Catholics of the U.S., the three Carrolls, together with Fitz-Simons and the New Yorker Dominic Lynch,subsequently presented a letter of congratulation to George Washington on his election as first President of the newly unified state. In his reply Washington politely lays down the law to Catholics, who are expected to continue to cooperate with the ideals of the Green Dragon, being now firmly committed to them:

"As mankind become more liberal, they will be more apt to allow, that all those *who conduct themselves as worthy members of the community* are equally entitled to the protection of the civil government. I hope ever to see America among the foremost examples of justice and liberality. And I presume that your fellow-citizens will not forget the patriotic part which you took in the accomplishment of their Revolution, and the establishment of their government; or the important assistance which they received from a nation in which the Catholic religion is professed," — alas, poor France! These words of Washington are of a piece with those in his Farewell Address where he warns against "the insidious wiles of foreign influence," which some students of the period feel more than included the Vatican.

PART II: *Americanism Enters the Church*

Catholics would be tolerated in the new republic as long as they proved useful and subservient. Daniel Carroll's co-operation, it seems, went even deeper than the other two Carrolls: According to the records of Masonic Lodge No. 16 of Baltimore, he received the degree of Entered Apprentice in May, 1780, was admitted the following July, and in May, 1781 became a Master Mason. As a member of the Craft and one of three Commissioners chosen to lay out a site for the artificial state's new capital, he played a star role in the Masonic ceremonies which laid the cornerstone of the District of Columbia near Jones' Point in 1791, and later that of the U.S. Capitol in 1792. This last now stands on land owned by another Daniel Carroll, which he transferred to the new government. (Strangely enough, in 1663 it had belonged to a man named Pope who called his estate "Rome".)

In an account of the cornerstone laying, the U.S. Capitol Historical Society's *"We, the People"* imparts, "As President, war hero, and Acting Grand Master of Maryland's Grand Lodge, Washington had the lead role, supported by a uniformed and decorated cast from the Alexandria Volunteer Artillery and Masonic lodges of Maryland, Virginia and the District. A parade began with the President's arrival on the Virginia shore of the 'Grand River of the Patowmack', crossed to the Maryland side, and moved on to the President's Square, collecting additions at each meeting place. 'The procession marched two abreast,' an observer reported in the September 25 issue of the *Alexandria Gazette*, 'in the greatest solemn dignity, with music playing, drums beating, colours flying and spectators rejoicing.' Skirting 'the great Serbonian bog' that was then Pennsylvania Avenue, the marchers followed a new post road, broke ranks to step from stone to stone to teeter over a single log across Tiber Creek at the foot of Capitol Hill, and proceeded to the hilltop building site. There, Washington, wearing a Masonic apron reported to be 'the handiwork of Mrs. General Lafayette,' conducted the ceremony with a marble headed gavel and a silver trowel."

In *Washington and His Masonic Compeers*, written by Sidney Hayden in 1866, further details can be found concerning the long ritual, which was punctuated by 15 volleys of artillery and crowned by a feast of barbecued ox. The inscription on the stone read, "This southeast cornerstone of the Capitol of the United States of America, in the City of Washington, was laid on the 18th day of September, 1793, in the thirteenth year of American independence, in the first year of the second term of the presidency of George Washington... in the year of Masonry, 5793, by the President of the United States, in concert with the Grand Lodge of Maryland, several lodges under its jurisdiction, and Lodge 22 from Alexandria, Virginia." On the cornerstone was set a plate "on which was deposed Corn, Wine, and Oil, when the whole congregation joined in reverential prayer, which was succeeded by Masonic chanting honors. . . "

Joseph Clarke of the Maryland Lodge delivered an oration in

which, imploring the blessing of "the Great Architect", he expressed the "hope that this work may be remembered for many ages to come, as a similar work has from the commencement of time to this remarkable moment; I mean, *the work of laying the corner-stone of our ancient, honorable and sublime order.* . . Brethren, although I have neither wishes nor pretensions to divinations, yet I venture to prophesy. . . that all I have suggested to you will soon come to pass; when we shall all hail Blessed Territory Columbia, — favored land, soon, very soon, indeed, shall the shores of thy peaceful and delightful city be visited by the commercial interests of the *united world* . . . And he concludes with the Masonic Amen, "So mote it be."

Historians admit that George Washington was not the most fervent of Masons, but it is hard to deny his affiliation in the face of the evidence. There have been attempts, one of the most telling being that of Governor Joseph Ritner of Pennsylvania in a communication to the House of Representatives in 1837, but this was delivered at the height of the anti-Masonic movement, and had regrettable political overtones. Stories of Washington's secret conversion to Catholicism also continue to circulate, with details of how Fr. Leonard Neale, S.J., future Archbishop of Baltimore, swam the Potomac to Mt. Vernon with the Sacraments literally in his teeth. All that is known for sure is that he had an interview with Washington shortly before he died. The truth is that in the funeral oration Bishop Carroll delivered for Washington he states clearly that he was not of the Faith. And who could have known better than he?

Of like substance is the tale of Washington's "vision" at Valley Forge, where he was presumably visited by a mysterious lady who prophesied America's future to him in three extraordinary tableaux. Some will even imply this lady was the Mother of God, despite the fact that both her message and her appearance have a decidedly Masonic flavor. The fact remains that Washington was, by his own consent, inaugurated into the Presidency by the Grand Master of New York, and took the oath of office on a Bible belonging to St. John's Lodge No. 1 — a Bible later used, incidentally, for Warren Harding in 1921 and Dwight Eisenhower in 1953, also Masons.

It's hard to see how Daniel Carroll, a Catholic, could have actually taken part in Masonic ritual. Even as an Apprentice, he would in veiled symbols have renounced all supernatural faith. Masons themselves are at a loss to explain him. Brother Ronald Heaton, in a Masonic Service publication dated 1961, "Masonic Membership of the Signers of the Articles of Confederation," is constrained to quote a Catholic apologist who offers lamely, "Carroll's membership as a Catholic in the Society was not unusual in that period, due no doubt . . . to the lack of knowledge concerning the Society." Such an explanation is hard to accept, for Daniel Carroll was no ignorant backwoodsman, but like his two relatives, a polished gentleman educated both here and abroad far beyond the average Protestant he consorted with.

It is inconceivable that he was unaware of Clement XII's Constitution *In Eminenti*, delivered back in 1731, which states that for the faithful to belong to secret societies "is, before the eyes of sensible and honorable persons, to stain themselves with *the sign of complete perversion.*" Perhaps the sign of the Green Dragon? Could he never have heard of the Constitution *Providas* of Benedict XIV? It renewed the warning in 1751 that "what takes place in those Masonic meetings is against the established order, be it religious or political!" His ignorance is unlikely, especially with a Jesuit younger brother who once taught moral theology in a European college and who was even now administering the whole Church in the U.S.

In the American Bishops' Pastoral of 1810, even this brother was forced to "enjoin on all priests exercising. . . faculties for the administration of the Sacraments, not to admit to those of Penance and the Blessed Eucharist such persons as are known to belong to the association, commonly called of Freemasons, unless these persons seriously promise to abstain forever after from going to their lodges, and professing themselves to belong to their society: and Pastors of Congregations shall frequently recommend to all under their care never to join with or become members of the said Fraternity." From these words it is evident that the evil must have been so rampant in the new republic that it had come to the attention of Rome.

Cardinal Rodriguez of Chile, in *The Mystery of Freemasonry Unveiled*, writes, "The hatred of North American Masonry against religious teachings, especially Catholic teaching, is the same as that of all the lodges of the world. Because of it they have dictated the law of only public and compulsory teaching; and of course it is atheistic in several states . . . However, this does not mean that the campaign does not go on, to prepare the land, to transform the Constitution and reach what in that country is called liberty. We already know too, that according to the explanation given by the most noted Masons in the United States, the god of Masonry is not the God worshiped by the Christians, or the Mohammedans, or the Jews; it is a pagan god; any god, Nature, sun, flesh, etc., anything except the real God, the Personal God, different from the world, and the Creator of Christianity.

"It is true that the Grand Lodge Masons of New York have declared that they do not want affiliations with lodges which do not acknowledge God or the Bible, but that does not mean an absolute breach at all." And he quotes William A. Rowan who in *The Builder* wrote, "There is only one God, Father of the human race; there is the rock over which we build; the Holy Bible is the Great Cross in Masonry. . . On these principles, I dare say, our Great Jurisdiction will be in union with all the Great Jurisdictions of the Universe, with a view to better reciprocal understanding, closer relations, and a common action to realize the Masonic unity and make the spirit of Brotherhood progress." All types of Masonry, says the Cardinal, "are serving as a base . . . to that mysterious pyramid, in which at the top, Satan is worshiped and Jesus Christ and God are renounced, and where there is taught as an ideal, universal rebellion and absolute licentiousness."

Can Daniel Carroll have been blind to all this?

• • •

With the help of his two relatives, John Carroll accomplished an extraordinary tour de force. Uniting all Catholic nationalities in the U.S. firmly under his sole politically sanctioned jurisdiction with the approval of Rome, he led them to peaceful, respectable cooperation with all the other elements rounded up under the sign of the Green Dragon. It had been necessary, of course, to convince large numbers of Catholics that the irreconcilable conflict between their religion and the principles of the Revolution was only apparent and need only be correctly understood to disappear completely.

That he succeeded is a tribute to his genius, for along with Masonry, modern secular democracy had already in his day been condemned by two Popes. Pius VI, who had made him Bishop, had excoriated separation of Church and state and sovereignty of the people in *Caritas Quae,* speaking of "the fury of the Tiers Etat" who fabricated "that baleful constitution separated and cut off from the Catholic religion." And long before him, the Angelic Doctor himself had denied that all men are created equal, laying down that the very notion of order "chiefly consists in inequality" (ST I, Q96, a3).

Soon Gregory XVI, in *Mirari Vos* and *Singulari Nos,* would speak out against the "insanity" of believing "that the liberty of conscience and of worship is the inalienable right of every citizen, ... that the citizens have the right to manifest openly and publicly their ideas by word of mouth, through the press, or by any other means." And again, "The barrier must be erected against the wild license of opinions and speech . . . the condemnation of an absolute liberty of conscience."

Today we have the benefit of the fulminations of at least five more Popes, even the liberal Leo XIII, and especially St. Pius X, who in his admirable letter on the Sillon Movement laid down: "Those who preside over the government of public affairs may indeed, *in certain cases*, be chosen by the will and judgment of the multitude without repugnance or opposition to Catholic doctrine. But while this choice marks out the ruler, *it does not confer upon him the authority to govern;* it does not delegate the power, it *designates* the person who will be invested with it. Moreover, if the people retains the power, what becomes of authority? A shadow, a myth; there is no more law properly so called, no more obedience." Authority does not come from below, as the Dragon would have it.

"There is an error and a danger," St. Pius warns, "in binding down Catholicism, by principle, to any particular form of government. Such error and danger are all the greater when one associates religion with a kind of democracy the doctrines of which are erroneous." This kind of democracy he defines as one "which goes to such lengths in its wickedness as to give sovereignty to the people, and which presses for the suppression of classes and for their leveling down." He calls "liberty, equality and fraternity" a "theory opposed to Catholic truth, warping the essential and fundamental notions which regulate social relations in every human society. . . By separating fraternity from Christian charity thus understood, democracy, far from being progress, means a disastrous set-back for civilization."

As for constructing artificial nations, he says, "No, civilization does not have to be invented, nor the New City built in the clouds. It has been already; it is here. It is Christian civilization, the Catholic City. The only problem is to keep setting it up and restoring it on its natural and divine foundations against the ever-recurring attacks of the unhealthy utopia of revolt and impiety." He begs, "Let not the Priesthood be misled by the miracles of a false democracy into the maze of ideas; let them not borrow from the rhetoric of the worst enemies of the Church the high-flown phrases full of promises which are as high-sounding as they are unrealizable!"

Pius XI echoed the same sentiments, declaring in *Divini Redemptoris*, "It is utterly untrue and mere empty talk, to say that all citizens have equal rights!" We tend to forget that modern democracy never entered the world by way of the Church, but by means of men who had long ago forsworn the true faith. Even Nietzsche saw that democracy would eventually "nurture a human type prepared for slavery in the most subtle sense of the term."

Papal quotations on the subject are legion. Nearer our own day, Pius XII in a radio message on Christmas Eve, 1944 said, "The State does not contain in itself and does not mechanically gather within a given territory an amorphous agglomeration of individuals. The State is, and must be in reality, the organic and organizing unity of a true people. . . Equality degenerates into a mechanical leveling, into a drab uniformity: the sentiment of true honor, personal commitment, respect for tradition, dignity — in a word, all that gives life its true value — little by little sinks and disappears."

• • •

What, exactly, is an "American?" What is an "American Catholic?" Wave after wave of foreign Catholic immigrants arrived in the U.S. to be recycled and absorbed into the establishment prepared for them by the Carrolls and their Green Dragon friends. "The Catholic Church of the Carrolls," writes Fr. Greeley, "was a native American church presided over by leaders lay and clerical who yielded to no one in being respectable members of the American establishment." There were many anguished protests to Rome, as in the Baltimore and Philadelphia "schisms," but Rome seems to have been powerless against the *fait accompli*, and was soon reduced to making the best of a bad situation.

During the great influx of immigrants from Germany and Italy, not to mention Ireland, in the 19th century, the problem reached crisis proportions. In 1895 a French visitor, Marc Leclerc, wrote *Choses d'Amerique*, in which he quotes John Carroll as saying, "It was never in our doctrine that salvation could be obtained only by those who are in actual communion with the Church." Apropos of this he goes on to write, "It is he who expressed the desire that the liturgy be allowed to employ English for the greatest good of the poor people and the illiterate negroes. Cardinal Gibbons, the present head of the American Church *(sic!)*, has faithfully continued to teach the same doctrines. He never speaks of the Protestant sects as irreconcilable enemies; he calls them rather 'our separated brethren,' 'our dissident brothers.'" He condemns in a dogmatic book, *The Faith of Our Fathers*, the Inquisition and persecutions.

Leclerc goes on to note approvingly, "In this land of liberty the Catholic Church has realized that she should preach and practice tolerance; likewise, she has made a point of proving that she is not an aristocratic organization, that she is, on the contrary, sincerely devoted to democracy... She wishes to be called American; she has entered into the spirit of the nation; but she has sensed, indeed that she has very much to do, more so every day, to transform and assimilate the heterogeneous elements who come to her without ceasing from Europe" — but who, we might add, possessed the unity of faith when they arrived.

This writer was not blind to the probable consequences: "The American civilization is profoundly materialistic. When the new settlers, *when the sons of the docile recruits of the Catholic Church have been imbued with the American spirit, will there remain a place in their hearts for the precepts of Rome and of the Faith?*

"Already the strong and solemn voice of the Anglo-Saxons has made itself heard and harkened to in the councils of the Church; it is that voice which thrusts upon Rome, *by threatening an appeal to the people*, the solicitude about social problems, and an *inexorably democratic policy*... The American Church, after having been a simple external appendage of the Church of Rome" has become one of the inmost motive forces... The ten million (in 1895) American Catholics have, on several memorable occasions, weighed heavier in the scales of the Holy See than the hundreds of millions of faithful in old Europe." Has the American Church actually been the Green Dragon's instrument to infiltrate the Church in Rome and destroy the remains of political Christendom? Let history judge.

In 1884 the Americanist Bishop of St. Paul, John Ireland, had proclaimed, "I would not utter one syllable that would belie, however remotely, either the Church or the Republic, and when I assert, as I now solemnly do, that the principles of the Church are in thorough harmony with the interests of the Republic, I know in the depths of my soul that I speak the truth." In 1909 Cardinal Gibbons wrote in the North American Review that Catholics preferred their country's form of government " before any other. They admire its institutions and the spirit of its laws. They accept the Constitution without reserve, with no desire as Catholics to see it changed in any feature. They can with a clear conscience swear to uphold it."

These protestations were calculated to silence violently anti-Catholic organizations like the infamous Know-Nothings and the American Protective Association, which, enemies as they were, publicly pointed out the intrinsic opposition between the Faith and the Masonic dogmas of the state. Before the Catholic John Kennedy captured the Presidency, he declared during his campaign in Houston, "I believe in an America where the separation of Church and State is absolute... where there is no Catholic vote." In West Virginia he promised "he would not take orders from any Pope, Cardinal, Bishop or priest, nor would they try to give me orders. If any Pope attempted to influence me as president, I would have to tell him it was completely improper. If you took orders from the Pope, you would be breaking your oath of office and commit a sin against God."

• • •

In 1871 an international organization called the St. Raphaelsverein had been founded to help preserve the faith of uprooted emigrants. Protesting their treatment in America, it presented to the Pope in December 1890 a document signed by representatives of seven countries which stated, "The losses which the Church has suffered in the United States of America number more than ten million souls." A report submitted to an international Congress in Liege the previous September by a French-Canadian priest of the Albany diocese, Alphonse Villeneuve, contended that out of 25 million immigrants to the U.S., 20 million had been lost to the Church. Exaggeration, perhaps. but so much smoke must mean quite a fire.

The St. Raphael report, published in full in the New York *Herald*, pled for separate parishes and schools for emigrant groups, administered by priests of their own nationality "wherever their numbers and means make such a practice possible." In a desperate attempt to stem the losses by freeing these flocks from the iron grip of the establishment Church, it was deemed advisable that they have their own episcopacy, so that "in the assemblies of bishops, every immigrant race would be represented, and its interests and needs would be protected." Also requested were special seminaries to train missionaries for emigrants, and the establishment of St. Raphael societies under a Cardinal Protector in Rome.

Needless to say, the Green Dragon would not brook any such returns to the natural order, even for purely spiritual ends, for he was not interested in saving souls, but only in forging docile Catholic "masses." As Pius XII observed in the aforementioned talk, "People and amorphous multitude or, as one says, the 'masses,' are two different concepts. A people lives by its own vitality; the mass is inert in itself, and can only be moved from without. A people lives by the fullness of the life of the men composing it, each of whom —

at his own post and in his own way — is a person conscious of his own responsibilities and his own convictions. The mass, on the contrary, waits for an impulsion from without, is an easy toy in the hands of whoever would exploit its instincts or emotionality, ready to follow in turn, today this, tomorrow that flag. . . In the ambitious hands of one or several individuals, joined artificially by their selfish tendencies, the State can, with the support of the mass reduced to a mere machine, impose its arbitrary will on the better part of the true people."

Ignoring Rome, which they taxed with "Curial ignorance" of the true needs of America, the Americanists continued regardless with their procrustean program. In some cases they even indulged in a kind of ecclesiastical "bussing", deliberately shifting foreign pastors to congregations of a different nationality in order to hasten the progress of both in English. Of all the foreign Catholics, only three of the Eastern Rites — Melkite, Ruthenian and Ukrainian — ever succeeded, after much suffering and humiliation, in securing Bishops independent of the American hierarchy. The other easterners continued under the jurisdiction of the local Roman Rite ordinary.

Myron Kuropas, in *The Ukrainians in America,* says "Today the Ukrainian Catholic Church enjoys the distinction of being the only wholly national Catholic Church in America sanctioned by the Holy See in Rome. What is even more significant, however, is the fact that, with the exception of a married clergy, the basic elements of Ukrainian Catholicism have been preserved."

Otherwise all "ethnicism" was officially frowned upon, for what flourished since 1776 was not the Catholic Church of the Apostles so much as the Americanist one of the Revolution. There was no place in the U.S. for a Church which unequivocally respects national cultures as God ordained them. David Boyce of the English Counter-Reformation League put it bluntly: "The America of 1776 started out on a foundation that was intrinsically inimical to the Catholic Church, so that it has *never* been part of Christendom."

• • •

Holy souls like St. Frances Xavier Cabrini, St. John Neumann and St. Vincent Palotti threw themselves and their resources at the service of the immigrant "nationals", but the policy of the American Church only grew stronger, soon supported by an unequaled educational system.

The groundwork for this too had been laid by John Carroll,

who in colonial days had already dreamed of a Catholic college in America on the lines of his old alma mater St. Omer in Belgium, and which had been planned a century before him by the Jesuit Thomas Copley of Maryland. This organ for the intellectual formation of American Catholics turned out to be Georgetown Academy on the Potomac, founded in 1789. That it bore no saint's name and its seal is an imitation of the Great Seal of the U.S. attests to its democratic inspiration. In 1796 George Washington addressed its students. The first three Archbishops of Baltimore were intimately connected with it, Carroll as founder, Leonard Neale as President, and Maréchal as professor.

The education it dispensed was to be scientific and liberal in every way. The prospectus read: "Agreeably to the liberal Principal of our Constitution, the Seminary will be open to Students of every religious profession." The Founder soon found fault with his coadjutor Bishop Neale's administration of discipline, for in 1802 he wrote, "Its president, my coadjutor, and his brother Francis . . . both of them as worthy men as live, deter parents from sending their sons thither by some rigorous regulations not calculated for the meridian of America. Their principles are too monastic . . . they deny that liberty which all here will lay claim to."

Desiring to keep Georgetown in step with the world, he deplored stringent discipline on the ground that "on being delivered from it, young men burst out of confinement into licentiousness, and give way to errors and vices, which with more acquaintance with the manners and language of the world, they would have avoided." Thus he subscribed fully to the strange modern idea that the best antidote against vice is immersion in the world! This sort of permissiveness gained momentum with Cardinal Gibbons, who protested the Holy See's condemnation of the works of the socialist Henry George with the following:

". . . In dealing with so practicable a people as the Americans, in whose genius bizarre and impracticable ideas quickly find their grave, it seems to me that prudence suggests that absurdities and fallacies be allowed to perish by themselves, and not run the risk of giving them an importance, a life and an artificial force by the intervention of the tribunals of the Church." There must be no condemnations.

Georgetown has formed and educated several generations of America's Catholic elite in this strange spirit, spawning numerous other colleges and universities in its image. In 1888 it was ably seconded by the Pontifical Catholic University of America, also established in the nation's capital, and whose *ex officio* Chancellor is the Archbishop of Baltimore. Its chief promoters were two Americanists: Fr. Isaac Hecker, founder of the Paulists, who is probably also the founder of Catholic pentecostalism by his doctrine of the Holy Ghost acting independently of the Sacraments and spiritual direction; and Bishop John Lancaster Spalding of Peoria, later forced by the Apostolic Delegate to resign his see in scandalous circumstances. The University's first rector, another Americanist Bishop, John Keane of Richmond, was summarily dismissed in 1896 as a liberal whose orthodoxy in religious matters was highly suspect.

Despite all, the "official" Catholic schools in America continued taking their cue from, and trained many of their teachers in such educational centers, with the result that even ethnic parochial schools were soon parroting the same political mythology as the government and the establishment pulpits. The emphasis was not so much on being a perfect Catholic as one-hundred percent American. The flag was placed next to the altar and very nearly worshiped. Generally subscribed to was the credo promulgated by the famous convert Orestes Brownson in the pages of his review "The American Republic" in 1865: "The United States, or the American Republic, has a mission, and *is chosen by God for the realization of a great idea.*" Bishop Ireland, who upheld compulsory education in all its rigor, was he who proclaimed, "An honest ballot and social decorum will do more for God's glory and the salvation of souls than midnight flagellations and Campostellan pilgrimages!"

In 1857 Americanism made connections overseas by the establishment of an American College at the University of Louvain in Belgium, an ancient, partly state supported, independent institution which had long been a seat of liberalism. Erasmus had been closely associated with it, as had the Michael Baius whose heretical doctrine on sin and justification had laid the foundations of Jansenism. In our day it contributed many of the Vatican II reformers, among them Leo Suenens, who as Cardinal of Malines became its *ex officio* Chancellor. Bishop John Spalding, a Louvain graduate, had used this institution as inspiration for the Catholic University in Washington, D.C.

His uncle, Martin John Spalding, Bishop of Louisville and later Baltimore — who at the First Vatican Council defended Fr. Hecker and also drew up a postulatum urging a definition of papal infallibility by implication rather than by outright affirmation — had first conceived the idea of an American college at Louvain while touring Europe recruiting clergy, thinking to train priests there for the American ministry. He and Bishop Lefevre of Detroit ultimately provided the financial support, and eventually it became a center where American clergy went abroad to study and absorb the more advanced ideas.

The College at Louvain was strenuously opposed by conservative Bishops like Francis Kenrick of Baltimore and Archbishop Hughes of New York, who had long desired an American College in Rome for training clergy under the direction of the Pope and a board of U.S. Bishops. A general collection was taken up on the feast of Our Lady of Guadalupe in 1858 to build on land donated by Pius IX, and the College opened the following year, with Mass celebrated on the same feast. A side altar was dedicated to Our Lady of Guadalupe, Patroness of the Americas. Many Bishops hoped the North American College in Rome would offset the influence of the Louvain-trained ecclesiastics, but it was a losing battle, for in due time it too became infected.

• • •

In America democracy had been too solidly entrenched in the Church from the beginning. An ardent believer in the power of government by consensus, John Carroll had convened his first synod in 1791, where 22 priests of five different nationalities were brought together to lay down uniform discipline for the new Church without reference to different national origins. During the suppression of the Jesuits he had established chapters of an organization he called "Select Body of the Clergy" whereby he and his fellow erstwhile Jesuits might continue to operate corporately, own property and even found Georgetown University. Two years after becoming Archbishop he laid plans for a National Council to be held in 1812, but this was frustrated by the War with England. The first of seven Provincial Councils was nevertheless held in Baltimore in 1829 after his death. These legislated for the entire U.S. until 1852, when Pius IX granted permission for a Plenary Council.

This First Plenary Council imposed the "Baltimore Ceremonial" on the whole Church in America without exception, besides ratifying the pronouncements of the previous provincial councils, so determined was the American Church to maintain its control over all "foreign" elements, now forced officially to conform. It is noteworthy that when its decrees were submitted to Propaganda for approval, Rome deemed it necessary to warn the American Fathers — among other things — not to insist on conformity in customs unknown in the universal Church, *lest the appearance of a national church be introduced.* The Second Plenary Council of 1866, dealing largely with catechetical matters at the urging of Rome, was attended in its closing session by President Andrew Johnson. The Third Council, in 1884, was concerned with belatedly warning the American faithful against secret societies.

The existence of a National American Church being now evident to many Cardinals in Rome, on January 22, 1899 Pope Leo XIII was finally constrained to issue his famous letter to Cardinal Gibbons, *Testem Benevolentiae,* specifically outlining the heresy of Americanism "to put an end to certain contentions which have arisen lately among you, and which disturb the minds, if not of all, at least of many." The Pope condemned the Americanist practice of watering down the Faith in a false ecumenical spirit, of promoting the false "liberty" proclaimed by the Revolution, of placing natural considerations and methods above the supernatural, and fomenting disdain for the religious life.

He reproved the liberties taken by Americans in ecclesiastical matters in imitation of "that liberty which, though quite recently introduced, is now the law and the foundation of almost every civil community," in other words, the democratic peril. He concluded by declaring that Americanism "raises the suspicion that there are some among you who conceive of and *desire a church in America different from that which is in the rest of the world.*" In view of what has been pointed out thus far, this was a masterpiece of papal understatement.

The Americanist Bishops rushed to disclaim any such aspirations, Bishop Ireland being among the first, and the Pope was apparently satisfied. Others were not so optimistic. Speaking for himself and his French confreres, Louis Isoard, Bishop of Nancy, wrote on George Washington's "feastday", February 22, to thank His Holiness for his letter to the Bishop of Baltimore: "I am well enough acquainted with the sentiments and misgivings of many of my colleagues in the episcopacy to take the liberty of conveying to Your Holiness our common thanks on the occasion of this new and signal benefit." Bishop Isoard could see ahead.

Hardly perceived at the time, a significant development in America's national Church took place in 1917 with the formation of the National War Council. An organization devised to coordinate the activities of American Catholics in World War I, it was largely promoted by the Paulist Fr. John Burke, then editor of the Americanist publication "Catholic World". The group was deemed so useful that after the Armistice, in 1919, approval was received from Benedict XV for its continuance as an annual Bishops' meeting which would be called the National Welfare Council and administered by a standing episcopal committee.

The prophetic voice immediately raised against this hydra was that of Bishop Charles McDonnell of Brooklyn, who warned that the organization's powers exceeded by far the provisions stipulated in the Pope's authorization, and that the authority of the Bishops in their respective dioceses was bound to be undermined. So many concurred in his opinion that a request for dissolution was laid before the Holy See, and Cardinal De Lai had no difficulty persuading the Pope that the Council in question would provide all the machinery necessary for the final construction of a democratic national Church in the U.S. Pope Benedict agreed to a decree of dissolution, but died before he could sign it.

His successor Pius XI was preparing to do so, but was dissuaded by the pressure put on him by certain members of the American hierarchy, who immediately sent Bishop Schrembs as their representative to Rome. What these pressures were can be guessed. The Holy See was in financial straits at the time, and the American Church was very wealthy. Bishop Schrembs soon cabled happily from Rome: "Fight is won. Keep program Bishops' meeting September. Official notice will be cabled next week. Hard struggle. Complete victory."

Not to be overlooked are the strictures and limitations Pius XI sent along with his approval. He stipulated that meetings need not be held every year, and that even then no Bishop was obliged to attend. Minutes of the meetings were to be forwarded to the Holy See, and no decisions reached were to have force of law or bind in any way. Nor did the Holy Father approve the word "Council", suggesting it be changed to the less authoritative "Committee". Eventually "Conference" was adopted, and the first National Catholic Welfare Conference held in 1923.

"Meanwhile," ruled the Pope, "all should know that this organization however named, *is not to be identified with the Catholic hierarchy itself in the United States."* There must be no infringement of the canonical authority of any Bishop, and "on the due denunciation by a Bishop, and proof of interference in the internal management of a diocese by any agent of the Welfare Council, the said agent shall be summarily dismissed from office."

But the fatal breach had been made. The NCWC became the central coordinating agency of all the Church's official activities, with the gigantic bureaucratic possibilities we all are now familiar with. In 1967 its name became openly the U.S. Catholic Conference, and the National Council of Catholic Bishops was formed in accordance with the directives of Vatican II. In the decree *Christus Dominus* these laid out for the whole world the democratic plan first tested in America under the sign of the Green Dragon:

"An episcopal conference is a kind of council in which the bishops of a given nation or territory *jointly exercise their pastoral office* ... Decisions of the episcopal conference, provided they have been made lawfully and by the choice of at least two-thirds of the prelates who have a deliberative vote ... are to have juridically binding force in those cases ... prescribed by common law or determined by special mandate of the Holy See, given spontaneously or in response to a petition from the conference itself ..." And there is added, *"Bishops of many nations can establish a single conference.* Moreover contacts between episcopal conferences of different nations should be encouraged ..."

Implementing this Decree, Paul VI on September 15, 1965, in the *motu proprio Apostolica Sollicitudo*, did "erect and establish in this city of Rome a body for the universal Church," with a permanent Secretariat. This is the Synod of Bishops "chosen from various parts of the world," and "constituted to be (1) a central ecclesiastical institution (2) representing the complete Catholic episcopate (3) by its nature perpetual," yet " (4) performing its duties for a time and when called upon ... *It may also have deliberative power,* when such power is conferred on it by the Sovereign Pontiff."

So now, the world, with democracy established at the summit of the Church! The Carrolls would be gratified to hear that the American NCCB officially adopted as the theme of Catholic observance of the Nation's Bicentennial in 1976: JUSTICE IN THE WORLD.

THE SHAMROCK
AND
THE EAGLE

PART I: *Americanism Wears The Purple*

On June 6, 1911, one of the most extraordinary celebrations in the history of the Roman Catholic Church took place, not at the Vatican, but at the Fifth Regiment Armory in Baltimore, Maryland. The President of the United States, William Howard Taft, former President Theodore Roosevelt, the Speaker of the House, the Chief Justice of the Supreme Court and most of the Cabinet, not to mention the British Ambassador and other dignitaries, had assembled to honor a smiling 77-year-old Catholic Cardinal, James Gibbons, Archbishop of Baltimore, on the occasion of his 25th anniversary under the red hat, his 50th as a priest. According to *The Washington Post*, the business of government had to be left to underlings that day, so depleted was the Capital of its higher echelons.

The guest of honor exuded pleasure and satisfaction, as well he might, for this triumph was a milestone on Catholicism's arduous climb to respectability in Protestant-Masonic society. From now on, Catholics had only to follow his inspired lead to be "in". The idea for this unique solemnity had originated with the editor of *The Baltimore Sun*, seconded by Maryland's Methodist governor, Baltimore's Episcopalian mayor, and last but certainly not least, by the eminently socially acceptable Protestant Episcopal Bishop of Maryland.

Apparently gone forever was all hope of martyrdom on these shores, where Know-Nothings, burned convents, pulled down crosses, the American Protective Association and the "awful disclosures" of Maria Monk had vanished with the last birth-pang of the new Americanist Catholic Church. In Americanism the Cardinal had found at last the formula for fusing the Mystical Body of Christ with Uncle Sam's. In his speech for the occasion, his friend Theodore Roosevelt (who had found the prelate's aid invaluable in settling such thorny problems as the disposal of the Spanish friars' lands in the newly acquired Philippines) revealed the secret of the Cardinal's success: " No church in the United States will ever have to defend itself as long as those standing highest in the church serve the people."

And the Cardinal did that. In his cathedral even his episcopal throne faced the people rather than the Altar, as did those of other prelates less in tune with democratic times. Yet he was regarded as keeping the Faith, for as another speaker, Senator Elihu Root, pointed out, "Our American doctrine of separation of church and state does not involve the separation of the people of America from religious belief," and he warmly congratulated the Cardinal on his fervent support of this revolutionary principle which eliminates all conflict by keeping religion in its place, and strictly private. These dicta were widely publicized, that all unenlightened Catholics might become acquainted with the norm of proper conduct.

James Gibbons, beaming and gracious, basked in the well-earned adulation. Already thirty years before, at a time when Catholics still held themselves scrupulously aloof from civic celebrations glorifying the tricolored revolution, he was urging parish organizations to march in the parades, and his policy had paid off. As Archbishop he had also assiduously promoted Thanksgiving Day, on which he especially wished public Masses to be offered, despite horrified opposition from the majority of the faithful and not a few of their bishops. One of these, Benjamin Keily of Savannah, fulminated, "Gibbons has out-Heroded Herod by wanting to recognize the damnably Puritanical substitute for Christmas. Maybe the poor man doesn't know any better!" All the while the *New York Herald* purred over "the first Catholic prelate to direct observance of the holiday."

• • •

So effective and benign a tool the sons of '76 could hardly have found in their own ranks for keeping a growing, potentially intractable papist population harnessed to the wheels of liberty, equality and fraternity. The Cardinal's conversion to modern democracy was total, and tragically sincere: " If I had the privilege of modifying the Constitution of the United States," said he at the installation of Catholic University's third Rector, "I would not expunge or alter a single paragraph, a single line or a single word of that important instrument. The Constitution is admirably adapted to the growth and expansion of the Catholic religion, and the Catholic religion is admirably adapted to the genius of the Constitution. They fit together like two links in the same chain."

A dozen years later he waxed even more eloquent in *The North American Review*, constituting himself spokesman for all the faithful without exception: "American Catholics rejoice in our separation of church and state, and I can conceive no combination of circumstances likely to arise which would make a union desirable for either Church or state." He would presumably have agreed with his friend Archbishop Ireland, who habitually informed startled audiences that "The Catholic Church, I am sure, has no fear of democracy, this flowering of her own most sacred principles of the equality, fraternity and liberty of all men, in Christ and through Christ," and that "Christ made the social question the basis of His ministry."

Gone were the days when a fellow Irishman like Archbishop John Hughes of New York might tactlessly proclaim in St. Patrick's Cathedral that the Catholic object was " to convert all pagan nations and all Protestant nations, even England with her proud Parliament and her imperial sovereign. There is no secrecy in all this. It is the commission of God to His Church and not a human project. . . Everyone should know that we have for our mission to convert the world, including the inhabitants of the United States, the people of the cities, the people of the country, the officers of the Navy and the Marines, commanders of the Army, the legislatures, the Senate, the Cabinet, the President and all!"

The Cardinal had progressed far beyond so crude an approach. The year following the Armory testimonial he was invited to deliver the invocation at the Democratic convention which nominated Woodrow Wilson, and when war broke out Gibbons immediately appealed for an absolute and unrestrained obedience to the country's call for volunteers. On his birthday he urged, "Be Americans always. Remember that you owe all to America, and be prepared, if your country demands it, to give all in return." Never did Christian serve Caesar more unconditionally. The League of Nations, soon hatched by the war, received his equally enthusiastic support.

Not so absolute, apparently, was his allegiance to Christ's Vicar. Back in 1909 he had already explained that if the Pope were to issue commands in purely civil matters, "He would be offending not only against civil society, but against God, and violating an authority as truly from God as his own. Any Catholic who truly recognizes this would not be bound to obey the Pope, or rather his conscience would hold him absolutely to disobey, because with Catholics conscience is the supreme law which, under no circumstances, can we ever lawfully disobey."

His enchantment with American Caesarism waxed with age. Shortly before his death he wrote in *The Catholic Review* for Washington's Birthday, "As the years go by I am more than ever convinced that the Constitution of the United States is the greatest instrument of government that ever issued from the hand of man. That within the short space of one hundred years we have grown to be a great nation is due to the Constitution, the palladium of our liberties and the landmark in our march of progress." Only the word "holy" is lacking from this eulogy.

Stricken at the home of his lifelong friends the Shrivers with what proved to be his final illness, the Cardinal was anointed by his secretary Fr. Albert Smith. Then, approaching eternity, he asked to be read to from *The Constitutional and Political History of the United States* by Herman von Holst. He followed this by a discussion with one of his priests of two biographies he had recently read, one of John Marshall and the other of Andrew Jackson. Dying not long after in Baltimore, his last recorded words were, "I have had a good day."

Thus ended the course of this slightly built, urbane and witty ecclesiastic, who with amiable calculation moved easily in all walks of society, but mayhap best in the higher ones. Transparently vain, he had played to the grandstand with eminent success, winning applause from all but his scandalized Catholic opponents. His support of the labor movement, ecumenism, the vernacular and all the other planks of the liberalism of his day was unstinted. Hardly given to spiritual works, he nevertheless wrote a catechism called *The Faith of Our Fathers* which sold in the millions and was for a time the *de facto* official Americanist text.

Not least was his part in establishing the Catholic University, whose cornerstone he laid in Washington, D.C. with the assistance of the President of the United States and the Cabinet, to the strains of John Philip Sousa's Marine Band. This institution — vigorously denounced by another son of Erin, Bishop Bernard McQuaid, who wanted diocesan seminaries built first — was soon preponderately staffed by clergy and professors of Americanist persuasion; and until Washington, D.C. became a separate diocese, its chancellorship was reserved by papal decree to the Archbishop of Baltimore. Through its agency the spores of liberalism soon made their way throughout the entire Catholic educational system even down to the parish levels, with the results seen today.

The Cardinal was easily recognized by alarmed conservatives as the shining exemplar of the Americanist heresy described in *Testem benevolentiae*, the apostolic letter addressed to him personally by Leo XIII. He received the papal censure obediently, but simultaneously disclaimed it as inapplicable to himself or his clergy. Indeed it is possible he intended never to divulge it to the faithful, for until the American press began publishing parts of it culled from *L'Osservatore Romano*, it remained quietly on his desk.

Although he denied the heresy in word, there is no getting around the fact that he lived it in deed, his whole life illustrating the false principle Leo condemned: "that, in order the more easily to bring over to Catholic doctrine those who dissent from it, the Church ought to adapt herself somewhat to our advanced civilization, and relaxing her ancient rigor, show some indulgence to modern popular theories and methods, even to pass over certain heads of doctrines, as if of lesser moment, or to soften them that they may not have the same meaning which the Church has invariably held."

• • •

A ruthless, velvet-gloved administrator who remained on top once he rose there, he was also a born politician. Priding himself on the "masterly inactivity" which exasperated even his best friends, he excelled at knowing when to do nothing while a situation took shape, and then, with an unerring sense of timing, strike deftly and unexpectedly at a momentarily exposed target. A case in point was the speech he delivered in the very heart of Rome in 1887 when he took possession of his titular church, Santa Maria in Trastevere. To an astounded congregation of diplomats and others awaiting the inoffensive platitudes such an occasion usually elicited, he boldly held forth on the benefits of separation of Church and state. Delivered in the very teeth of Leo's *Immortale Dei*, promulgated only two years before, Gibbons' words proved powerful explosives in the hands of the European revolutionaries then at work dismantling the remains of Christendom.

A like sensation had not been produced by an Irishman since 1847, when the Great Emancipator himself, Daniel O'Connell, on pilgrimage abroad while famine and typhus raged at home, had with his high sense of "good theater" died in Genoa and directed that his heart be sent on to Rome. His Requiem at S. Andrea della Valle turned into an unforgettable political demonstration, Italy herself then being in the throes of revolution."I was surprised at my own audacity, the Cardinal confessed later, but it was in me and I had to say it. . . But I was careful to save myself by applying my remarks only to this country."   He was aware, of course, of the novelty of his doctrine, but it was a full decade before he was formally reprimanded by the letter *Testem*.

This kind of well planned impulsiveness seems to have been a childhood characteristic. When he was being prepared for Confirmation in Ireland, he and his mother were informed by the pastor that he did not consider the boy ready for the Sacrament that year. Making no protest, James bided his time, and when the day arrived, simply walked into church with the rest of the class and after the doors had been closed, walked up to the Bishop and was confirmed before he was detected. Such devious directness served him well. His sworn antagonist, the convert journalist Ella Edes, friend of Archbishop Corrigan, pronounced the Cardinal "capable of anything," and " an intriguer and *ambizioso* of the first water, for all his pretended sanctity."

His see, often referred to as "the little Vatican at Baltimore", was substantially a perfected version of the old ecclesiastical dictatorship set up there originally with the approval of the Masonic government by the first U.S. Bishop John Carroll. The historian John Gilmary Shea rightly remarked of the Baltimore See, " It has more than a Catholic interest, moreover, its origin is intertwined with the separate national life of the United States as an independent power, and is part and parcel of the national heritage. The growth of the Church in Baltimore compares with the growth of the United States since it threw off the fetters of the Old World." In other words, both marched in the same revolution to the same tune.

From this stronghold, Gibbons as ranking U.S. prelate continued, like Carroll and his predecessors, to act as sole official channel of communication between the U.S. and Rome, privy to all moves from either side unless some private means could be found by his hapless clergy or the members of the Roman Congregations. He succeeded until 1893 in preventing the appointment of an Apostolic Delegate from the Holy See who would assume this function as in other countries. Even a delegate with limited powers to attend the Third Plenary Council in Baltimore had been blocked. In 1895, in *Longinqua oceani* the Pope was still trying to placate Baltimore, assuring the Americanist hierarchy that the new Delegate would in fact be no "detriment to the ordinary power of the bishops, " but on the contrary would "rather bring an accession of stability and strength."

Suggestions that the U.S. government send in turn its own delegate to the Vatican was met with like enthusiasm. At the close of World War I an American diplomat's wife, Maria Longworth Storer, used her influence to try to persuade the American bishops to appeal to President Wilson to admit a Papal representative to the Peace Conference. Gibbons roundly excoriated the lady's *meddling in ecclesiastical affairs,* and nothing more was heard of the matter.

The Cardinal had become so influential by this time, both here and abroad, that his friends felt he had only the Papacy left to aspire to. Few in Europe took the threat seriously, but a French newspaper, *L'Eclair,* publicly accused the Americanizers of plotting within the Sacred College to make him Leo's successor, so proverbial had American arrogance become. According to Archbishop Ireland, "The work of Catholics in America is . . .to solve for the Church Universal the problems with which religion is today confronted." Regarding our Lady's appearance at Lourdes, one American prelate explained to his foreign colleagues that there were no such apparitions in America because they were simply not needed!

For, as Leo XIII would note in his letter on Americanism, "the Holy Ghost, they say, pours greater and richer gifts into the hearts of the faithful now than in times past, and by a certain hidden instinct teaches and moves them with no one as an intermediary." This dangerous delusion, which eventually opened the door wide to pentecostalism and contributed heavily to the corruption of religious life, the Holy Father condemned as "not a little rash."

• • •

Although Cardinal Gibbons was the acknowledged star of the Americanist show, it must be conceded he had a very strong supporting cast. Before he made his entrance in history two talented actors had already played the all-important mood-setting opening scenes. The curtain had parted first on the aforementioned John Carroll, whose episcopal appointment Rome had delayed a full five years, well knowing his dangerous democratic tendencies and the problems in missionary territory; but as he had insisted that his own clergy elect him, and he had the approval of his powerful Masonic friend, Benjamin Franklin, no likely substitute was ever found. And it was of course deemed incompatible with the triumph of the revolution for Catholics in America to remain subject to a Superior in England as had been the case until then.

Any doubt concerning Carroll's view of his office is quickly dispelled by one close look at the new episcopal seal he chose: On it appears what might be termed the Americanist Madonna, for the ring of stars surrounding the figure of our Lady bearing the divine infant are not the traditional twelve with which she is crowned as essential symbol of the Church in the Apocalypse — as the unwary Catholic would naturally assume if he didn't count them. They in fact number thirteen, presumably representing — certainly not the twelve Apostles nor the twelve tribes of redeemed Israel — but the original thirteen states of the new Masonic republic! Gnostic doublespeak has hardly been so ingenious since the days of the Albigensians. Here our Lady herself would seem to sponsor the first civil government of modern times deliberately constituted without reference to the order laid down by God for His world under Christ the King!

Between John Carroll and James Gibbons there stretched a non-Americanist interregnum of some 35 years in Baltimore, broken only in 1851 by the accession of Bishop Francis Kenrick and Bishop Martin Spalding in 1864. During this time three conservative Sulpician-trained prelates with ultramontane views - the Frenchman Ambrose Maréchal, the Englishman James Whitfield and the Maryland convert Samuel Eccleston - attempted to steer the Church into the ancient path. The liberal offensive, however, far from languishing in the interim, merely shifted for the time being to the Carolinas, from whence it was brilliantly and devastatingly led until 1842 by John England, who had been secretly appointed Bishop of Charleston without Maréchal's knowledge. But that's another story.

Consecrated in Ireland by Francis Moylan, Bishop of Cork and brother of George Washington's aide General Stephen Moylan, Bishop England by dint of preaching in Protestant pulpits soon rose to a social prominence much like that later achieved by Cardinal Gibbons. Indeed many of the latter's utterances could have been quotes from England, who once assured a Protestant minister whose congregation he agreed to address, "I can promise you that nothing shall be said or done which you or your congregation will disapprove."

Invited to speak to the Congress in 1826, he proclaimed,"I would not allow to the Pope, or to any bishop of our Church outside this Union, the smallest interference with the humblest vote at our most insignificant balloting-box." It would be "wisdom and prudence and safety to continue the separation" of Church and state. "If that tribunal which is established by the Creator to testify to me what He has revealed... shall presume to go beyond that boundary which circumscribes its power, its acts are invalid: my rights are not to be destroyed by its usurpation; and there is no principle of my creed which prevents my using my natural rights of proper resistance to any tyrannical usurpation." He furthermore maintained, as did later Bishop Ireland, that the Catholic Church herself was the inspiration for the American political experiment.

The first bishop to draw up a Constitution for his diocese, he was, needless to say, one of the most zealous promoters of a Provincial Council for all of the U.S., convoked in 1829 to legislate "uniform discipline" on the divergent nationalities after Roman opposition had been weakened. His see lacked the primacy of Baltimore's, so that, unlike Carroll and Gibbons, his influence might not have been nationwide but for another "first": a publication directed to the general public called *The United States Catholic Miscellany*. It earned him the title of "Father of the Catholic press", and opened the way to the Americanist capture of the Catholic anglophone media. A weekly devoted to political and religious polemic, it failed twice for near total lack of support from the scandalized faithful, but by dint of private help flourished in the red until the Civil War, disseminating the Americanist tenets as if it were the voice of Rome itself.

In passing it might be noted here that Catholics inhabited the Carolinas from earliest colonial times, the abortive settlement at Port Royal in 1568 under de Gourges having in fact been responsible for naming Charleston after Charles IX of France. And contrary to popular belief, it was not Lord Baltimore's colony in Maryland which was the first haven for persecuted English Catholics in the New World, but the famous "lost" colony on Roanoke Island, which then formed part of the Carolinas and not Virginia. With the connivance of the English government Catholics had been permitted to join the other settlers there, only to vanish mysteriously with them without a trace. It is even likely that Virginia Dare, America's first born and baptized English child, was a Catholic.

Since those days the colonial Established Church of England had driven the Faith underground, and unknown numbers of Catholics began attending Protestant services. It turned out that one of Bishop England's peculiar duties when traveling his extensive territory was revealing secret Catholics to one another who had been neighbors for years without suspecting they shared the Faith. In 1832 he estimated these cases to be "four times as numerous as the actual number of those who belong to the Church."

Bearing in mind what joyous hopes their own Catholic bishop

in a newly formed see must have raised in these abandoned hearts, it becomes most significant that when John England died he left a diocese burdened with enormous debts; for popular as he became with Protestants, he was never able to enlist the financial support of his flock for his innovations (among less offensive ones, the peremptory abolition of pews), and managed to keep going only by repeated trips to Ireland to beg funds. Nor was he any more acceptable to his fellow bishops, whom he did not neglect to advise on how to run their sees. Rome itself had to bear with his unsolicited advice on how to keep abreast of the times. When James Whitfield was raised to the episcopal throne of Baltimore, England was not even invited to the ceremony.

From the foregoing it is easy to see that Americanism, like all successful revolts against authority, was not a popular movement in its beginnings, but one painstakingly rendered so by rebels high in the ranks. Once established, however, anguished appeals to "tradition" were soon voiced by the rebels themselves, as if tradition had always been liberal, and no opposition to their regime had ever existed — or could exist in future without culpable disobedience.

After the Civil War the Americanist characters began appearing on stage in numbers suggesting a mob scene. It would be impossible to outline even sketchy biographies of them all, but the ring-leaders were few and well-known. Foremost and noisiest was the French-educated John Ireland, Archbishop of St. Paul, with whom Gibbons became intimate at the First Vatican Council, and who gave Europe many reasons to expect he would soon be heading a new American schismatic church. And there was their friend John Joseph Keane, Archbishop of Dubuque, former Bishop of Richmond.

Although not mentioned till now, this is not because Keane did not play an important, albeit more hidden role. Recipient of an honorary doctorate from Harvard, he often lectured there, and twice preached to the U.S. Senate. After dismissal by the Vatican from the rectorship of Catholic University, Keane served for a time, along with Archbishop Ireland, as an indefatigable lobbyist and foreign correspondent for their cause in Rome, where he was a Canon of St. John Lateran. These two were ably assisted by Bishop Denis O'Connell, who had been similarly dismissed for good reason as Rector of the North American College in Rome, but was kept in the Eternal City by Cardinal Gibbons as his Vicar at Santa Maria in Trastevere. There are few pertinent quotations from Archbishop Keane, for he, Ireland and O'Connell had made a pact to destroy all their papers relating to Americanism, rather than risk the judgment of posterity. Keane, with characteristic probity, kept his part of the bargain whereas the other two did not.

It is regrettable, for in many ways he emerges as the most straightforward of the lot. He was in fact the writer of a famous fearless letter still extant in which he tells his friend Cardinal Gibbons, "I find to my intense regret that an impression has taken shape in Rome to the effect that your Eminence is changeable in views, weak and vacillating in purpose, anxious to conciliate both parties on nearly every question; that it is hard to know, therefore, upon which side you stand concerning any important question. Hence I find a growing inclination to look elsewhere than to your Eminence for reliable information and judgment, — a tendency not only here, but among Bishops of the United States, to look to New York," — where the dreaded anti-Americanist bishops Corrigan and McQuaid held sway — "rather than to Baltimore for the representative and leader of our Hierarchy." He then proceeded to cite examples of the Cardinal's failings.

Gibbons, Ireland and Keane formed a powerful triumvirate about whom a bevy of other high ecclesiastics played, or had played, secondary but indispensable roles. Besides Denis O'Connell, there were the two bishops Spalding, uncle and nephew: Martin John Spalding, a predecessor of Gibbons in Baltimore and former Bishop of Louisville; and John Lancaster Spalding, Catholic University's third Rector, who shone as the theoretician of what was a singularly non-intellectual movement. Although its adherents seem to have been eloquent spellbinders without exception, theirs was not highly reasoned oratory, if we are to judge by the specimens left behind.

Despising theory generally, Americanists prided themselves on being *practical*. Holding, according to Leo XIII's diagnosis, that the so-called "passive" virtues were suited well enough to past times, but that "active" virtues are more in keeping with the present, they did not distinguish themselves for either spirituality or erudition. In his historic speech at Santa Maria, Cardinal Gibbons gravely opened by telling his hearers his basilica dated from St. Callixtus, apparently unaware that it was founded only a hundred years later by Pope Julius I. Bishop O'Connell, warmly endorsing the recently published French edition of the hotly denounced *Life of Father Isaac Hecker* as " the supernatural philosophy of the whole movement — given out by a saint! " later admitted he had found it too long and never read it.

In the 1940's the judgment of D.W. Brogan of Cambridge

University was disputed by none: "In no Western society is the intellectual prestige of Catholicism lower than in the country where, in such respects as wealth, numbers, strength of organization, it is so powerful." Much of the blame for this can be laid to the Americanists, who laid so exclusive an emphasis on action and organization and whose unwritten censorship strangled free expression. There were Catholic scholars and spiritual men in the U.S., but being unable to swallow the Americanist contradictions, and discouraged from voicing the whole Catholic truth about anything, they to all practical purposes vanished from the scene.

It would be tedious and unnecessary to list all the Americanist prelates: the Paulist Bishop Thomas O'Gorman of Sioux Falls, whose father had been a friend of Archbishop Ireland's father in Chicago; Bishop Patrick Riordan of San Francisco; Bishop Edward Fitzgerald of Little Rock; Archbishop Peter Kenrick of St. Louis should be enough. By now the most unobservant reader cannot have failed to notice that all these Americanist Bishops, from Carroll on down, seem unaccountably to have been Irish. Several, like Keane, Ireland and O'Connell, were born in Ireland; and Gibbons, except for what he himself called a lucky accident, would have been. Many seem to have received at least part of their education there, and most traveled to Ireland frequently. Despite their protestations of unalloyed Americanism, the truth is they never severed the cultural ties with the old homeland which they expected other nationalities to sever.

Is there some connection between Americanism and the Emerald Isle?

Although it might seem that all these Americanists were Irish, this does not mean that all the Irish here were Americanists. Indeed some of their bitterest adversaries were Irishmen like themselves, who boasted their own triumvirate of Bishops: the aforesaid Michael Augustine Corrigan of New York and Bernard McQuaid of Rochester, ably thirded by Patrick Ryan of Philadelphia. These were pitted against the Americanists on almost every issue, openly rejoicing at the promulgation of *Testem benevolentiae*. It is therefore no simple matter of equating the Irish with Americanism, any more than the French can be equated with Gallicanism, but numbers alone would lead us to suspect that a connection of some kind does in fact exist in the one case as in the other.

What could it be?

PART II: *The Irish Connection*

Bishop Riordan's dismissal of Americanism as a problem which "existed only in the imagination of three or four Frenchmen" indicates the French had been quick to detect its affinity to Gallicanism, an error which had persisted among them since Carolingian days and come to full flower with Louis XIV's Declaration of 1682. It had incurred papal condemnations as early as 1296, when Boniface VIII issued *Clericis laicos* against Philippe le Bel, who maintained that as French king he was independent of Rome in the temporal sphere, and that papal authority was subject to councils.

Licet iuxta doctrinam followed from John XXII in 1327, with additional proscriptions by Eugene IV and Leo X. In 1690 Alexander VIII condemned the Sun King's Declaration denying the priesthood any power over civil rulers. Innocent XII and Pius VI continued the battle, which culminated in Pius IX's *Syllabus* and the great *Pastor Aeternus* which formally defined papal infallibility at the First Vatican Council. This last was furiously opposed by the Americanist bishops, who left Rome before having to vote on it, with the exception of Bishop Fitzgerald of Little Rock, who cast one of the only two dissenting ballots at the conclave.

Although he may not have realized it, Cardinal Gibbons' view of the spiritual and temporal domains was roughly that of the Gallican theologian Honoré de Tournély, a professor at Douai and later at the Sorbonne who died in 1729. As both student and professor at St. Omer, the future Bishop John Carroll would certainly have been exposed to his teachings. An inductive, pragmatic theologian working outside the deductive scholastic tradition, Tournély refused the Church even the "indirect" power over civil authority insisted on by Cardinal St. Robert Bellarmine and other orthodox theologians following St. Thomas, who laid down:

"The secular power is not subject to the spiritual power universally and from every point of view. . . but if anything in temporal affairs constitutes an obstacle to the eternal salvation of his subjects, the bishop who intervenes by a command or a prohibition . . . acts by his own rightful divinely constituted authority. Where the salvation of men is at stake, all secular powers are subject to the spiritual power."

The voice of truth was never silent. Centuries later, in Gibbons' lifetime, Pius IX in Article 24 of his *Syllabus* condemned the proposition that, "The Church has not the power of using force, nor has she any temporal power, direct or indirect." Anyone doubting that the Church founded on Peter is the source of both temporal and spiritual power under Christ the King need only have looked up at the famous 8th century mosaic on the wall of the Leonine triclinium in St. John Lateran, first cathedral of Christendom. As one of its Canons, Archbishop Keane, for one, could not have avoided doing so, and he would have seen there represented St. Peter, with the Keys on his lap, bestowing at one time the pallium on Pope Leo II with his right had and entrusting the standard to Charlemagne with his left.

The spirit of Tournély flared anew in America in our own day with the "new formulations" of Fr. John Courtney Murray, S.J., who sought to reconcile the principles of revolutionary democracy with the traditional ultramontanism held by all the saints without exception through the ages. In an article on "The Church and the Democratic State" in 1952, Fr. Murray's disciple Fr. Gustave Weigel, S.J., summarized the two contradictory positions. He prefaces, "We need only read American history to see that Catholicism has had some part in the rise and growth of the United States of America. However, despite what Catholics themselves feel about their allegiance, history will also show that Catholics have always been accused of being disloyal citizens by some of their compatriots because of their religious affiliation. . . Notice that the attack is centered not on the fact of Catholic loyalty to America, but rather on the logicality of the Catholic way of acting in the light of authoritative Catholic doctrine on Church and state relationships."

Alas, the lack of logic in the Americanist position has ever been more apparent to the Church's enemies than to her faithful. Traditional theologians, whom Fr. Weigel designates as "the static expositors", maintain "that the state has the objective obligation to recognize the Catholic Church as the true religion. Therefore the state must defend the Catholic Church even to the point of suppressing, if necessary, freedom of speech in this area. Moreover, the state has to legislate in the light of the doctrine of the Catholic Church and the natural law. Even more, the state must profess the Catholic religion and render acts of cult according to the Catholic scheme, although it is admitted that the state cannot force non-Catholics into the Catholic Church."

It must be noted, however, that these are "objective obligations from which the legislators can be freed by their ignorance, and such a condition must be tolerated by the Church, but such toleration must recognize that the restriction in the Constitution whereby governors as such are deprived of the power to profess the Catholic religion and to defend it, is an error." Leo XIII laid down, nevertheless, that it is right at times to permit what is speculatively wrong, given the expediency of pursuing the common good.

The Americanists, whom Fr. Weigel dubs "the dynamic expositors", get around Leo XIII and his otherwise "static" teaching by their tried and true device of maintaining that times have changed: "The historical situation must be taken into account when considering papal teachings, whether they be those of Boniface or those of Leo." Like cardinal Gibbons and Bishop Carroll before him, Fr. Weigel considers the traditional teaching "not immediately pertinent to the concrete American governmental situation. . . " There is no real problem, "because of the lack of American state-worship."

Pope St. Pius X in *Vehementer* would appear to have thought otherwise: "That the Church and State ought to be separated is an absolutely false and pernicious error. Based as it is on the principle that the State should not make profession of any religious worship, this doctrine is first of all a grave insult to almighty God. For the Creator of mankind is also the Founder of human societies, and He preserves them just as He maintains individuals in existence. To give Him due honor we owe Him then not only private veneration, but public and social ownership. Besides, this thesis involves the unconcealed denial of the supernatural order. It limits the action of the State exclusively to the pursuit of public prosperity during this life, though this is only the proximate *raison d'être* of political societies."

Arguing on the purely "pragmatic" level Americanists love so well, it might be further pointed out that a genuine separation of Church and State did in fact exist in the Middle Ages, but it was properly a distinction of function, and not of principle. Because they rule the same subject, namely the citizen, Church and State must cooperate; and they do, whether they like it or not. Today the situation is entirely reversed, however, for where Masonic theosophical universal brotherhood is the *de facto* religion of the State, the separation does not exist in fact, but only in principle. But then, according to Fr. Weigel, "Philosophy is not a pragmatic norm for government in the concrete." Or, as Pilate once put it, "What is truth?"

The religious indifferentism to which political indifferentism inevitably leads was already far advanced here by the time of the Civil War. Edward Dicey, American correspondent for London's *Spectator* in 1862, related to his readers the level to which religion had sunk at Harvard: "The prayers, which are very short, are worded so as to contain nothing offensive to the tenets of any Christian sect, and I must fancy, in consequence be curious commonplaces." Americanists adhered scrupulously to this code when praying or preaching publicly, and Cardinal Gibbons openly boasted that his catechism contained not a single line which might offend Protestants. *Ad rem* the words of *Immortale Dei:* "It is unlawful to follow one line of conduct in private life and another in public, respecting privately the authority of the Church, but publicly rejecting it; for this would amount to joining together good and evil, and to putting man in conflict with himself; whereas he ought always to be consistent, and never in the least point not in any condition of life to swerve from Christian virtue."

• • •

The tap roots of the Americanist distemper are uncovered easily enough in the history of Ireland. As in France, where orthodox Catholics existed alongside Gallicans, it would seem that from earliest times there were also two kinds of Irish, one of them indistinguishable in America from the Americanist. He might be called the Hibernian, the Irish counterpart of the Gallican.

He emerged openly in 1757 when the Irish hierarchy formally abjured the opinion that Popes could depose monarchs, as St. Pius V had Queen Elizabeth, or authorize executions of heretics. They also disclaimed papal infallibility, not yet defined at the time, along with any intention of dislodging the Established Church of England in Ireland; and eventually Bishop Coppinger published a catechism embodying these and other accommodated notions. By 1816 liberals and ultramontanes were clashing in the episcopal synods, and in 1831 Bishop Doyle was openly advocating common schools for Protestant and Catholic children.

These lines had been laid, however, at the very dawn of the Reformation, for all the Irish chiefs but one had sworn allegiance to Henry VIII's new supremacy, despite the fact that the bulk of the friars and the common people held their ground — so true is it that revolutions always begin from above. In 1541 a parliament met wherein 23 prelates and 20 peers acclaimed Henry as King of Ireland, who hitherto had held only the title of "Lord" of Ireland under the Pope. The next year saw many abjure the Pope, like Con O'Neill, who received the Earldom of Tyrone as his recompense. When the Spaniard D'Aguila landed 50 years later with 4,000 men at Kinsale to liberate Ireland he gave up in disgust at the disunion and treachery he met with. Protestant historians like Oliphant have been led to conclude that the Irish are characterized by "an incurable love of disunion."

Governed from earliest times by "kings" elected by the people, Ireland had a long democratic tradition, with "political" priests apparently fixtures predating Christianity on her shores. As late as 1542 an O'Kelly was chief of his clan as well as hereditary Cistercian Abbot at Knockmory near Tuam. Never did Ireland form politically a part of Christendom, nor was she ever governed by the feudal laws to which the rest of Europe subscribed. From the time the first missionaries reached her she had remained under the tutelage of the Papacy, retaining a tribal culture distinct from the other Catholic countries. In the 12th century she was entrusted to England by papal grant to Henry II from Nicholas Breakspeare, the only English Pope Adrian IV, for the express purpose of extirpating vice and ignorance among the natives, but more significantly, of bringing her into closer relations with the Holy See. It is clear Henry never sought the charge, because for many years he put off doing anything about it.

Severe measures were apparently called for. The Venerable Bede in his famous *Ecclesiastical History* makes no mention whatever of St. Patrick, although he inserts his name in the martyrologies. This has led historians to suspect that the great Patron of Ireland, who in turn never refers to the Pope or to the Holy See in his *Confessions,* may in fact have been heading an ecclesiastical establishment operating on its own quite apart from Rome. The great controversy over the date of Easter which raged between Ireland and Rome during the 7th and 8th centuries offers further evidence that till then there had been no close rapport between the Irish and the rest of Christendom as existed between the other Catholic countries. It would seem that Ireland had a native Church which was growing in isolation and loving it, but with the sad consequences which eventually provoked Adrian's Bull. This document has never been revoked, but the Irish are pleased to hold that if it ever really existed, it became null when Queen Elizabeth violated her Coronation oath by forsaking the Faith.

It is an error to think that the strip of coast known as the "Pale", seat of English government in Ireland, dates only from Elizabethan times, for it had been established in the days of the Bull. Outside the Pale native princes continued to rule much as they pleased under the old pagan laws of the *brehons* without reference to the rest of Christendom. Curiously enough the Pale was originally a wall of defense, not offense, against the Irish, who were excluded from its confines only because the English who were allowed to mix with them unaccountably tended to turn against the government. The English generally tried to keep the Irish from Church preferment for the same reason, for at no time in Ireland's history was her native clergy noted for close ties with the Roman organization. Then as now it seems to have been a matter of "obey the Pope and do what you will."

These conditions pertained long before the Reformation, in the days when both Irish and English shared the same Faith, so it must be acknowledged that the endemic conflict between them was not essentially religious, as the rest of the world would later be led to believe, but rather racial and political. The famous revolt of "Silken Thomas" against Henry VIII merely happens to be the last of a long succession of pre-Reformation Irish uprisings against their English regents. Later, when Henry repudiated his Spanish Queen and exacted the famous Oath of Supremacy from his subjects, the Catholic English in Ireland refused it along with the native inhabitants. Only after Elizabeth did their differences begin taking on the distinctive religious coloration they now enjoy, to their enormous embitterment.

· · ·

The international occult forces promoting revolution throughout Christendom lost no time in exploiting the situation. Hatred and resentment of England were made almost a way of life for the Irish, a revolution in their very blood. Through all the snarls of their painful history the demonic desire for independence in this fallen world assumed more and more the aspect of a holy crusade. Under cover of Catholicism Irish revolutionaries, many like Wolfe Tone under direct Masonic inspiration, blinded the people to the great truth later so ably proclaimed by Joseph de Maistre, that no nation can confer liberty on itself. At best it can recover a liberty it already possesses, which had been conferred on it from above.

Amply fed by real injustice and cruelty on the part of an apostate England in panic, victim of a revolution of her own, Irish hatred of England transposed itself easily to the New World, where it contributed materially to the success of the American Revolution, many of whose so-called Irish Catholic patriots were Catholics in name only. (Not that the Irish were the only offenders. The Masonic battle flag carried by the Polish Catholic General Pulaski is today a cherished relic of the lodges. He is one example among many, like the "Catholic" General Lafayette.) Similar tactics were used in the revolution in the Church, which kept pace with the political, to the point that Paul VI was reported by several churchmen to have privately voiced his fears of an autonomous American church even during his pontificate. Some feel it exists in fact.

Experts admit our war for independence was not the work of ordinary citizens, but of a handful of very rich colonials who hoped to become richer once relieved of English taxation. At the outset the only Catholics who subscribed to it were wealthy and well-educated Irishmen like the Carrolls, for whom one of the great attractions here was remoteness from England and its established church, and mayhap also from Rome. Although even in the Colonies they were subject to the harsh English penal laws against Catholics, the English-speaking Irish had very early begun assuming leadership in the Church, under America's Vicar Apostolic residing in England. By language and culture they were far better equipped to settle into the Anglo-Saxon ambience than the Catholics of other nationalities, although these at first out-numbered them.

For the most part staunch Tories not interested in revolt, the other Catholic nationalities would most likely have remained British subjects but for the fact that in 1778 they suddenly saw Catholic France, eldest daughter of the Church, under the political imperative of weakening her mortal Protestant enemy, take sides with England's rebellious subjects. The Carrolls and the founding Fathers exploited this turn of events to the utmost, all the while dangling before Catholic eyes freedom of worship if they joined the revolutionary cause. As we know, John Carroll was a member of a commission sent to persuade Catholic Canada to fall in with them. By the time George III showed himself willing to grant freedom of worship, as already given to Canada by the Quebec Act, American Catholics had been irrevocably committed to the revolution, a direction in which great numbers remain headed to this day.

Hoping to forge a native American Church conforming as closely as possible to the burgeoning artificial secular state, the new Bishop Carroll held his "foreign" faithful in tight check, and had Rome permitted, he would even in that early day have imposed a vernacular liturgy — the vernacular being, of course, exclusively English. As it was he made it mandatory to the limit allowed, even in the dispensation of the Sacraments, to the great discomfort of the non-Irish, and to the great natural advantage of the English-speaking Irish and faithful. John Carroll was not untrained for his task, for although born in Maryland, he had returned there only at the age of 40 after 27 years abroad, where he was closely associated with institutions deeply dyed in liberalism. As evident from his episcopal seal, the direction he took was deliberate.

So was John England's, who arrived on the scene in 1820 soon after Carroll's death, bringing with him two priests he had ordained in Ireland. He had much valuable experience behind him in his native country, where he refused the oath of allegiance to Britain on the strength of his intention of becoming an American citizen as soon as possible. His grandfather had spent four years in prison and his father a year as a fugitive because of their revolutionary activities; and England, a law student before entering the seminary, continued the fight not only as a priest, but as editor and trustee of the *Cork Mercantile Chronicle*, member of a three-man committee dealing with the Veto controversy and in other capacities. It has been said of him that next to the fabled Daniel O'Connell's, "his influence was the greatest in the agitation which culminated in Catholic Emancipation." O'Connell himself testified, "If I had John England at my back, I would not fear the entire world before me." (He also made the famous remark, "I am a Catholic, but not a papist.")

This background England brought with him to the U.S., where he served the same political ideals he had deemed so worthy at home. His only obstacles, besides his own disenchanted congregations, seem to have been his superiors: Ambrose Maréchal and Maréchal's successor James Whitfield, who, as the luck of the Irish would have it at the moment, happened to be two of the very rare non-Irish bishops who graced the See of Baltimore. Their incurably old-fashioned orthodoxy found England's democratic innovations unbearable, but apparently impossible to restrain in so vast an expanse as the Carolinas.

To his friend Bishop Rosati of St. Louis Whitfield wrote concerning the vacant See of Cincinnati in 1832: "If possibly a good choice can be made, let an American born be recommended, and (between us in strict confidence) I do really think we should guard against having any more Irish bishops. . . This you know is a dangerous secret, but I trust it to one in whom I have full confidence." On occasion the Irish hegemony acted from Ireland itself, to the point that even Bishop Carroll had complained of it when the Dominican Archbishop of Dublin sought to engineer the appointments of two of Carroll's suffragan bishops. "Intrigue must have been very active," he notes.

As for Maréchal, he had been wont to express himself in

French regarding the *canaille irlandaise,* or in elegant Latin, on the subject of *sacerdotes Hiberni intemperantiae aut ambitioni dediti.* In point of fact, the See of Baltimore was already exhibiting certain disturbing similarities to the ancient See of Armagh, primatial seat of St. Patrick, which for two hundred years remained the exclusive possession of one family — some of them not even priests — until St. Malachi managed to get himself appointed to it.

• • •

Thus exposed is the background of the terrible dissension which was to rack the Church in America for the remainder of the century, during which the bulk of the non-Irish (and some of the Irish) Catholics struggled vainly to break the stranglehold being slowly but surely clamped upon them by the nationalist Hibernian heresy imported long ago from the Old Sod, and which was transformed into *Americanism.*

"These strains within the Catholic body," writes Msgr. Tracy Ellis in *American Catholicism,* "constantly changed according to circumstances of time and place. . . At first the French and Irish bickered in the East and in Kentucky, but as time passed it became a contest between Irish and Germans in the East and Middle West. In Louisiana the earlier clashes of French against Spaniards often gave way after the purchase of 1803 to a combination of the two against the more recent arrivals, the American and the Irish. In a major conflict in Buffalo at mid-century, French and Germans were arrayed against the Irish. It is unnecessary to emphasize here what European immigration up to 1850 meant by way of determining the character of the Catholic Church in the United States. By that date the federal census-takers reported 961,719 Irish in the country. Many of these, it is true, were North of Ireland Protestants, but the greater number had come from the famine-ridden counties of southern Ireland, which were largely Catholic."

After the Civil War in 1866, according to Msgr. Ellis, "the number of bishops born in Ireland, or of Irish descent, disproportionate to the general Catholic population and to bishops of German and other foreign strains, marked the period as one of an increasing Irish ascendancy in the American hierarchy, a fact which would bring severe strains before the end of the century," when the Irish were being numbered in the millions.

The influx had been accelerated by positive recruitment on the part of the Irish already here — as seen in a famous letter to one John

Francis Maguire, member of parliament from Cork, who incorporated it in his book, *The Irish in America*. The letter had been written in 1867 by the then Bishop of Charleston Patrick Lynch, a close friend of Cardinal Gibbons. A loyal supporter of the Confederacy like his predecessor John England, Bishop Lynch had acted as Jefferson Davis' envoy to Pius IX in the attempt to secure formal diplomatic recognition from the Vatican. He quite understandably wished to attract his emigrating countrymen to the South, and the picture he painted apparently proved well-nigh irresistible.

Following a glowing description of the agricultural enticements, he promised them "a church and priest of their own, and Catholic schools for their children. Appealing to their ethnic instincts, he also explained, "This invitation to emigrants from Ireland is but a repetition of what was done over a hundred years ago, when there was a large immigration of Irish Protestant farmers to South Carolina; and with them must have come many Catholics who in those days when there was neither priest nor Catholicity in the country, soon lost the Faith. This Irish immigration almost took possession of the State. Irish family names abound in every rank and condition in life; and there are few men, natives of the State, in whose veins there does not run more or less of Irish blood.

"South Carolina is, probably, the most Irish of any of the States of the Union. While its inhabitants have always had the impetuous character of the Irish race, nowhere has there been a more earnest sympathy for the struggles of the Irishmen at home; nowhere will the Irish immigrant be received with greater welcome, or be more generously supported in all his rights... I believe that all these points will be presented with due details to those who wish to leave Ireland to better their fortunes in America by a special agent who may be sent out; and also that proper arrangements will likewise be provided for the passage of those who wish to emigrate from Ireland to South Carolina."

This may have been a bit over-enthusiastic, but it brought results, if some disillusionment. As Bishop Lynch implies, America was fast losing the aspect of a foreign country where the Irish were concerned.

• • •

For many years the other Catholic nationalities had been petitioning in vain for parishes and schools of their own, and their frustrations culminated in what came to be known as the Cahensly affair. In 1886 Fr. Peter Abbelen, representing the Germans of Milwaukee, had gone to Rome to protest the policy of enforced Americanization which, now suddenly become a rule of faith, was endangering the salvation of thousands still not at home in English, nor among the Irish. He was the bearer of a letter of recommendation to Cardinal Simeoni, Prefect of Propaganda, from Cardinal Gibbons — who, according to Bishop Keane, at the same time quietly wrote to the Roman authorities against the mission.

Fr. Abbelen's efforts aroused the interest of Peter Paul Cahensly, a selfless, devout German merchant of considerable means who was Secretary General of the St. Raphaelsverein, a society formed to promote the material and spiritual welfare of Catholic immigrants the world over. Following an international meeting in Lucerne, Switzerland in 1891, the Society presented Leo XIII with a document signed by delegates from seven different countries pleading for consideration for those who had emigrated to America.

"It seems necessary," it read among other recommendations, "to grant to priests devoting themselves to the emigrants all the rights, privileges and prerogatives enjoyed by the priests of the country. This arrangement, which is only just, would have the result that zealous, pious and apostolic priests of all nationalities will be attracted to immigrant work," and stem the tide of defections to the Church which "in the United States of America number more than ten million souls." And, "It seems very desirable that the Catholics of each nationality wherever it is deemed possible, have in the episcopacy of the country where they immigrate, several bishops who are of the same origin. It seems that in this way the organization of the Church would be perfect, for in the assemblies of the bishops, every immigrant race would be represented, and its interests and needs would be protected."

This perfect organization of the Church is hardly what the Masonic founding Fathers had had in mind. Needless to say the Americanists rose as one man in righteous indignation against this threat of *foreignism*. Archbishop Ireland loudly decried this "impudence in undertaking under any pretext to meddle in the Catholic affairs in America." He felt that any immigrant "who does not thank God that he is an American should in simple consistency take his foreign soul to foreign shores and crouch in misery and abjection beneath tyranny's scepter." Americans who saw nothing wrong with American intervention in Cuban affairs against Catholic Spain accused Herr Cahensly of being the agent of a Prussian plot against the U.S.

The Germans, who happened to be numerically the greatest threat to the Irish Americanists controlling the Church, bore the brunt of their ire: "The liberals' offensive against the Germans stemmed in part from nothing more exalted than the desire to eliminate the only significant resistance to the Irish-American domination of the hierarchy," writes Robert Cross in *The Emergence of Liberal American Catholicism,* " but in an era when pan-Germanism was alarming a good deal of the world, the persistence of a group of the faithful in proclaiming that their Catholicism and their Germanism were closely linked gave the liberals a more exalted justification for their crusade."

And a crusade it was, defined in no uncertain terms by the lone 'intellectual' among them, Bishop John Lancaster Spalding. In *The Religious Mission of the Irish People* we read: "This is the second home of the Irish people. Here their descendants are to dwell; here their blood is to mingle with that of all the races of Europe. Here they are to fulfill their great mission" — of spreading the Faith, which, according to him, was a task especially entrusted to them in the modern world: "Irish Catholics are the most important element in the Church in this country, and that their present surroundings and occupations" — in crowded cities and menial tasks — are for the most part a hindrance to the fulfillment of the mission which God has given to them... this is the object and aim of the Irish Colonization Association of the United States," formed to re-locate the growing Irish population on the cheap lands of the west. "There is not a priest in the whole country who may not become an active worker in this cause."

This colonization program had its Irish opponents even before the Civil War, when it was ridiculed as quixotic and unrealistic by Archbishop Hughes of New York: "Our confidence in the wisdom of the advice thus offered to the Irish is considerably diminished by the fact that some at least of those who have taken a leading part in the movement have hardly proved themselves competent to manage their own affairs." Whatever the reason, the Irish showed no inclination to return to massive farming. They could never be dislodged from the crowded cities in any numbers, and the colonization program failed.

Alas for the Church, Hibernianism did not. According to Archbishop Spalding it was to be in the U.S., that the sons of Erin would morally and finally defeat England: "Whatever the fate the future may have in store for the Isle of Destiny, the past cannot be undone. Ireland is henceforth forever united to England by bonds

that are stronger than any political union. Her language is English."
And that, apparently, was the adhesive in the Irishman's fatal
Americanism. Had the Irish been still speaking Gaelic, we might
reasonably expect them to have formed a most vociferous segment
of the St. Raphael Society they condemned as *foreign*.

But even so, Ireland's "laws are English, and would remain so
even if England should cease to exist. The bravery of her sons has
borne a great part in spreading the power of England throughout the
earth, and all this and much besides cannot be undone by any
possible revolution. Here in America is a Greater England, and here,
too, must Ireland do her highest work. The cause in the old home is
sacred, and all who love justice and liberty must give their hearts;
deepest sympathy to those who there are struggling upward to the
light and free air. But here, too, is an Irish cause which is Catholic.
Shall we never understand that our people even here are not yet free,
and shall we neglect the work which lies at hand?"

This is what the German, French, Belgian, Polish, Spanish,
Eastern Rite Catholics and others were up against in their own
Church in the New World. The Hibernians, whose own ethnic
attachments and foreignism happened to be cloaked by the English
language and familiarity with English law-forms and general culture, which they had long ago adopted as their own, would brook
no leadership but theirs in an English-speaking Church. Although
such factionalism is certainly valid politically speaking, in the
Church it constitutes a sect, and that is very dangerous.

Bishop Spalding admits, "Our victory is in no way assured;
but the Lord hath regarded our lowliness and hath wrought great
things upon us. There are few among us who are great, who are
noble, who are learned, who are powerful, but such as we are, we
stand in the open light of day and on God's battlefield in Ireland, in
England, in Scotland, in America, in Australia, in every part of the
wide earth where the English language is spoken; and we are in all
probability today the greatest and most living religious fact in all
these lands, and so recognized to be by those who are able to
interpret without passion or prejudice the signs of the times. . .

"If now we turn to explain this rebirth of Catholicism among
the English-speaking peoples, we must at once admit that the Irish
race is the providential instrument through which God has wrought
this marvelous revival. As in another age men spoke of the *gesta Dei
per Francos*, so may we now speak of the *gesta Dei per Hibernos*."

And as in another age men spoke of French Gallicanism, so
may we now speak of Irish Hibernianism. Both are revolutionary

nationalism become a religion. . . wearing the garb and using the vocabulary of religion: "With the passing away of the real powers of royalties and aristocracies, the course of events is inevitably tending to bring about greater sympathy between [the Church] and her people." Is it possible that Bishop Spalding was implying that there is no salvation outside democracy? Outside the Americanist heresy?

Fr. Anton Walburg of Cincinnati, who held quite unashamedly the traditional view of native culture as the Faith's natural protective covering, but without seeking to impose his own on others, certainly spoke for most of the Germans when he warned his flock at St. Augustine's: "A foreigner who loses his nationality is in danger of losing his faith and character. When the German immigrant, arriving in this country, seeks to throw aside his nationality and to become 'quite English, you know,' the first word he learns is generally a curse, and the rowdy element is generally his preference to the sterling qualities of the Puritan. A German aping American customs and manners is in his walk, talk and appearance an object of ridicule and contempt."

To which Archbishop Ireland, apparently entirely blind to his own Irishness, would retort, "No encouragement must be given to social and political organizations or methods which perpetuate in this country foreign ideas and customs." As if all English culture here were not an importation! "Efforts to concentrate immigrants in social groups and to retard their Americanization should be steadily frowned down."

Comparatively few Irishmen had time to entertain the grander Hibernian delusions, but it's hard not to sympathize somewhat with Bishop Henni of Milwaukee, who vowed, "No Irish bishop will ever sit on my throne!"

PART III: *The Consequences*

From Rome Denis O'Connell reported with alarm to his friends that the Vatican considered the Germans the only reliable Catholics in America, and the Irish extremely dangerous. He wrote that the Prefect of Propaganda had declared that "the Irish in America are a bad set, and the sooner the Propaganda takes hold of them the better." Their attacks on "foreignism were seen as attacks on the universality of the Church and even on papal authority."

It is true there was talk now of forcing the Germans to adopt instantly the language of their new homeland, a measure never proposed in her entire history by the universal Church, who until after Vatican II had imposed no vernacular on anyone anywhere. On the contrary, all cultures found themselves at home in her maternal bosom. She proved herself to be the only power on earth capable of welding together the most varied races, who were not only allowed to keep what was distinctly their own, but encouraged to do so, finding it enormously enhanced and developed under the influence of divine grace.

Modern nations had come into being as the result of the unifying grace of Catholicism. This was especially evident in England, where Christianity brought warring tribes almost immediately under one king. The only common language ever imposed was Latin, a sacred tongue mystically dead to the world but alive in worship and international centers of learning, and this without detriment to the vernaculars, which flourished with new vigor. Today the nationalizing and internationalizing action of the Church has been supplanted by an artificial force operating apart from God and His Church and seeking a one-world, man-made unity of its own. It began operating in America and was immediately espoused by the kind of Catholics called Americanists.

English was not required even by the U.S. government, whose Constitution nowhere declared it the official language or more "American" than others spoken here. Only the self-constituted Americanist *bloc* exacted English. President Grover Cleveland, appealed to by a New Jersey priest whose request for a separate diocese for Slavic Catholics had been refused by Cardinal Gibbons, could make nothing of the petition and simply turned it over to the prelate in bewilderment. Yet in the face of this neutral official attitude in Church matters, the Americanists continued to make the government rather than the Holy Ghost the Church's bond of unity in America.

Accused of being un-American and "stirring up the people" (Luke 23:5), a group of Germans were re-assured by their Irish friend Archbishop Corrigan: "Enough for us that we have been born here, or that we have voluntarily made it our home, that our patriotism should not be challenged without good reason." Fearing the Holy See might approve Cahensly's proposals, however, some of the Americanists launched a propaganda campaign in the press to alert America generally to the threat of Germanism.

In their biography of Cardinal Gibbons, Arline Boucher and John Tehan show to what lengths this was carried: "It was later discovered that, without the knowledge of Gibbons, Archbishop

Ireland and Denis O'Connell were responsible for manufacturing a number of inflammatory news cables, which were unjust and exaggerated attacks on Cahensly, clearly designed to stir up public opinion in America, but which only served to further rend the unity of the Church in the United States. Of these dispatches Ireland wrote O'Connell, 'They are so cleverly put and they always hit the nail on the head. They are creating a tremendous sensation and effecting more than aught else could have done Catholic public opinion.'

"Later he cabled O'Connell: 'Send more, send all! Miracles of good done! Great disturbances, danger of schism and persecution unless Rome denounce Cahenslyism and denounce once and for all, and for time being name no German bishops.' Continuing this rabble-rousing technique, Ireland wrote O'Connell, 'I think we have the country well worked up now and we will be able to begin reaping the harvest. I sent an 'alarming' cable to you yesterday. You may be able to show it around. As a matter of fact, Americans are most angry and I am sure that in the next Congress Cahensly will get an airing.'"

Thus was anti-Catholic sentiment aroused by the Americanists against their fellow Catholics, to achieve their own ends. Whatever other factors may have been involved, in this kind of warfare the logical, sober Germans were no match for the highly articulate, theatrical and imaginative Irish, who were furthermore distinguished by a high tolerance for inconsistencies on the theoretical level. A race which produces poets, playwrights and politicians rather than philosophers and scientists is singularly qualified to handle its own publicity and detect what has most appeal to the audience. They would, furthermore, be quite untroubled by the analytical distinction a Frenchman like Maurras would make between one's *legal* country and one's *real* country — the distinction which has to be made between the United States and America if a Catholic here is to think at all clearly and act in accord with right reason.

s s s

Americanism, characterized by its tendency to soften or omit certain doctrinal principles in favor of action yielding quicker results, proved fatally attractive to thousands of Irish not deeply instructed in their faith due to the English persecutions. Yet their prowess in journalism, oratory and the other communicative arts insured their capture of the English speaking media set in motion by

Bishop England, which was beamed as much to the general public as to Catholics. It became almost impossible for anyone to become acquainted with any but Americanist views on any issue unless one could read the German language papers or foreign periodicals. Today Catholic textbooks are compiled in good faith by authors who have only the work of Americanist historians to draw on, there being hardly any others in print in English.

The net result, among other fatal consequences, is that Catholics in the U.S. generally have little or no cognizance of previous Catholic cultures here, not only the German and Slavic,but especially the French, Indian and Spanish, which had taken root over far vaster areas of the continent than were ever occupied by the English colonies. These have been nearly obliterated from Catholic consciousness, to be replaced almost exclusively by what was essentially the impoverished Anglo-Saxon Protestant way of life which had already stunted the Irish themselves back in Ireland. Hispanic tradition no doubt suffered the most, monarchical Spain being the natural foe of Masonry and a national enemy in two "wars". How many school age Catholics today would know of Ven. Anthony Margil? Or that Spanish missionaries were martyred in Virginia? Or anything about the miraculous catechizing of the Southwest by Venerable Mary of Agreda? Even now that she has been declared Empress of all the Americas by papal pronouncement, Our Lady of Guadalupe hardly gets a hearing as anything but a local Mexican devotion.

To return to our story, the scare tactics used in the media by the Americanists worked perfectly. Discussing Cahensly with Cardinal Gibbons at the presidential cottage at Cape May, Benjamin Harrison remarked pointedly, "Foreign and unauthorized interference with American affairs cannot be viewed with indifference. I was very much pleased with the opinion you expressed publicly in the matter . . . This is no longer a missionary country like others which need missionaries from abroad. It has an authorized hierarchy and well-established congregations. Of all men, bishops of the Church should be in full harmony with the political institutions and sentiments of the country." The Hibernians qualified. Other Catholic nationals were now potential subversives. Any demur on their part would be "divisive" to both national and Church unity.

The Holy See, reluctant to lend support to a movement deemed inimical by the U.S. government, formally rejected the Cahensly petition. Still, well aware of the real dangers pointed out by the proposal — of too rapid, enforced Americanization of foreign Catholics — Rome saw fit to disregard Cardinal Gibbons' and the Americanists' nominations to the See of Milwaukee on the death of Archbishop Heiss, who had succeeded Henni. Still another German, Frederick Katzer, was appointed. Archbishop Ireland pronounced him "thoroughly unfit to be an archbishop," and apparently unaware of any historical absurdity, declared Katzer "knew less about America than any Huron!" The more subtle Gibbons, with both Church and state now behind him, availed himself of Katzer's installation ceremony to deliver a severe warning to the Germans against further dissension on any level. Today all Germans and Hurons here speak English, even at Mass.

There were other forces at work. Of record is Cardinal Gibbons' trip to Rome to defend the American secret societies, for he shared the prevailing Americanist view of American Masonry and its affiliates as "different" from continental varieties and essentially benign. He was even known to preach in Masonic lodges. He would have agreed with San Francisco's Archbishop Riordan, who believed "we should treat such organizations in as large a spirit as the discipline of the Church will permit us," and with Archbishop Ireland, who favored allowing Catholics as much liberty "as is at all consistent with Catholic principles" in their contacts with the fraternities. One of the great *coups* of the Gibbons regime was his successful reversal of the Vatican's condemnation of the Knights of Labor, a union two-thirds Catholic, largely modeled on Irish political secret societies of Masonic inspiration, and even in that day known to be heavily larded with Communists. Its approval opened the whole Catholic working class in the U.S. to the machinations of the left.

Such complaisance would seem to be nothing new, however, for a number of the Carrolls had never seen any conflict between Masonry and Catholicism. William J. Whalen, in *Christianity and American Freemasonry*, says, "Daniel Carroll, brother of the first American bishop, was active in Masonry, and apparently Bishop Carroll did not consider the papal ban applicable to this country until some time after 1800. For example, the bishop discussed the various censures of the Holy See on the lodge question in a letter to a layman in 1794. He added, 'I do not pretend that these decrees are received generally by the Church, or have full authority in this diocese. . .' Masons laid the first cornerstone for St. Mary's Church, first Catholic church in Albany and first cathedral in that diocese." Catholic sightseers in Baltimore should find Bishop Carroll's first cathedral worthy of notice, for it was designed by the Masonic architect of the Capitol, Benjamin Latrobe, and is an especially fine example of the "Enlightenment" style then being popularized by the sons of Hiram Abiff.

It may occasion surprise that, whereas some Catholics all over Europe continued to join the lodges after the first papal condemnation *In eminenti* in 1738, this was particularly true in Ireland. According to Fr. Whalen, "Some served as Worshipful Masters, and some lodges were composed entirely of Catholic priests and laymen. Even the Irish patriot Daniel O'Connell served as Master of Dublin Lodge No. 189 after his initiation in 1799," although "in 1837 he testified that he had renounced the lodge some years before." In Cardinal Gibbons' day, Masonic membership had been confined largely to the Protestants, but "at the end of the eighteenth century the Craft counted more lodges in Ireland than in England."

The Masonic historian Robert Freke Gould writes, "The roll of Irish lodges probably reached its highest figure about the year 1797, when scarcely a village in the Kingdom was without its 'Masonic Assembly'. Afterwards, however, a period of dormancy set in." Gould's source of information, Chetwode Crawley, explains that the large number of Irish Masons is due to the fact that the Catholics found in the lodges a refuge from the social disabilities visited on them by the English penal laws. As late as 1829, according to a letter written by Col. Claude Cane, Deputy Grand Master in Ireland, to the *Irish Times* on March 22, 1929, sixty percent of Irish Freemasons were Roman Catholics on the records and registers, "which have been accurately kept by the Grand Lodge of Ireland for nearly two centuries."

The Irish priest Fr. E. Cahill estimated that in the 1920's, whereas "the U.S.A. is by far the most Masonic country in the world . . . there are more Freemasons in Ireland (without counting the members of the Orange Society) than in any continental country except Germany and France, and immensely more in proportion to the population than in any country of Europe or South America." Persons acquainted only with Irish clerical writers who are anti-Masonic, like Fr. Cahill, Msgr. Dillon or Fr. Fahey, may find this unbelievable. It becomes necessary therefore to remind the reader of the two types of Irish Catholics, the orthodox and the Hibernian, and that both types are found equally in Ireland and the U.S. As we have shown, the Hibernians, politically orientated to revolution and preoccupied with natural rather than supernatural ways of spreading the Faith, formed an abnormally large segment of the Americanist cabal which assumed control of the Church in the U.S.

The I.R.B., Irish Republican Brotherhood, a secret society known as the Fenians, was founded simultaneously at Dublin and New York in 1858. Nearly all its founders had been connected with the 1848 Irish uprising in that great year of revolutions unleashed throughout Europe by occult forces. Almost its entire membership were Catholics dedicated, like our Americanists, to separation of Church and state. *The Course of Irish History*, published in Cork and edited by two Irish professors, T.W. Moody and F.X. Martin, informs us that the I.R.B. "drew its support not only from the Irish at home but also from the new Ireland that emigration had created in Britain and the U.S.A. The special function of the American body was to aid the home organization with arms and officers. Considerable numbers of American officers, trained in the Civil War, came to Ireland in 1865 when that war ended; and it was only because, owing to a conflict of view among American Fenians, the promised arms did not also arrive, that the rising intended for 1865 was postponed ... The I.R.B. survived to take a leading part in 1916 in an insurrection of the kind it had aimed at in 1865."

In the interim in the 1870's the Fenian Michael Davitt had gone to America, "where in collaboration with John Devoy, the dominant personality among the American Fenians, he formulated. . . a common revolutionary front." Not that American help to the revolutionary Irish was anything new. Back in the eighteenth century the revolutionary Wolfe Tone once noted in his diary, "Called on the American Consul, who gave me 50 pounds. I am now ready to march."

• • •

Some American bishops had not been slow in querying Rome for directives regarding the Fenians, whose U.S. branch even organized an army and soon marched into Canada against the British! On July 13, 1865 the Editor of the *Actae Sanctae Sedis* footnoted the reply of the Holy Office to the bishops with, "If one takes into consideration the immense development which these secret societies have attained; the length of time they are persevering in their vigor; their false principles it professes; the persevering mutual cooperation of so many different types of men in promoting evil; one can hardly deny that the 'Supreme Architect' of these associations (seeing that the cause must be proportioned to the effect) can be none other than he who in the sacred writings is styled the Prince of the

World; and that Satan himself, even by his physical cooperation, directs and inspires at least the leaders of these bodies, physically cooperating with them." The Fenians were formally condemned January 12, 1870.

Of like dark inspiration were the succeeding *Clan na Gael* and the *Ancient Order of Hibernians,* the latter degenerating as it did into the criminal "Molly Maguires" who terrorized the Pennsylvania coal fields for two decades. Such organizations were responsible not only for many unsafe streets, but for anti-Catholic reactions of a kind till then unknown among the general American public, for whom, with the help of the media, *Irish* and *Catholic* had become synonymous.

These Irish-American societies were lineal descendants of earlier ones in Ireland. "The American Revolution had its effect upon the oppressed of Ireland, and when the French Revolution broke out," writes Fr. Peter Rosen in *The Catholic Church and Secret Societies,* "the people of Ireland hailed it as the dawn of their own independence." An early Catholic society called the *White Boys,* so called because they wore white shirts over their ordinary dress as disguise, became the *Right Boys* in 1787, and became *quite powerful in political affairs.* There followed the *Defenders* and the *United Irishmen,* who became in turn the *Ribbonmen* and eventually *St. Patrick's Boys.* Their oath was, "I swear that my right hand be cut off and be nailed to the door of the prison at Armagh, rather than to deceive or to betray a brother; and to persevere in the cause to which I deliberately devote myself; to pardon neither sex nor age, should it be in the way of my vengeance against the Orange men." Needless to say, this occasioned the formation of rival societies among the Protestants, who became the *Heart of Steel,* the *Threshers,* and the *Break of Day Boys.*

There was parallel development in America, where the secret organization known as the Sons of Liberty was formed in Maryland in 1764 to further the revolutionary cause, giving rise to rival Tory organizations like the St. George, St. Andrew and St. David societies. The *Sons of Liberty* claimed the patronage of an undoubted American, an Indian chief named Tamina... They called themselves the *Sons of St. Tamina,* afterwards *Tammany.* From all this it is not hard to see how the Irish came to form the backbone of the Knights of Columbus, fashioned as this organization was with ritual so resembling the Masonic.

As for organizations like the *Odd Fellows, Knights of Pythias* and *Sons of Temperance,* "The position of Gibbons," says Fr. Andrew

Greeley in *The Catholic Experience*, "was that there was no certainty of any positive evil in the societies and hence no reason for a general mandate forbidding them, while on the other hand, if such a mandate was given, a great deal of offense would be taken by non-Catholic Americans." In view of the well-known Irish propensity to alcoholism, the remedy offered by the *Sons of Temperance* was understandably attractive, but hardly Catholic. Rome condemned all in 1894, directing that, ". . . the American bishops be notified to warn their people against such societies, adding that if Catholic members persisted after being warned, they were to be deprived of the Sacraments. Gibbons. . . persuaded the archbishops of the country to decide that the promulgation of the decree was inopportune, largely because of the bitter campaign the American Protective Association was waging. However, the archdiocese of New York and the diocese of Brooklyn — both headed by non-Hibernian Irishmen — promptly promulgated the decree, and eventually the Holy See insisted that the other bishops do the same. Gibbons reluctantly agreed."

The Holy See had been long aware of the Irish weakness for secret societies, and Leo XIII, although politically a liberal, made no concessions in that quarter. In 1882 and 1883 he wrote several letters to the bishops of Ireland in which he warned them, "It is a matter for serious thought that the most righteous cause is dishonored by being promoted by iniquitous means. Justice is inconsistent not only with violence, but especially so with any participation in the deeds of unlawful societies, which under the fair pretext of righting wrong, bring all communities to the verge of ruin. Just as our predecessors have taught that all right-minded men should carefully shun these dark associations, even so you have added your timely admonition to the same effect. As, however, these dangers recur, it will become your watchful care to renew these admonitions, beseeching all Irishmen by their reverence for the Catholic name, and by their very love for their native land, to have nothing to do with these secret societies. . . The secret societies, as we have learned with pain during these last months, always persist in putting their hope in the commission of crime, in kindling into fury popular passions, in seeking for the national grievances remedies worse than the grievances themselves, and in pursuing a path which will lead to ruin instead of to prosperity."

Unjust and oppressive as British rule may have been, the English cannot be made to take the blame for the potato famine, which arrived in 1846-47 on the very heels of our Lady's warning at

La Salette; nor were the English responsible for the later one in 1879, occurring the year of the ominous apocalyptic apparition at Knock in County Mayo. With fine Italian tact, the Holy Father implied that God might not be entirely pleased with His Irish people, and that if they would only seek first the kingdom of God and His Justice, " ... they will be free to seek to rise from the state of misery into which they have fallen. They surely have a right to claim the lawful redress of their wrongs. . . nevertheless, even the public welfare must be regulated by the principles of honesty and righteousness. . . Divine Providence enables the just to reap at last a joyful harvest from their patient waiting and their virtuous deeds, whereas the evil-doers, having run their dark course to no purpose, incur the severe condemnation of both God and man."

When the famous "Propaganda Circular" arrived in Ireland in 1888 condemning as immoral before the world the Plan of Campaign and the nationwide boycott of the English landlords, it was obediently accepted by orthodox Irish bishops like Bishop Dwyer of Limerick, but indignantly rejected by the Hibernians, who even solicited Protestant assistance against the Pope. London's Catholic *Tablet* for May 5 of that year believed a good effect of the decree would be to "separate the revolutionary and irreligious section from the law-abiding and legitimate element in the National party. Bishops, priests and all good men in Ireland have received with fear and anxiety the admixture of the American revolutionary influence in the national movement. . . Sympathy with Ireland has been very general throughout the Church," but whether this continues, "will in the future depend on the kind of obedience shown in Ireland to the instruction given by the Holy See." Resistance was strong, and the following July the *Tablet* reported that the recalcitrants were judged "no better than an Irish wing of the continental revolution; the people may still be Catholic, but such political leaders as these will be their ruin."

Cardinal Moran of Australia's Irish colony was quoted as saying, "If the Pope were to condemn the national movement, I do not hesitate to say that the Irish people would be perfectly within their right in disregarding even the command of the Holy See." This has a curiously Americanist ring. Like utterances were commonplace with Cardinal Gibbons and Archbishop Ireland, and later with Al Smith and John Kennedy. When the Irish primate Cardinal McCabe died, Leo XIII restored himself to the good graces of the Hibernians by appointing in his place Dr. Walsh, President of Maynooth, despite every effort on the part of the Curia to have this liberal's appointment set aside. Thenceforth the clergy was wedded to the Nationalist movement, and the Irish Church began exhibiting much the same aspects as its American cousin.

It seems superfluous to add that in Ireland, Hibernian approval of its American colony was unqualified. One has only to glance through, say, the long chapter on *The Church in America* as found in the Maynooth professor Fr. James MacCaffrey's *History of the Catholic Church in the Nineteenth Century*. The section on the Church in the U.S. reflects entirely the Americanist viewpoint, its heroes extolled and its enemies either damned or ignored. One looks in vain for even a mention of the anti-Americanist Irish Bishops McQuaid or Corrigan, whereas Fr. Isaac Hecker, founder of the Paulists and an Americanist-canonized saint, is referred to as "a man of great sanctity and zeal, more dependent for his spiritual guidance upon his own communings with the Holy Spirit than upon the teachings of theologians, and like his patron St. Paul, burning with the desire of bringing all men within the fold of Christ." As in the U.S., the papal condemnation of the Americanist heresy is praised, but pronounced inapplicable to the prelates in question, who "had never held the doctrines that had been condemned." Maynooth, forsooth!

• • •

Catholics who now find themselves saddled with the results of the Americanists' aberrations tend to pass harsh judgment on them, but there is no way of knowing what the state of the Church would be had their opponents won, who were as human and fallible as they. We can only bow to God's secret judgments and make the best of it, reminding ourselves that nothing happens which He does not permit for the greater good of those who love Him.

Perhaps the most disturbing element of the Americanist make-up was their exuberant sincerity in the rightness of their cause; their certainty that they were doing God's will, and in Archbishop Keane's case at least, their exemplary resignation to it when for the moment things did not go their way. And they worked so hard! They exhibited the kind of confidence which only the deepest ignorance can ordinarily bestow. Firm in their delusion that the U.S. and the whole world would become Catholic as soon as the Church was democratized and rid of her reactionary, dogma-ridden watchdogs, they were oddly preoccupied with converting the masses without evincing any real concern for the problems of the individual, or groups of individuals. And whatever they did, it was always with one eye on the non-Catholic grandstand. The German paper *Herald des Glaubens* sputtered helplessly at "American priests in this country who would rather see several million Germans go to hell than forego the opportunity to convert a few hundred Yankees." And as for the Hurons, well. . .

Actually theirs was a war of the heart, ever blind, against the head — the problem of Adam and Eve all over again. And now, again, we are seeing the results of what happens when Adam "hearkens to the voice of his wife." (Gen. 3:7), and the intellect takes its orders from below. But that, of course, is the very essence of democracy. Ironically enough, Americanism's own messianic prophet Orestes Brownson inadvertently best described the psychology of the malady he himself was helping to spread when he wrote:

"Heresies originate in the spirit and tendency of their epoch, and in the effort to develop the Church and carry her, in her doctrines and practice, along with them. . . The heresiarch does not set out with the deliberate intention of founding a heresy. No man ever rises up and with deliberate forethought says, 'Go to, now, let us devise and found us a heresy.' The heresiarch is the man of his times — if not, for his times — and is the one who, better than any other, embodies or impersonates their dominant ideas and sentiments. He begins by taking his standard of truth from the ideas and sentiments which he finds generally received, and with which he is filled to overflowing; these, he says, are true, and therefore the Church, if true, must agree with them. He then proceeds to develop the Church, to explain her doctrine and practice in their sense. . . "

Nevertheless, the naive good intentions — or, let's say it, the ignorance and unscrupulous ambition — of the Americanists cannot be blamed entirely for their far progress along their chosen path. Their triumph could not have been so complete without highly-placed connivance in Rome, itself infected with Modernism. For instance, back in 1834 Bishop John England had taken it upon himself to send Rome a long memorial in which he laid most of the problems of the Church in America to foreign (i.e., non-English-speaking) priests who dared among other deficiencies "declare their preference for foreign institutional methods." His report received unusual notice at the Vatican, but would very likely have been passed over had it not been summarized and sponsored by Cardinal Weld, who happened to be a member of the Curia. It happens that Weld's family were close friends of the Carrolls, and as a youth the

Cardinal himself had served as an altar-boy at John Carroll's episcopal consecration. From the beginning Americanism had good friends at court. Reporting from there in 1896 to Archbishop Ireland, Archbishop Keane spoke of the powerful friends he found in Bishop Carl Mourey, the French representative in the Curia; Fr. David Fleming, a Franciscan consultor in the Inquisition; and the two Cardinals Vanutelli: "So the phalanx is a good strong one, and I think it is bound to do work that will tell," said he.

There was sustained behind-the-scenes help from Cardinal Rampolla, Vatican Secretary of State, as might be expected. Even then being planned by occult forces in Europe, his election as successor to Leo XIII would be blocked only by a last minute courageous intervention on the part of the Austro-Hungarian Emperor, who threatened to exercise his ancient veto power. Rampolla used his influence to have Keane appointed Archbishop of Dubuque after his dismissal in disgrace from Catholic University, giving the impression that Rome approved of the former rector after all. Just before the letter on Americanism appeared, he had promised Archbishop Ireland that he would do all he could to spread the view "that the words of the Letter allow us to say that the things condemned were never said or written in America, not even by Hecker, but were set afloat in France as 'Americanism' at the occasion of the *Life* [a biography of Fr. Isaac Hecker, written by the Paulist Fr. Walter Elliott], and especially of its translation, and of interpretation given in foreign languages." This is the official version still given out today in American Catholic school texts. The Cardinal also did what he could to minimize the effect of Fr. Maignen's excellent polemic against that heresy, while getting Archbishop Ireland published in *L'Univers*.

Besides active support of this kind, there was also weakness on the part of those whose duty it was to check the recalcitrants. Cardinal Ledochowski, Prefect of Propaganda and friend of the Germans, who, it is said, seeing that the Americans resented the slightest foreign influence, let them run their Church as they pleased rather than risk worse divisions. Even the Pope may have helped. Although he reprimanded their more exuberant excesses, he was dependent on Peter's Pence, and the Americans were brilliant and generous money raisers. Nor did these scruple to use their advantage. When Cardinal Gibbons was pleading for the red hat for his friend Archbishop Ireland in the course of a visit to Leo's successor Benedict XV, he himself ingenuously reports, "I gave the Pope $5,000 additional in gold." But Ireland was never made a Cardinal, nonetheless.

What restraints had been applied to the Americanists seem to have originated principally in the Curia, for it is an open secret that Leo XIII, a political liberal, agreed with them on some of the advantages of democracy. We owe to Archbishop Keane the information that the Pope privately believed that a republic would be a better form of government for the Italians. This could hardly have been published without the Pope's knowledge. Immediately aware how this could "prove favorable to Americanism," Keane made the most of it. As for the heresy itself, the American diplomat's wife, Maria Longworth Storer relates in her husband's biography that Ireland told her in Rome on August 5, 1900: "The Pope told me to forget that letter on Americanism, which has no application except in a few dioceses in France!"

• • •

It would be a serious mistake to underestimate the role played by Americanism in the growth and influence of the U.S., the world's first purely secular state. There were in America no temporary restorations of monarchy, constitutional or otherwise, no sporadic religious revolts to cope with as in Europe. Except for the Civil War, from which the U.S. emerged more consolidated than ever, with states' rights forever gone, progress towards lock-step *nirvana* seems to have been uninterrupted. The only segments of the population which might have provided any real resistance to the creeping totalitarianism were the multi-national Catholics. Without their help or connivance, the Spirit of '76 might have had a rough time of it, especially after the Civil War, when their numbers became so overwhelming.

As we know, however, these potential counter-revolutionists were gradually harnessed to the wheels of the New Republic, not by the U.S. government, and certainly not by Rome, but by their own adoptive hierarchy. Not only did these not oppose the revolutionary secularism, they actively promoted it, ostensibly for a freedom of worship already guaranteed to all without exception by law! Had these different national strains been allowed to polarize around the Faith rather than around the Constitution, how would American history read today? How would the laws read? Would abortion be legal? Would godless public education, divorce and usury be running rampant? The direful "Catholic vote" so dreaded by the WASP has yet to materialize, but it still holds its terror for the Church's enemies, who have had experience of the supernatural power of the unity she alone possesses as the Mystical Body of Christ.

An article in *Smithsonian* magazine relates that the Know-Nothing *Almanac* for 1856 and a 1929 issue of the Masonic *New Age* featured the *San Patricios* as characteristic examples of Catholic disloyalty to the U.S. These were a company of soldiers, preponderately Irish and some of them deserters from the American forces, who fought the *Yanqui* invaders in the Mexican War under a green banner displaying St. Patrick, the harp of Erin and the shamrock. They numbered about 200, but the Mexican generals had expected thousands of Irish, French and German-Americans to come over to their side because of the many Roman Catholics among them and the strong anti-immigrant feeling then current in the U.S. Except for the *San Patricios*, nothing of the kind happened.

These fought fiercely in defense of the convent of San Mateo at Churubusco, thus prompting this Mexican account: "Their deportment deserves the greatest eulogies, since all the time the attack lasted they sustained the fire with extraordinary courage. A great many of them fell in action; while those who survived, more unfortunate than their companions, suffered soon after a cruel death or horrible torments, improper in a civilized age, and from a people who aspire to the title of illustrious and humane." Strange to relate, of the 50 captured and sentenced to hang by General Winfield Scott as deserters, only 7 acknowledged themselves Catholics on the scaffold and were later buried in consecrated ground. Where were the Catholics, so counted on by the Mexicans, so distrusted by the Americans?

Back in 1940 the illustrious Irish-American scholar and historian William Thomas Walsh had this to say of America in *Characters of the Inquisition:* "Here on the last edge and twilight of the world, the stage is set for the re-enactment of an ancient tragedy — or can it this time be a comedy? Here are all the actors who have appeared over and over again in that tragedy in Europe. Here we have most of the Freemasons of the world, most of the Jews, most of the gold and its masters. . . men gathered together from all nations under the sun, speaking one language, leading a common life; and among them heirs of all the isms and heresies that the Catholic Church has denounced throughout the centuries, and some millions of good bewildered folk who have ceased to believe much in anything. . . and scattered among these millions with their roots in the movements of the past, some twenty-five millions of Catholics.

"Now, either the Catholic body will come into sharp conflict with those about them or they will not.

"If they do not, it will be the first time in history that the Mystical Body of Christ. . . has not aroused violent and unreasoning antagonism. This has been so uniformly a characteristic of the life of Christ and the life of the Catholic Church, that when persons calling themselves Christian or Catholic do not meet with opposition, one may well begin to wonder whether they are profoundly Christian and truly Catholic. Perhaps then it is a reflection upon us Catholics that we have inspired so little antagonism (comparatively) thus far. Perhaps we have not been telling our neighbors the truth, the strong truth, the hard saying they will not like. . . "

Perhaps we have all become Americanists.

(Maybe not all of us. An editorial in the *Wall Street Journal* for December 14, 1978 took note of "A New Catholic Bigotry" on the horizon.)

THE
STAR-SPANGLED
CHURCH

PART I: *Karl Marx, Yankee*

Is a Communist a public sinner? Should he be classed among those designated by the Codex as the excommunicated, prostitutes, usurers, couples openly living in sin, blasphemers and the like? At least as late as 1925 this was no idle question. The French canonist Fr. Durieux, more liberal than many, held that a radical or a socialist would not, strictly speaking, be considered so. Nevertheless, "he would have to be refused Communion where people might look upon such a concession as approval of his error, or where he himself might be seeking this as a means of disguising the danger of his doctrine."

So rigorous an opinion draws indulgent smiles in chancery offices today, when freedom of conscience — and therefore error — soars above every commandment. After Pope John XXIII broke all precedent by officially receiving a Communist leader for the first time, with Paul VI following suit in 1967 by entertaining at the Vatican no less a personage than the President of the Soviet Union, the world has watched with little surprise the formation of a new political monster in the ranks of the faithful: the Christian-Communist. Like his predecessor the Christian-Democrat, who grew to maturity in the last century under the benevolent eye of the liberal Leo XIII, he is a walking contradiction pledged to irreconcilable allegiances. Doomed to serving two masters, like the Christian-Democrat he inevitably comes to love the one and to hate that Other. Needless to say, he is abundantly recruited from among those "moderates" who find virtue in compromise.

Not that papal pronouncements against Communism are lacking. Every instructed Catholic is familiar with Pius IX's definition, released two years before the Communist Manifesto: "That infamous doctrine of so-called Communism which is *absolutely contrary to the natural law itself,* and if once adopted would utterly destroy the rights, property and possessions of all men, and even society itself." Even Leo XIII, who finally opted for the "proletariat" as against the surviving monarchies, characterized Communism as "the fatal plague which insinuates itself into the very marrow of human society only to bring about its ruin." Pius XI declared, "Communism is *intrinsically evil,* and no one who would save Christian civilization may collaborate with it *in any undertaking whatsoever.* "

After Pius XII, silence on this subject on the part of the Popes. As we know, a petition from bishops at the Second Vatican Council formally to condemn Communism came to nought. On the contrary, official and semi-official dialogues between Catholics and Communists began immediately thereafter in Salzburg in 1965, followed by those in Assisi and Heerinchimsee the next year, and are now commonplace. Paul VI, addressing a Taiwanese delegation, extolled Chairman Mao's cultural revolution as "the dawn of the new times."

How well did the apostate priest Roca prophesy a hundred years before that, "The Vatican's convert will not need, according to Christ, to reveal a new teaching to his brothers. He will need to push neither Christianity nor the world into fully new paths, other than the paths followed by the peoples under the secret inspiration of the spirit, but simply to confirm them in this modern civilization. . . Because of the privilege of his personal infallibility, he will declare canonically *urbi et orbi* that the present civilization is the legitimate daughter of the holy Gospel of social redemption!"

Bishop Matagrin of Grenoble therefore explains, "There is no longer any question of excommunicating Christians adhering to Communism. The Church of Vatican II wishes to be attentive to the action of the Holy Spirit wherever it works." From this Council Roca had predicted there would come something which would stupefy the world: "This thing will be the demonstration of the perfect accord between the ideals of modern civilization and the ideals of Christ and His Gospel. It will be the consecration of the new social order and the solemn Baptism of modern civilization."

So now, in an article in *The New Catholic World,* (May-June, 1977) Catholic prelates like Dom Helder Camara of Brazil can openly exhort the faithful to "the study of the problem, at first sight contradictory and absurd, of the Christian-Marxist... If we regret to admit that in the past religion was and sometimes still is presented as an alienating force, nowadays there are, not only in Christianity but in all great religions groups which, far from accepting religion as an alienation, seek to live and bring religion to life as a liberating force for the oppressed and as a moral liberating pressure exercised upon the oppressors. This fact compels those who do not read Marx as a dogma to take a totally new attitude toward religion. Besides, nothing is more anti-Marx than the servile attachment to what he said and did, instead of trying to do and say what he would have said and done, faced with new situations." And so begins the Imitation of Marx.

• • •

Let us therefore see something of "what he said and did," this prophet of World Revolution, Freemason and Satanist, grandson of a Cologne Rabbi, son of a freethinking Jew named not Marx but Mordecai, co-author of the Communist Manifesto, wet nurse to the International, and personal friend of the leading occultists and revolutionaries of his day.

He himself quipped, "I, I am not a Marxist!" Indeed not, for like Masonry, Marxism was merely an instrument forged to secure a larger goal. He began his career as a member of the Jewish Union for Civilization and Science, whose purpose is well described in a passage quoted by Fr. Fahey in *The Mystical Body of Christ in the Modern World:* "The Jewish people taken collectively shall be its own Messias. Their rule over the universe shall be obtained by welding together the other races, thanks to the suppression of frontiers and monarchies, which form the bulwark of national peculiarities... In this new organization of humanity, the sons of Israel now scattered over the whole surface of the globe... shall everywhere become the ruling element without opposition. This will be particularly easy, if they succeed in imposing on the masses of the working classes the guidance of one of their number. The governments of the nations forming the Universal or World-Republic shall all thus pass without any effort into Jewish hands, *thanks to the victory of the proletariat.* "

This opens a vast subject, which we shall limit to the little-publicized part Marx played personally in the affairs of the United States, and the means Marxism used in that day to enlist the aid of the Catholic Church here. He correctly foresaw that our synthetic nation would easily "go Communist," for he knew better than anyone that Communism is the natural consequence of modern Democracy, on whose evils the red Revolution feeds. The false democratic principles condemned by the Popes from the beginning were specifically treated by Pope St. Pius X in his famous letter on the Sillon movement in France, leveled against the Christian Democrats; but it proved one of the last attempts to shut the Pandora's box opened to Communism by his predecessor Leo XIII.

It was too late. The Dom Helders would soon tell Catholics, "Fortunately, nowadays the Church no longer has power against heretics and anti-Christians," rejoicing that, "Karl Marx challenges our courage because he is a materialist, a militant atheist, an agitator, a subversive, an anti-Christian."

• • •

A contemporary of Abraham Lincoln near the same age, Marx took more than an academic interest in the Civil War and the "new birth of freedom" the President promised at Gettysburg, whereby "government of the people, by the people and for the people" condemned by Christ's Vicars "shall not perish from the earth." Aware that the outcome would affect the destiny of the whole world, Marx called it "the first grand war of contemporaneous history." A letter of congratulation to Lincoln on his re-election which Marx wrote on behalf of the General Council of the International Workingmen's Association, shows he recognized the Civil War as nothing else than the continuation of the American Revolution, whose Declaration of the Rights of Man "gave the first impulse to the European revolution of the eighteenth century."

By these "rights" the Revolution had relieved the thirteen colonies of their sovereignty and the independence from one another they had heretofore enjoyed, and reduced them to "states." By the Civil War these states in turn lost the last of their autonomy in the face of the juggernaut of despotic centralized government — including their right to withdraw from the Union. Marx specifically designates the Confederacy's "revolt" as a *counter-revolution*, seeing very well from his own world perspective that it was not the South, but the North — the Union — who were the revolutionaries. Ideologically, the Confederates were the lineal descendants of the faithful Tories who had fled by the thousands to Canada after 1776 and populated Ontario.

Marx' letter reads, "The workingmen of Europe feel sure that as the American War of Independence initiated a new era of ascendancy for the middle class, so the American anti-slavery war will do for the working classes. They consider it as an earnest of the epoch to come, that it fell to the lot of Abraham Lincoln, the single-minded son of the working class, to lead his country through the matchless struggle for the rescue of an enchained race and the reconstruction of a social world."

What Lincoln stood for was clear from the outset. When elected he did not receive a single vote from 10 of the 11 southern states. We can cite the authority of a prominent abolitionist, Wendell Phillips, to the effect that the Republican party, on whose ticket Lincoln ran, was "the first sectional party ever organized in this country. . . It is not national. The Republican party is a party of the North against the South."

Abolition was indispensable to Marx — not for any humanitarian reasons — he called slaves "niggers" repeatedly in his private correspondence — but because he saw it as the quickest way to destroy the American bourgeoisie. As opposed to 23 states in the North with a population of 22,000,000, the South had only 9,000,000, one third of whom were slaves. Once freed, these blacks might not only be turned against their Southern masters, but easily manipulated in their new role as "proletariat." Slavery was furthermore an insuperable obstacle to the militant labor movement needed to spark the next phase of the revolution. Not only did Marx feel that slavery threw manual labor into disrepute, but that it hindered the rise of man-made factories which were to re-make society in man's image. By destroying the primacy of agriculture, farming would be subordinated to industry. The new artificial system the latter was spawning was a veritable de-creation, where God's creatures would be inexorably replaced by man's fabrications. Its end can only be sterility and death, for "What is more wicked than that which flesh and blood hath invented !" (Ecclus. 17:30).

• • •

Unfortunately at this juncture in history, slavery was the only means, regrettable as it may have been, whereby an agricultural economy could hope to compete with an industrial one, and it was an institution supported as much by the North as by the South. The *London Economist* could not forbear noting that Abolitionists were persecuted as much in the North as in the South, and reminded its readers that the U.S. federal government had consistently impeded

English efforts to stop the slave trade on the African coast, slave trade clippers being "built with Northern capital, owned by Northern merchants and manned by Northern seamen." The North would have permitted the South to keep its slaves had it agreed to remain in the Union. The Civil War was not fought over slavery.

The U.S. has never achieved anything more than an appearance of unity, being an artificial association of disparate elements where, by the very nature of Democracy, the stronger merely impose their will on the others. In 1860 this became extraordinarily clear. Few Americans think of the Mason-Dixon line as an iron curtain, but the fact remains that the inhabitants south of it had to be kept in the "free and independent union" at gun point.

Even fewer realize that this was equally true in the North. The liberal Comte de Chambrun, an unofficial emissary to Lincoln paid by underground French forces with secret funds, writes to his wife in June, 1865, "To judge impartially. . . if New York, where the 'copperheads' (Southern sympathizers) were all powerful, if Philadelphia, if Washington had not been subjected to terrible pressures, civil war would have erupted in the North. It was inevitable. In 1864, while Lincoln was being re-elected, New York was threatening. Heavy precautions had to be taken; also, discretionary power was given to Butler, who has an iron hand; 30,000 men were concentrated in the city; 'monitors' with guns were brought into the harbor; before this display of force, the election was held very peaceably; nevertheless the results were wretched — a majority of 39,000 against Lincoln! The South is prey to a social revolution whose scope no one can measure yet. . . For myself, I sincerely believe only one kind of government is possible in the South at this hour: that of the sword, a military regime."

• • •

While pointing out that the Constitution provided for no right to secede from the Union, as a lawyer even Lincoln had to admit publicly that the federal government had no power under the same Constitution to compel a state to return. Southerners rested their case on the "right to revolution" guaranteed by the Declaration of Independence. In his inaugural address as President of the Confederacy, Jefferson Davis appeals to "the right solemnly proclaimed at the birth of the States, and which has been affirmed and re-affirmed in the bills of rights of the States subsequently admitted to the Union of 1789. This "undeniably recognizes in the people the power to resume the authority delegated for the purposes of government. Thus the sovereign States here represented proceeded to form this Confederacy; and it is by the abuse of language that their act has been denominated revolution." Even Marx's friend Engels put the Southern "rebellion" in quotation marks.

Impartial modern historians like Edward Channing of Harvard prefer to call the Civil War "the War for Southern Independence." Charles A. Beard, closer to Marx, called it the Second American Revolution. All agree today that slavery was an issue secondary to the graver and truer ones of states' rights and which way of life would be extended to the new western territories. Would they be agricultural or industrial? Conservative Catholic churchmen like Bishop Patrick Lynch of Charleston naturally sided wholeheartedly with the South. In 1861, in an exchange with Archbishop Hughes of New York, friend of Lincoln, he retorted, "The separation of the Southern States is *un fait accompli*. The Federal Government has no power to reverse it. Sooner or later it must be recognized. Why preface the recognition by a war needless and bloody?"

Alfred Iverson of Georgia, in his speech on Secession before the Senate in 1860, put it more bluntly: "Disguise the fact as you will, there is enmity between the Northern and the Southern people that is deep and enduring, and you can never eradicate it, never! Look at the spectacle exhibited on this floor. How is it? There are Republican Northern senators upon that side. Here are the Southern senators on this side. How much social intercourse is there between us?. . . Yesterday I observed that there was not a solitary man on that side of the chamber came over here even to extend the civilities and courtesies of life; nor did any of us go over there. Here are two hostile bodies on this floor; and it is but a type of the feeling that exists between the two sections. We are enemies as much as if we were hostile States. I believe that the Northern people hate the South worse than ever the English people hated France; and I can tell my brethren over there that there is no love lost upon the part of the South. . . I ask, why should we remain in the same Union together?"

This was plain speaking about a situation existing here from earliest colonial times, when the on-going English revolution between Roundheads and Cavaliers was transported wholesale to America. The Roundheads, with their short haircuts and clean-shaven faces, established themselves in the North, which became the seat of a tight-lipped, calvinist theocracy where Capitalism founded on rampant usury could flourish unhindered in a basically manichaean culture. Sex and alcohol were regarded as intrinsically evil, and virtue was rewarded by God with material prosperity. It was the logical terrain on which to begin Marxist agitation. In the South, alongside the Catholic cultures established by the French and Spanish in Louisiana and Texas, English Cavaliers and Jacobites, curled, bearded and unashamedly fun-loving (according to song and story) settled by instinct. Although most were Church of England, as in Virginia, these were far from considering themselves Protestants, whom they detested.

We must beware of separating North and South unilaterally into "bad guys and good guys," for Masonry was prevalent in both camps, even in the first days of the one English Catholic colony of Maryland — named after Henrietta Maria, French Catholic wife of Charles I. But facts are facts. One aspect of the Civil War which has been studiously ignored by establishment historians is its character as a *war of religion*. Protestants found themselves pitted against Catholics and Anglo-Catholics in a death struggle over two incompatible ways of life. The South retained far more vestiges of the old hieratic Christendom than did the North. Long before Iverson, Thomas Jefferson had predicted the Civil War in his Memoirs, noting the two incompatible cultures. Even in his day the South had resisted the movement toward the Constitution and had desired a Confederation, deeming the Constitution totalitarian and disparaging of states' rights.

The bulk of American Catholics at that period of our history were Southerners. Today one thinks of Catholic population concentrations as a Northern phenomenon, forgetting that these occurred only as a result of the heavy post-Civil War immigrations. Before that the reverse was true. Even in the North most Catholics were Southern sympathizers. "In a general way," wrote de Chambrun, "I believe the Catholic clergy. . . instinctively follow the European clergy; they have been conservative and South-oriented as much as can be imagined, and that for two reasons: the first is that the South was more favorable to Catholics than the Puritan areas; the second is that the clerical leaders espoused wholeheartedly the monarchical and aristocratic ideas of the slave-owners."

Catholic priests not tainted with Americanism, like the feisty Redemptorist Confederate Chaplain James Sheeran, had no hesitation in identifying the Faith with the Southern cause. Preaching the two together, he records in his Journal how he ministered to a detachment of Yankees burying their dead: "In my conversation with these men I found many of them were Catholics. These misguided, poor fellows on finding out who I was, were rejoiced to see me and seemed to forget for the moment that they were in the hands of the enemy. I conversed long and freely with them, disabusing their minds of many wrong ideas they had entertained with regard to the war and the people of the South."

On an another occasion he took "about an hour of my time" to introduce a Yankee captain "into a world of ideas altogether different from that in which he had hitherto been traveling. He denied that he was in favor of Lincoln's administration, maintaining that he was fighting only for the preservation of the Constitution. My parting advice to him was this: 'My very good man, before going to bed every night try and recall to your memory the number of times Abe Lincoln has perjured himself by violating the Constitution since his introduction into office; then put your hand to your breast and ask yourself in the presence of God, if in fighting for your perjured President, you are fighting for the Constitution of your country!'"

Karl Marx saw all this in terms of class struggle, the automatic dynamism of revolution and evolutionary change. He never called the opponents by their real names: the adulterated remnants of Christian society under God (still actually Catholic in many areas like Texas, Louisiana, Kentucky and Maryland), versus the one-world centralizing forces of the City of Man. He rarely used the word Christian, which for him was merely an outmoded stage of evolution.

According to Catholic teaching on true democratic institutions, power once delegated by the people cannot be retained by them, for they are not the authors of power, as both St. Thomas and St. Pius X declared. Although in their acts of Secession the Southern states invoked this false principle guaranteed them by the Declaration of Independence, the Confederacy was a true counter-revolution insofar as it opposed the Revolution's further progress by clinging to the remains of natural law. "Counter-revolution begins," says Jacques Vier, "when we re-integrate the Order which God assigns us once and for all in the universe."

South Carolina, first state to secede, dismissed the Constitution as "an experiment that failed." As the Chinese say, a wise man may sit on an ant-hill, but only a fool will stay there. Although the South had strayed from the truth, harboring Masonry and growing labor unions within its body, it remains that neither the Masonic eagle nor the Egyptian pyramid of the Illuminati ever figured on its seal as they did on the Union's. Furthermore the Confederate flag, the beloved "Stars and Bars", forms a *cross*, an emblem glaringly absent from all official U.S. iconography.

The success with which the North has since imposed its will upon the South, and the degree of homogeneity and cooperation now existing between these disparate sections of the country is a bald indication of the ruthless progress made here by the Revolution since Appomattox. We hear it said that the South has now become industrialized to the point where she might win if she tackled the North today, but what is left of her society worth fighting for?

• • •

AND WHERE WAS MARX IN ALL THIS? Believe it or not, one place he could be found was the columns of the *New York Tribune*. This daily's erratic founder Horace Greeley, whose brilliant political inconsistencies marshaled some 300,000 readers before he died insane, believed the South should be allowed to depart peacefully. This did not prevent him from preaching violent abolitionism and enforced temperance, nor from hiring Marx as a foreign correspondent and political analyst.

Their association dated from 1851, when the Tribune, hoping to gain German-American readers, asked Marx, then living in England, for a series of articles on Germany, still recovering from its abortive revolution of 1848-9. Marx accepted eagerly. He had been heavily involved in the German revolt, largely planned by him and his friends, and this was an opportunity to disseminate his ideas freely in a coming theater of operations. Few Americans know how many of these professional revolutionists subsequently fled to the U.S., learned English and then set to work here. The majority, if not all, were Jews like Marx. Needless to say, all threw their weight against the South, promoting the Union cause in every possible way here and abroad.

Among them was Friedrich Sorge, the German Communist who took part in the Baden uprising of 1849 and eventually became Secretary General of the International. He was in constant correspondence with Marx and Engels after coming to the U.S., where he was prominent in the labor movement. Hard-cores like Sorge were joined by bourgeois liberals like Frederick Kapp and the well-known Carl Schurz. This last was in communication with the secret French envoy de Chambrun, who speaks of him along with a Siegel and a Sedwich as revolutionists who in Germany "had distinguished themselves by the wildest opinions; forced to emigrate, they left for the United States, and fifteen years later, they hold substantial positions in the army because of their ardent abolitionism. I've had occasion to meet them and I was struck at seeing how much they feel at ease in the American constitutional regime... Thus here are men who were strangling in European irons, who suddenly realized their dream on entering the American society, without having to give up any of their ideas. These enemies of the established order in Prussia or Austria are quite unmolested here." Later he speaks to his wife of "the famous General Schurz, one of the highest placed of the radicals, a future senator, maybe even future Secretary of State..." Schurz did eventually become a senator from Missouri and Secretary of the Interior under President Hayes.

Some of these revolutionaries with military experience had indeed enlisted in the Union army, in which both factions of the old Communist League were represented, men like Bernstein, Anneke, Steffen, Willich and Weydemeyer, who wielded swords as well as pens. Marx said, "Without the considerable mass of military experience that emigrated to America in consequence of the European revolutionary commotions of 1848-9, the organization of the Union army would have required a much longer time" than it did. August Willich, a former Prussian artillery officer who resigned to join the German revolution, had pursued his activities in England, where he learned the carpenter's trade. Emigrating to the U.S. in 1853, he took up newspaper work, and at the outbreak of hostilities joined the Union army, made good and became a general. Marx wrote of him in *Revelations concerning the Communist Trial in Cologne:* " In the Civil War in North America Willich showed that he is more than a visionary." Indeed so. After the war he entered government service and occupied high positions in Cincinnati.

Joseph Weydemeyer, another former Prussian artillery officer, was also a writer who published in several German periodicals. He arrived in New York in 1851, where the next year he began a German language paper called *Die Revolution.* Only two issues appeared, but one contained the first printing of Marx' famous "Eighteenth Brumaire of Louis Bonaparte." The next year Weydemeyer helped form the Workingmen's League. He wound up a colonel in the Union army.

• • •

Correspondence between Marx and Engels recently published in English reveals how closely the subversives kept in touch. July 1, 1861, Marx reports to Engels, "In Missouri the defeat of the Southerners seems to be decisive, and the terrible 'Colonel Bernstein' has now turned up there too. According to a private letter to Weber, Colonel Willich is at the head of a corps from Cincinnati. He does not seem to have gone to the front yet." Like Willich — with whom Engels had fought in the Baden uprising — Bernstein was also an old '49-er. The Weber referred to was a Berlin lawyer friend of Marx.

By May 6, 1862, Marx exclaims to Engels, "Schurz is — a brigadier-general with Fremont!" A fortnight later Engels replies, "Anneke is with Buell's army, and from today is writing in the *Augsburger*. . . Willich is a colonel (the eternal colonel!) and commands the 32nd Indiana Regiment." On June 4 Engels says, "At last, then, we learn from Anneke's letter that counting Pope and Mitchell's forces, Halleck had rather more than 100,000 men and 30 guns on April 26, and that he was waiting for the arrival of Curtis and Siegel with further reinforcements. Up to April 29 the condition of the army seems to have been passable on the whole; A[nneke] says nothing about sickness." There follows a detailed analysis of the Union campaign.

" For the rest, Monsieur Anneke appears in his letters as the same old grumbling fault-finder who judges the army not according to circumstances and not according to the adversary either, but by the old, schooled European armies, and not even by these as they are, but as they should be. The blockhead ought, however, to think of the confusion that he himself must have experienced often enough in Prussian maneuvers." By September 10 Marx can write Engels, "Willich is a brigadier-general and, as Kapp has related in Cologne, Steffen is now to take the field also. It seems to me that you let yourself be swayed a little too much by the military aspect of things."

If the North didn't win right off, it certainly wasn't for lack of foreign help. On reading the foregoing correspondence, one can't help wondering whether any native Americans had any real say in Northern campaigns. It is estimated that tens of thousands of foreign born served the Union. Not all were former European revolutionaries, but a disturbing percentage of the upper echelons were, even apart from Marx' friends. No less than six major generals were born abroad, among them the cavalry expert Julius Strahel, winner of the Cross of Bravery in the Hungarian revolution and later of the Union's Congressional Medal of Honor. At least 19 brigadier generals were foreign-born. Curiously enough, the 82nd Illinois Regiment, commanded by Edward Salomon, had a company composed entirely of Jews, from which Salomon rose to his command. Sponsored by Chicago businessmen, it was the wealthiest in the army.

We might mention in passing that the play of international Jewish interests in the Civil War has long been known but little publicized. In 1959 a publication prepared by a Union War Veterans organization for the War's Centennial, particularly exposing the influence of the Rothschilds, made the headlines and drew fire from B'nai B'rith and the Anti-Defamation League. A descendant of General Grant's, who had approved its circulation, was induced to make a formal retraction of the charges cited, disclaiming any anti-Semitism.

There was also the Garibaldi Guard, the 38th New York, whose Colonel was the Hungarian George Utassy and whose ranks were a veritable foreign legion of European veterans. It flew the revolutionary Hungarian flag of red, white and green, and its regimental colors were some Garibaldi had planted in Rome in his attack against the Papal States. Utassy too had been offered a Union commission, as was General George Klapka, another hero of the Hungarian revolt. There were many others, including a Russian, General Ivan Turchin, who captured Huntsville, Alabama, fought at Chickamauga and commanded a cavalry division in the Army of the Cumberland.

The Confederacy also had foreigners under arms, but in nowhere such numbers, and their political persuasions were very different — apart from traitors like the Hungarian Adolphus Adler, who was eventually imprisoned and escaped to the North. The majority were Irish and French, many of the latter titled nobility with royalist backgrounds like Prince de Polignac, who managed to command an exceedingly wild bunch of Texans who called him "Polecat," but grew to love him after he, in retaliation, ordered them over rough country in search of these animals. Louisiana and the deep South had so many French in its ranks that in practice two official languages had to be recognized. To meet the needs of both, General Beauregard, himself of French extraction, coined an epithet both could use: *sacredamn.*

• • •

Despite the Union's initial military reverses and the sympathy of Christian Europe with the Confederacy, Marx never doubted the North would win in the end, for he correctly judged that the economic factors at play — not to mention the occult forces at work in every chancery — would prevent any European government from actually coming to the aid of the South. Our Civil War threatened panic in France and England, whose industries were by then almost totally dependent on our exports. Lack of cotton and grain drove France into crisis and further indebtedness to the Rothschilds. The Comte de Paris, the Duc de Chartres and Prince de Joinville, all liberals, actually went to America to fight for the Union.

Marx told *Tribune* readers (November 7, 1861) that these gentlemen were trying to curry favor with the French masses, who "connect the fight for the maintenance of the Union with the fight of their forefathers for the foundation of American independence. . . With them, every Frenchman drawing his sword for the national government appears only to execute the bequest of Lafayette." Marx' contempt for them is palpable. The *London Times* noted dourly that these Orleanist nobles "will derive no increase of popularity with the French nation from stooping to serve on this ignoble field of action." Which didn't stop the Comte de Paris from writing a book on the Civil War ten years later.

England's conservative government, which under Lord Palmerston, Lord Russell and Gladstone came near to declaring war against the Union over the Trent affair, was deterred — as Marx predicted — by England's greater need for the North's wheat than for the South's cotton, added to the huge anti-South "peace" demonstrations mounted by the English labor unions. Although these last stood to suffer most from a cotton shortage, and a Southern victory would have resulted in breaking the Northern blockade of Southern ports, professional organizers were able to persuade them of the contrary. In every country the policy of the unions was pro-Union, even within the Confederacy. In the North they filled the ranks of the militia and in some cases an entire labor organization would enlist as a body. One in Philadelphia passed the following resolution: "It having been resolved to enlist with Uncle Sam for the war, this union stands adjourned until either the Union is saved or we are whipped." Naive, and pathetic.

• • •

In a letter to Weydemeyer back in 1852 Marx had explained that "bourgeois society in the United States has not yet developed far enough to make the class struggle obvious and comprehensible." Eight years later he could tell Engels, "In my opinion, the biggest things that are happening in the world today are on the one hand the movement of the slaves in America started by the death of John

Brown, and on the other the movements of the serfs in Russia." Now at last the proletariat was nucleizing!

In October 1862 he writes, "The fury with which the Southerners have received Lincoln's Acts proves their importance. All Lincoln's Acts appear like the mean pettifogging conditions which one lawyer puts to his opposing lawyer. But this does not alter their historic content. . . Of course, like other people, I see the repulsive side of the form the movement takes among the Yankees; but I find the explanation of it in the nature of 'bourgeois' democracy. *The events over there are a world upheaval* ." In the same letter he observes astutely, "There is no doubt at all that morally the collapse of the Maryland campaign was of the most tremendous importance." Not only was Maryland one of the strategic border states upon whose control all depended militarily, but — a fact Marx elaborately ignores — Maryland was the citadel of official Catholic authority in the U.S., domain of the ranking prelate, the Archbishop of Baltimore. Catholicism, the hidden supernatural power deep in the Southern cause, was and still is Marxism's only real enemy.

A dispassionate reading of political oratory before the Conflict reveals the South had every expectation of withdrawing from the Union without a shot, but if the worst happened, she knew she had the nation's best professional soldiers, with a united people behind them. She was also aware that she had the moral support of every monarchy in the world and fully anticipated at least their financial aid, with perhaps a direct invasion of the North on the part of Mexico. Over and above all this, the South knew what it was fighting for, which the North as a whole did not, anti-war sentiment in the North being one of the greatest obstacles the Union had to contend with.

But Marx knew that humanly speaking an agricultural nation could not win against an industrialized one like the North. On this conviction he staked his whole theory of the means of production as the sparking agent in the class struggle which feeds revolution. The devil must be given his due. His articles in the *Tribune* during 1860-61 are masterpieces of political analysis. Not as proficient in English as his friend Engels, he asked the latter to write some of the articles for him, and sometimes incorporated whole sections from Engels' personal letters, especially regarding the military situation. As a former adjutant and serious student of military science, Engels was highly qualified in this area.

Marx writes him on one occasion, "I should be glad if you supplied me *this week* (by Friday morning) with an *English* article on the American War. You can write *entirely without constraint.* The *Tribune* will print it as the letter of a foreign officer. *Nota bene:* The *Tribune* hates McClellan." General McClellan, first chief of the Union forces, was relieved of command by Secretary Stanton, says Marx, for his Southern sympathies, being averse to fratricidal warfare and against Lincoln's arbitrary Emancipation Proclamation. In a Counter-proclamation to his army, McClellan forbade demonstration against Lincoln's measure, unpopular among many Yankees who thought Southerners should at least be reimbursed for the confiscation of their slaves, but he maintained, "The remedy for political errors, if any are committed, is to be found only in the action of the people at the polls." Obviously, McClellan had to go.

• • •

As a military strategist Engels was fascinated by the Richmond campaign and admired both General Grant and Grant's former professor at West Point, General Robert E. Lee, now opposing his erstwhile pupil on the battlefield as General-in-Chief of the Confederate forces. Engels dubbed Lee "an excellent example for the Prussians to study," and Stonewall Jackson "by far the best chap in America," who could win for the South if he had real support. The Union's General Pope he characterized as "the lousiest of the lot." "The lads in the South, who at least know what they want," writes he to Marx in 1862, "strike me as heroes in comparison with the flabby management of the North."

Berating Northern slackness and its want of true revolutionary spirit, he wrote again on November 5, 1862, "The defeats do not stir these Yankees up. . . Cowardice in government and Congress. They are afraid of conscription, of resolute financial steps, of attacks on slavery, of everything that's urgently necessary. . . In addition, the total lack of talent. One general more stupid than the other." And again, "I cannot work up any enthusiasm for a people which on such a colossal issue allows itself to be continually beaten by a fourth of its own population, and which after 18 months of war achieved nothing more than the discovery that all its generals are asses and all its officials rascals and traitors."

Engels paints the picture of a basically decent nation being driven to fight a war it knew was unjust, and which was unwanted except by a determined fanatical minority. It was the American Revolution all over again. One can't help sympathizing with the Union draftee more than with the Southern recruit. "The lads in the

South at least know what they want," is well put. By November he rages, "It is mortifying that a lousy oligarchy with only half the number of inhabitants proves itself just as strong as the unwieldy, great, helpless democracy. They [the North] are even capable of proclaiming Jeff Davis President of the United States forthwith and to surrender even the whole of the border states, if there is no other way to peace. Then, goodbye America!" Indeed America would have been lost to Marxism had the South won.

It is clear from such letters that war fury had to be artificially whipped up north of the Mason-Dixon line. As Jefferson Davis pointed out, "An agricultural people whose chief interest is the export of a commodity [cotton] required in every manufacturing country, [the Confederacy's] true policy is peace, and the freest trade which our necessities will permit. . . There can be but little rivalry between ours and any manufacturing or navigating community such as the northeastern States of the American Union" (Inaugural Address, 1861). There was no valid reason why North and South could not exist peacefully as separate entities.

● ● ●

Engels' contempt for America in general is as plain as Marx', the war for him being merely a phase of the Great Revolution, and the Northerners the best tools at hand for the moment: "One financial measure more lunatic than the other. Helplessness and cowardice everywhere, save among the common soldiers. The politicians in like case — just as absurd and devoid of counsel. And the *populus* is more helpless than if it lingered 3,000 years under the Austrian scepter. For the South, on the contrary — it's no use shutting one's eyes to the fact — it's a matter of bloody earnest." He particularly admired Southern diplomatic prowess, as well he might, for at first it looked as if all Europe would be drawn to their side. "Besides," he admits honestly, "they fight quite famously."

To these complaints Marx, the political expert and student of Clausewitz, rejoins that the North will win in the end, despite the fact that the Southerners "acted as one man from the beginning." He explains, "The long and short of the business seems to me to be that a war of this kind must be conducted along revolutionary lines, while the Yankees so far have been trying to conduct it constitutionally." The Yankees, it seems, didn't take to subversion naturally. But then, says Engels, "The manner in which the North wages war is only to be expected from a bourgeois republic, where fraud has so long reigned supreme. . . It is possible that it will come to a sort of revolution in the North itself first. . . If there were only some proof or indication that the masses in the North were beginning to rise as they did in France in 1792 and 1793, then it would all be very fine!"

• • •

This proved unnecessary. As early as 1862 the North was being trained "along revolutionary lines" by its imported leadership. Burke Davis, in *Our Incredible Civil War*, relates the following regarding the taking of Athens, Alabama by the aforementioned Russian General Turchin: "When the occupation was complete, Turchin assembled his cavalrymen in the town square and in his heavy accents advised them on Total Warfare: 'Now, boys, you stop in this rebel town this night and I shut mine eyes for von hours.' Soon afterward, seeing no signs of trouble, Turchin sent for his adjutant to ask if the place was being set afire. When the soldier reported that there had been no arson, Turchin said insistently, 'Well, tell the boys I shut mine eyes for von hours and a half.' At last the troopers fell to work, burned and looted the town. There were numerous reports of atrocities there, including rapine. Turchin fell into disrepute when the story was circulated, and he was court-martialled and dismissed from the service. His charming wife, however, was yet to be reckoned with. 'Mama' had already come to fame by commanding the regiment in battle when her husband was wounded. She took her case to Washington, and by a personal plea to Lincoln had Turchin restored to command, and advanced in rank."

The South had much sad experience of such tactics by the time General Sherman began his infamous march through Georgia to the sea, burning and pillaging everything in his path like a true forerunner of the Russian Cheka. Richard M. Weaver, in *The Southern Tradition at Bay*, points out,". . . There remains considerable foundation for the assertion that the United States is the first government in modern times to commit itself to the policy of unlimited aggression. This was one of the many innovations which came out of the Civil War" — along with "unconditional surrender" at Appomattox. "Generals Hunter, Sheridan and Sherman put themselves on record, both by utterance and practice, as believing in the war of unlimited aggression, in the prosecution of which they received at least the tacit endorsement of the Lincoln administration. . . a matter of prime importance. . . because the war of unlimited aggression strikes at one of the bases of civilization: " It eliminates rules in warfare. Specifically anti-Christian in character, it is a return to the barbarity reigning before the Incarnation.

A good example of the unregenerate reasoning behind "total war," now accepted as American on principle, is found in Sherman's answer to Atlanta's Mayor Calhoun's plea for the life of the city: "I . . . shall not revoke my orders, because they were not designed to meet the humanities of the case, but to prepare for the future struggles in which millions of good people outside of Atlanta have a deep interest. We must have peace, not only at Atlanta, but in all America. To secure this, we must stop the war that now desolates our once happy and favored country." President Truman reasoned in much the same way when he gave orders to drop the first nuclear bomb on what happened to be the most Catholic areas in Japan.

"You might as well appeal against the thunderstorm," said Sherman, "as against these terrible hardships of war. They are inevitable, and the only way the people of Atlanta can hope once more to live in peace and quiet at home, is to stop the war, which can only be done by admitting that it began in error and is perpetuated in pride." Thus were the conquered divested even of the testimony of their own consciences. Could Nuremburg have been far behind? Well has the Civil War been called the last of the medieval wars and the first of modern ones, for along with immoral theory it ushered in countless other innovations, even submarines and aerial reconnaissance. The South actually launched a two-stage rocket in the direction of Washington, D.C. with Jefferson Davis' signature on its head!

Sherman, beginning his march by boldly cutting his own supply lines to allow complete freedom of movement, lived off the enemy in what amounted to modern guerrilla warfare in uniform. Of the pillaging of helpless civilians he says shamelessly in his Memoirs, "The skill of the men in collecting forage was one of the features of this march. . . Although this foraging was attended with great danger and hard work, there seemed to be a charm about it that attracted the soldiers, and it was a privilege to be detailed on such a party. No doubt, many acts of pillage, robbery and violence were committed by these parties. . . " but then, as he also said, "War is hell." The sacrosanct Union was thus preserved at the price of any semblance of unity, but these details do not appear in establishment textbooks.

• • •

Again foreshadowing modern times, the first "war criminal" was hanged after it was all over. He was, of course, a Southerner, and he was a Catholic: the Swiss-born Dr. Henry Wirz, who rose from a clerkship in a Richmond prison to command of the Andersonville military prison in Georgia. Like Mary Surratt, hanged in April, 1865 for alleged complicity in Lincoln's assassination, Wirz walked to execution in the Old Capitol prison yard the following November, flanked by two Catholic priests. When his sentence was read in court he had said, "I'm damned if the Yankee eagle hasn't turned out to be what I expected, a damned turkey buzzard!"

To the major who asked him at the gallows whether he had some last words, Wirz replied, "I have nothing to say to the public, but to you I say I am innocent. I can die but once. I have hope for the future." His neck did not break when he fell to the end of the rope, so that he struggled in agony for seven minutes before dying. First buried near the Lincoln conspirators in the arsenal yard, his body now lies in Washington D.C.'s Mt. Olivet Catholic cemetery. In 1960, at the time of the War Centennial, an anonymous South Carolinian set up a stone at his grave reading, "Captain, C.S.A. Martyr." No such fate was suffered by Union personnel, even at the Union military prison at Fort Delaware, an infamous place some of which was below the water line of the Delaware River.

• • •

After 1862 the war news had crowded Marx' contributions from the pages of the *Tribune,* but he and Engels continued their Civil War reportage in *Die Presse* of Vienna. It is extremely significant that two full years before Sherman's decisive march, which successfully cut the Confederacy in two and insured Union victory, this specific strategy had already been worked out and revealed in the *Presse.*

On the whole Marx had been pleased with the progress of the Revolution, disguised as a war for preserving the Union. Of Lincoln, whose re-election he had considered a foregone conclusion, he rightly predicted, "In conformity with his legal manner, the old man will then find more radical methods compatible with his conscience." He dubbed his assassination "the greatest piece of folly (the Southerners) could commit." Such great folly indeed that a century later few historians believe they had anything to do with it, for as Marx himself allows, Lincoln's successor Johnson "is stern, inflexible, revengeful, and as a former poor white has a deadly hatred of the oligarchy. He will stand less on ceremony with the poor fellows, and through the assassination he finds the temper of the North adequate to his intentions."

The rabid Northern contingent, realizing Lincoln intended leniency to the vanquished, and expecting ruthlessness from Johnson, had actually stronger motives for killing the President than the Southerners, and especially Southerners like Mary Surratt and her acquaintances who were hanged for the crime. Johnson's about-face on assuming office may have contributed materially to his impeachment. As it was, sentiment was high. The Comte de Chambrun wrote his wife, "The President's assassination has been an excuse for indescribable reprisals. Yesterday I met an officer coming from Sherman's camp: at the time the tragic news came out there were 400 rebels in the camp's prisons. The army, with no human force able to stop it, literally threw itself upon them; in a few moments only one survivor remained." As for Lincoln himself, the Comte opined he departed this life just in time to "save his halo." He would be hailed a martyr.

• • •

"After the Civil War phase," Marx writes Engels in 1866, "the United States are really only now entering the revolutionary phase, and the European wiseacres who believe in the omnipotence of Mr. Johnson will soon be disillusioned." Somehow, Marx always knew.

The lines for "the revolutionary phase" were laid without delay. The previous November a mass meeting of workers had adopted the following resolution at Faneuil Hall in Boston: "We rejoice that the rebel aristocracy of the South has been crushed, that ... beneath the glorious shadow of our victorious flag men of every clime, lineage and color are recognized as free. But while we will bear with patient endurance the burden of the public debt, we yet want it to be known that the workingmen of America will demand in future a more equal share in the wealth their industry creates... and a more equal participation in the privileges and blessings of those free institutions, defended by their manhood on many a bloody field of battle."

Thus, inspired and coached by Karl Marx and his lieutenants, thousands of hardworking Americans began laying the groundwork for a new slavery encompassing all creeds and colors which would some day make the slavery of the South look very humane and kindly by comparison. Universal economic slavery, now unhampered by the antiquated Christian ideals of the Confederacy, was to be the lot of all Americans.

By the turn of the century Lenin saw fit to congratulate them in his "Letter to the American Workers," praising them for their contribution to the great cause by their "war of liberation against the British in the 18th century and the Civil War in the 19th century." The bloody massacre of the South, last political foothold of Christ the King in the United States, Lenin called "world historic, progressive and revolutionary." He should know.

PART II: *Meanwhile, back at the Vatican. . .*

There is no getting around the fact that the only foreign power to recognize the Confederacy and receive its envoys was the Vatican, from whose vantage point in the already threatened Papal States the issues could be distinguished with excessive clarity. When the U.S. authorities remonstrated with the Vatican Secretary of State Cardinal Antonelli for providing asylum to Confederates, according to an official report the Cardinal replied that he "intended to take such rebels under his special protection." Mary Surratt's son John, sought for complicity in Lincoln's assassination, was even admitted into the Papal Zouaves. The Southern envoy Dudley Mann found the Cardinal "bold, resolute, and a great admirer of President Davis," and was told, "*Mon cher,* your government has accomplished prodigies alike in the Cabinet and in the field."

Bearer of a letter from Jefferson Davis to Pius IX, Mann, who was received in private audience, tells us he took care as it was being translated to His Holiness "to carefully survey the features of the Sovereign Pontiff. A sweeter expression of pious affection, of tender benignity, never adorned the face of mortal man. . . Every sentence of the letter appeared sensibly to affect him. At the conclusion of each he would lay his hand down upon the desk and bow his head approvingly."

In his reply to the "Illustrious and Honorable Jefferson Davis, President of the Confederate States of America," written in Latin, the Pontiff stated, "It has been very gratifying to Us to recognize, illustrious and honorable sir, that you and your people are animated by the same desire for peace and tranquility which We had so earnestly inculcated in Our aforesaid letter." [This communication, in which Lincoln was referred to as a tyrant and usurper, had been addressed to the Archbishops of New York and New Orleans.] "Oh, that the people also of the States and their rulers, considering seriously how cruel and deplorable is this intestine war, would receive and embrace the counsels of peace and tranquility!"

When J.T. Soutter, another Southern diplomat, told the Pontiff, "The Confederate Government was fully aware of what His Holiness had done in our behalf, and that no European power had evinced such *active* sympathy as he had shown from the beginning of the struggle," Pius rejoined that "he had done all that he could, and regretted that he had not been able to do more." When Soutter expressed the hope that papal pressure might be exerted to dispose other European sovereigns to recognize the independence of the Confederacy, the Pope replied that he "would not like to meddle in the affairs of other governments by any direct action, but that it would give him pleasure to state to the various Ambassadors here what his mind was on the subject of American affairs, that his great desire was to see an end of the horrid war now desolating America, and nothing he could do to obtain that object would be left undone."

Soutter "came away convinced that the Pope was our earnest friend, not only in the interest of humanity, but because he thought we had justice and right on our side." These quotations may be read at length in *Messages and Papers of the Confederacy.*

• • •

In October 1846, two years before the fateful "year of revolutions" which saw revolt breaking out not only in Germany, but simultaneously in almost every nation of Christendom, our Lord had appeared to Sr. Marie de St. Pierre, the Carmelite of Tours, France, to whom He had confided the devotion to the Holy Face, and foretold that He would now chastise the sinful world not by natural catastrophes, but especially by "the malice of revolutionary men." The previous month at La Salette, His blessed Mother had already predicted that by "the year 1864 Lucifer, together with a great number of devils, will be loosed from hell."

How much of the Union strategy Lucifer may have worked out with the help of his underlings can't be ascertained, but it's history that in 1864 the tide turned irrevocably against the South, and the only movement even approaching a counter-revolution in the U.S. was thrown decisively off course. In that same year it's also history that Karl Marx was instructed by the International to draft the seldom mentioned letter of congratulation to Lincoln on his re-election. It read, "The working classes of Europe understood at once, even before the fanatic partisanship of the upper classes for the Confederate gentry had given its dismal warning, that the slaveholders' rebellion was to sound the tocsin for the general holy crusade of property against labor, and that for the men of labor, with their hopes for the future, even their past conquests were at stake in that tremendous conflict on the other side of the Atlantic."

Whereas many Americans, especially in the North, had no idea of the global import of their domestic dissension or the true causes of it, all Christian Europe was watching the developments in America with horrified fascination. Already at the time of the Communist Manifesto Sr. St. Pierre related how our Lord told her that "the Society known as the Communists had so far made only one outbreak, but that they were working secretly to advance their schemes." He added, "Oh, if you only knew their secret and diabolical plots and their anti-Christian principles!"

Later Sr. St. Pierre says, "Our Lord commanded me to make war on the Communists because He said they were the enemies of the Church and of her Christ. He told me also that most of these wolfish men who are now Communists had been born in the Church, whose bitter enemies they now openly declare themselves to be." And again, "They are the ones who have dragged Me from My tabernacles and desecrated My sanctuaries."

The war Sr. St. Pierre was to initiate among the faithful would be spiritual, but hard, and of long duration. Indeed, during the reign of Pius IX, whose accession occurred the same year as these apparitions at Tours and at La Salette, Lucifer's troops had already gained a physical foothold in the citadel itself. The papacy was soon engulfed in it's own Civil War, the outcome of which was to be the irretrievable loss of its states and temporal sovereignty. Hailed as the liberal Pope so long awaited by the forces of progress, Pio Nono unfortunately reinforced this impression in the early years of his pontificate by granting blanket amnesty to previous political offenders and what amounted to a constitutional government with freedom of the press to the Papal States. The rumor dies hard that he had even been initiated into Italian Masonry in the over confidence of his youth, a calumny still circulated by Masons today, despite the fact that it has been disproved many times, and that Pius IX's formal, indignant denial is of record.

Forced to flee in disguise to Gaeta when Mazzini's revolutionaries occupied Rome and brutally murdered the papal Premier Count Rossi (apparently disregarding our Lady's injunction not to leave the Eternal City after 1859) he made a complete political about-face, having learned the hard way what trusting benevolence toward this kind of foe produces. "Universal suffrage, universal falsehood!" he would exclaim. Long before he died he had earned the title " Scourge of Liberalism," along with a reputation for sanctity.

Unfortunately the trend first set proved irreversible. According to the Marquis de la Franquerie, during the reign of Pius' successor Leo XIII, a Masonic Lodge was successfully established within the very confines of the Vatican itself by Leo's Secretary of State Cardinal Rampolla, which drew into the ranks of the enemy many sons of the Church even down to the present day. Now the post-Vatican II exposure of certain prelates as Masonic initiates, far from eliciting any official denials, has only resulted in the lifting of the 200-year ban of excommunication until now leveled against Catholics joining lodges.

• • •

It was also during Pius IX's pontificate, in the same dread year 1864 designated by our Lady, that the old Counter-Reformation came to a thundering close with the promulgation of the Encyclical *Quanta cura* and the famous *"Syllabus* of the principal errors of our time, which are censured in the consistorial Allocutions, Encyclicals and other Apostolic Letters of our Most Holy Lord Pius IX." It was dated appropriately on the Feast of the Immaculate Conception, whose dogma this Pope had defined ten years previously. To all appearances, the battle waged so valiantly for over 300 years against the modern Reformers by some of the Church's greatest saints and martyrs had failed. No St. Ignatius, no St. Teresa, no St. Robert Bellarmine had succeeded in really stemming the tide. Routed here and there in brilliant skirmishes, the enemy now loomed larger and stronger than ever, it would seem, turning the weakening soldiers of Christ in every greater numbers against their own brethren. The dragon of the Apocalypse had indeed been given power "over every tribe, and people, and tongue, and nation" (Apo. 13:7).

What had really happened, however, is that the Counter-Reformation had simply disappeared with the so-called Reformation. The battle was entering the decisive final stage we are becoming so familiar with today, for Pius IX brought the issues out into the open for all to see. Today still, it is by his telltale embarrassment at any mention of the *Syllabus* that the false Catholic betrays his affiliation to the Father of lies. How often has the world been assured by these false brethren that the *Syllabus* was a "mistake," an unfortunate political blunder, and that anyway it no longer applies to the current situation. Actually, of course, it applies more closely than ever.

Louis Veuillot, the great orthodox editor of *L'Univers,* exulted at the time," Rome is officially taking the reins into her hands!" In England Gladstone called the issuance of the *Syllabus* "the gravest event since the French uprising in 1789." The last four of its eighty condemned propositions certainly cut the ground once and for all from under the feet of "liberal Catholics", who, like the compromisers in every age, sought to serve two warring masters by presuming they would soon be one:

> *77. In the present day it is no longer expedient that the Catholic religion should be held as the only religion of the State, to the exclusion of all other forms of worship. (Allocution *Nemo vestrum,* July 26, 1855)
> *78. Hence it has been wisely decided by law in some Catholic countries that persons coming to reside therein shall enjoy the public exercise of their own peculiar worship. (Allocution *Acerbissimum,* Sept. 27, 1852)
> *79. Moreover, it is false that the civil liberty of every form of worship, and the full power, given to all, of overtly and publicly manifesting any opinions whatsoever and thoughts, conduce more easily to corrupt the morals and minds of the people and to propagate the pest of indifferentism. (Allocution *Nunquam fore,* Dec. 15, 1856)
> *80. The Roman Pontiff can, and ought to reconcile himself and come to terms with progress, liberalism and modern civilization." (Allocution *Jamdum cernimus,* Mar. 18, 1861)

By anathematizing those holding such opinions, Pius IX branded liberalism as a sin of mortal variety, "of the mind, and a supreme insult to God," as Fr. Denis Fahey later put it. "The direct result of liberalism is anarchy or tyranny." It is a "moral pestilence" according to Cardinal Merry del Val, and capable of hatching any evil. Politically it has engendered both Socialism and Communism, which Pius IX was the first Pope to mention by name. He warned the faithful against it in his inaugural Encyclical *Qui pluribus,* keynote of his entire pontificate, issued two years before the Communist Manifesto and still in his so-called "liberal" days: "Communism is completely opposed to the natural law itself, and its establishment would entail the complete destruction of all property and even human society" (September 11, 1846). Years later his successor Pius XI was still warning, "Bear in mind that the parent of this cultural Socialism is Liberalism, and that its offspring will be Bolshevism." And the famous words in *Quadragesimo anno:* "Religious socialism, Christian socialism, are expressions implying a contradiction in terms. No one can be at the same time a sincere Catholic and a socialist properly so called."

But these are details. Seven years after the *Syllabus,* Pius IX had exclaimed to a French deputation, "Believe me, the evil I denounce is more terrible than the Revolution, more terrible even than the *Commune.* I have always condemned liberal Catholicism, and I will condemn it forty times over if it be necessary!"

• • •

Christ's declared enemies found the *Syllabus* singularly clear and unambiguous in its terminology. They knew they had been recognized and that now the fight would gain in intensity what it had lost in extension after the Church's monumental losses in lands and numbers of fighting men. Some civil governments categorically forbade by law the reading of the *Syllabus;* others required special government permission to publish it.

In America, the Chicago *Tribune* saw only too well that the *Syllabus* was "directly in conflict with the Constitution of the United States and of every state in the Union" (January 19, 1865). In a dissertation entitled "American Public Opinion on the *Syllabus,* " Sr. Agnes Battersby, SSJ, noted in 1952 that the *Tribune* "pointed out that the Pope had required all civil governments to make a distinction between 'true religion and heresy.' This, the journal stated, meant between Catholicism on the one hand, and Protestantism and Judaism on the other. If the penalties of the law had to be inflicted on violators of the Catholic religion it would be in direct opposition to one of the most valued clauses of the Constitution, namely, that 'Congress shall make no law respecting an establishment of religion or prohibiting the free exercise thereof. . . ' Then the Constitution of the United States is Heresy, and no Roman Catholic can swear to support it, or can hold office, etc."

As might be expected, it was only the liberal Catholics who seemed to be unable to understand the *Syllabus*, indulging in endless qualifications and interpretations of its text. In January 1865 the Hartford *Daily Courant* quoted the Catholic imperial newspaper *La France* as saying, "The persons most devoted to the cause of the Holy See have asked themselves, with surprise and regret, what could have been the object of an act which would revive, in the 19th century, in the presence of the advancement everywhere made by liberal ideas, the doctrines of the middle ages on the subordination of the civil power to the supremacy of the Pope, and which condemns the first and most essential of liberties — religious liberty?" Of course *Quanta cura* had already excoriated this objection, "that the will of the people, manifested by what they call public opinion, or in any other way, constitutes the supreme law, independent of all divine and human right, and that, in the political order, *accomplished facts, by the mere fact of having been accomplished, have the force of right."*

The New York *Tribune*, whose columns had harbored Marx and Engels, could be counted on to locate the seat of major opposition to the *Syllabus*. At the close of the Civil War this paper ran an editorial labeled "American Ideas in Europe", in which its readers were told: "One of the most interesting features in the modern history of Europe is the conflict between this American notion (the right of every man to the untrammeled profession of his religious views) and the opposing views which formerly prevailed in every European country. The American principle has almost everywhere to record an uninterrupted series of successes. England has emancipated the Catholics; Sweden has revised her proscriptive laws; Switzerland is effacing from her code the last remnant of religious intolerance — her laws against the Jews. Holland and Denmark have gone nearly the whole length of the American principle. Religious toleration as a principle is admitted by every Protestant country. The Roman Catholic countries have remained but little behind the Protestant. Belgium has inscribed the principles of equal civil rights for all religious sects in her constitution, and in France, Italy and Austria, this principle has nearly secured an equal recognition. . .

"It is the process of this Americanization of Europe which the recent Encyclical of the Pope laments, condemns, and orders all the Bishops of Europe to combat. The free exercise of non-Catholic forms of worship are condemned in the most emphatic manner. Governments of entirely Catholic countries are reminded that immigration of Protestant settlers should not be encouraged by the offer of freedom of worship" (Feb. 9, 1865, quoted by Sr. Battersby).

Consternation reigned in the ranks of the Americanist Catholic clergy, for whom the "Americanization of Europe" as preached by the Catholic-convert-from-Unitarianism, Orestes Brownson, was very nearly an article of faith. Archbishop Ireland, a former Union chaplain dubbed "the Antichrist of the North" by the German-American faithful, wrote in panic to his nephew in Rome requesting him to ask Cardinal Antonelli for "clarification" of Propositions 55, 77, 78 and 79 — as well he might, for there was no getting around them as they stood. Proposition 55, drawn from *Acerbissimum*, condemned the notion that, "The Church ought to be separated from the State, and the State from the Church," — to which Americanists not only subscribed personally, but actively promoted among their flocks.

He expressed fear that the Pope's words might "be construed here as condemning our system of religious toleration, so advantageous. . . to religion," and that they would "furnish a pretext to the fanatics to persecute us." As if, suddenly, this were not the normal consequence of preaching the true Faith! He was only one of many who tried to explain away the *Syllabus* at the time. Bishop James Roosevelt Bayley, relative of Mother Seton, deplored the lack of distinction made between civil liberty and the choice of religion before God.

Archbishop Spalding of Baltimore, the ranking prelate, qualified the condemnation of freedom of worship by arguing that this referred only to "the right of introducing false religion into a country where it does not exist," that such freedom in itself is "not only not censurable, but commendable, and the only thing practicable in countries like ours." He maintained that he defended the Pontiff and his Encyclical, but did so "from the American standpoint." He held the *Syllabus* was not intended to apply to America with its free Constitution, but only to the "false liberalism" of Europe, that there was no opposition between our democratic institutions and the Roman strictures, etc., etc.

The New York Times, seeing the situation from its own avowed liberal position without ambiguity, told its readers that the Archbishop had openly declared his opposition to Rome. To our shame, in the next century an anti-Catholic writer like George Seldes was able to write, "It is a fact that American Catholics — and only Americans — claim that the *Syllabus of Errors* is not a law for members in any part of the world. . . It is only in the United States that the democratic principle is accepted wholeheartedly by the

Catholic Church, as well as its 21,000,000 Catholics" *(The Catholic Crisis)*.

This despite the fact that the *Syllabus* was delivered *ex cathedra*, its condemnations most solemn: "By Our Apostolic Authority, We reprove, We proscribe, We condemn, We desire that all children of the Catholic Church hold as reproved, proscribed and condemned, each and every evil opinion and doctrine pointed out in detail in these present letters." Not to be overlooked is that this pronouncement was renewed and confirmed by Pius' successor Leo XIII, who despite his compromising *praxis*, remained dogmatically irreproachable.

Many years later the Englishman Evelyn Waugh explained where the trouble lay in America. Following a visit to the U.S., he wrote in *Life* magazine for Sept. 19, 1949: "It could be quite plausibly argued that the people of the United States are resolutely anti-Catholic. Although most of the great adventures of exploration in the new continent were made by Catholic missionaries, the first colonists (everywhere except in Maryland) were Protestants whose chief complaint against their mother country was that she retained too much traditional character in her Established Church. School textbooks do not make much of the fact, which research abundantly proves, that it was the Quebec Act, tolerating Popery in Canada, quite as much as the Stamp Act and the Tea Duties, which rendered George III intolerable to the colonists. The Constitution-makers little thought that in separating Church and State they were laying their country open to the prodigious Catholic growth of the nineteenth century, and. . . the Supreme Court has shown in the McCollum case, that the phrase may be interpreted to the Church's injury [A 1948 decision barring religious instruction in any public school buildings]. In foreign policy, when religious questions were involved, America has usually supported the anti-Catholic side, particularly where she is most powerful, in Mexico. President Wilson did nothing to oppose the disastrous anti-Catholic prejudices of the peace-makers of 1919.

"Moreover the individual qualities that are regarded as particularly characteristic of Americans, their endemic revolt against traditional authority, their respect for success and sheer activity, their belief that progress is beneficent, their welcome of novelties, their suspicions of titles and uniforms and ceremonies, their dislike of dogmas that divide good citizens and their love of the generalities which unite them, their resentment of discipline — all these and others are unsympathetic to the habits of the Church.

"... The United States does not form part of Christendom in the traditional sense of the word. She is the child of late eighteenth century 'enlightenment' and the liberalism of her founders has persisted through all the changes of her history and penetrated into every part of her life. Separation of Church and State was an essential dogma. Government, whatever its form, was looked upon as the captain of a liner, whose concern is purely with navigation. He holds his command ultimately from the passengers. Under his immediate authority the public rooms of his ship are used for religious assemblies of all kinds, while in the bar anyone may quietly blaspheme ..."

• • •

By 1869, at the First Vatican Council, called to proclaim the dogma of Papal Infallibility, the ideological conflict in ecclesiastical America's upper air was approaching paroxysm. One American Bishop proudly declared at the Council, "Now I know of an assembly rougher than our own Congress." Four American prelates threatened to return home and publish their arguments against Infallibility if the dogma was proclaimed by acclamation as first proposed. A vote was duly taken supporting the definition, but even so, a large number of dissenters left Rome before the final solemnity rather than pronounce the public *Placet* traditionally required from all during the official ceremonies.

The old Counter-Reformation and its "constitutional" preoccupations had by now been left far behind. Parrying the movements of the enemy, it was now plunging into the "revolutionary phase" hailed by Marx with the outbreak of our Civil War. The Catholic Counter-*Revolution* had begun, the stage of struggle we are engaged in today, within the Church herself. Hand to hand, toe to toe, every man fights virtually on his own on a shifting terrain where boundaries have been obliterated and it becomes increasingly difficult to tell friend from foe. But with this difference, however: With the dogma of Infallibility defined, there now exists an infallible test whereby the simplest Catholic can detect a false Pope: He would be one who speaks heresy *ex cathedra*. Evidently the Holy Ghost foresaw there would be need.

During the Council Pius IX had pled, "Be united to me, and not with the Revolution!" He had deplored, "We are surrounded by great difficulties, for some, like Pilate when terrified by the Jews, are afraid to do right. They fear the Revolution. Though knowing the truth, they sacrifice all to Caesar, even the rights of the Holy See and their attachment to the Vicar of Christ. . . We have in the Council the organs of the Liberal party, whose word of command is to gain time by opposing everything, and to wear out the patience of the majority." Thus matters stood a century ago.

Louis Veuillot, fervent chronicler of the Council, had rightly predicted, "The day that the Council is convoked, *The Counter-revolution will commence.* . . Pius IX will open his mouth and the great word, 'Let there be light,' will proceed out of his lips. . . It will be a solemn date in history; it will witness the laying of the immovable stone of Re-construction. . . At the voice of the Pontiff the bowels of the earth will move, to give birth to the new civilization of the Cross . . . For centuries Rome has not seen the Pope in such splendor, nor has he so manifestly appeared in his character as head of the human race."

And so it proved, for the First Vatican Council was far from the failure its enemies would make it out to be. We need only quote a prejudiced Protestant divine like Geddes MacGregor. A Scot teaching religion at Bryn Mawr, he admitted as late as 1957 that the definition of papal infallibility, which he termed "the Vatican Revolution of 1870," had injected new vigor into the Church. "The new spirit, with its strongly Jesuitical preoccupations, transformed piety in all lands. Zealous Roman Catholics increasingly seemed almost to enjoy the idea of the Pope 'clamping down' on recalcitrant members, as if this reassured them of the vitality of the Church. . . There is no doubt that despite the defections and lapses that are a constant grief to the hierarchy, Roman Catholicism has flourished since 1870 in comparison with almost all other types of Christianity, especially among the masses.

"Since there are virtually no countries in the world where it could be shown that the fortunes of the Roman Church might have in any way suffered from the decrees of the (First) Vatican Council, and since the contrary is in many cases so abundantly evident, it is only to be expected that Roman Catholics should see, as they do, the hand of God in the Vatican decrees. The gloomy prognostications of the so-called Inopportunist party [those who opposed the definition] have seemed very ill-founded. "

The fervor sparked by the Council had to be dampened at all costs. " Christians in the United States of America are in a position of unique opportunity, " Dr. MacGregor noted, " for if the papalist program is defeated here it is unlikely it will be triumphant elsewhere, and the Roman Church throughout the world will be obliged to re-examine her own constitution. " This, of course, is precisely what happened. The Luciferian forces at the very gates of the Vatican had succeeded in interrupting the First Council, hailed by Veuillot as the opening of the Counter-Revolution. To this day it has been neither resumed nor officially terminated. Its business is still pending. Instead, a Second Vatican Council was convened in the fateful 1960's, a "pastoral" one whose impetus was destined to come not so much from the Rhine flowing into the Tiber, as sometimes alleged, as from the Potomac!

But Veuillot's words ring as true as ever: "It is Baptism which constitutes humanity, and all that has not been introduced into the Church by Baptism is, in reality, only a sort of raw material which as yet awaits the breath of life. " Civil power must be subject to the Church as the body to the soul. To reverse this order is subversion by definition, and the result is chaos. This great journalist also spoke of the Holy Stair in Rome and the *triclinium* where Charlemagne received the sword kneeling, designating the place and form of his throne : " When the world merits to re-enter on the path of unity, God will raise up a man, or a people, which will be Charlemagne. This Charlemagne, man or nation, will be seen here at the Lateran kneeling before the Pope, returned from dungeons or from exile; and the Pope will take the scepter of the world off the altar and put it into his hands."

Lest we forget, the Coronation of a Pope was traditionally accompanied by the words, " Take Thou the tiara adorned with the triple crown, and know that Thou art the Father of princes and of kings, and art the Governor of the world !" This why the Sacred Heart told Sr. Claire Ferchaud at the time of the First World War that there would be no true peace until His Vicar took part at the conference table.

• • •

Thus, as the astute French diplomat Joseph de Maistre once remarked, "The attacks against the Catholic edifice *always* grow stronger; one is *always* mistaken when one says that things can get no worse." His pessimism is being daily borne out. Now in each one of us the Church "is going up to Jerusalem" to be crucified. The "new civilization of the Cross" Veuillot foretold has indeed begun, through which the Church will be purified for battle.

Spotless bride of Christ, she conforms her life entirely to Christ's on earth, following the example of our Lady, her Mother and His. Because here below she re-enacts mystically all His mysteries from Bethlehem to Golgotha, she too must look forward to dying on the Cross erected by her enemies with the help of the secular power. Like her Lord, she will appear to have been destroyed by them. Marie-Julie Jahenny, visionary of La Fraudais, predicted that for a time there would remain " no vestige of the Holy Sacrifice, no apparent trace of faith."

As with Christ her Head, however, we can expect the Church to have her resurrection, and like His, it will be a historic, but entirely miraculous event, taking place when God wills and by His power alone. This would not be the end of the world, as some believe, for it is congruous in the Church's case to expect something analogous to Christ's own " forty days " on earth after the Resurrection, during which the faithful, supernaturally enlightened and rejoicing in His presence, can practice their faith unopposed amid the ever present unbelievers, who are never capable of seeing manifestations of Christ in the world, whether at the Tomb or on the shores of Tiberias.

We may piously believe that this is what our Lady meant when she predicted at Fatima that her Immaculate Heart would triumph, when the Apostles of the Latter Times revealed to St. Grignion de Montfort, Melanie of La Salette and others like Marie-Julie, would set to work re-evangelizing the world after the Church's purifying Crucifixion. Crushed and mutilated, bled and spent, she will destroy Antichrist the same way her divine Lord chose to destroy Satan's power on Calvary. And in her too will the same Messianic prophecy be fulfilled: "You shall not break a bone of Him" (John 19:30). Wounded only in her flesh, she will persist intact in her invisible structure. When she rises, the world will see that the " institutional" Church is quite as immortal as the " charismatic" one. Her final ascension to glory will spell the end of this foolish world. Our Lord told us this will be sudden, expected by no one, occurring while the world, as ever, goes about its business of marrying, tilling and grinding - as if time were eternity.

To hasten the day, our Lord told Sr. St. Pierre a year before her death (in the odor of sanctity) in 1848, what weapons she must use: "I have already told you that I hold you in My hands as an arrow. I now want to hurl this arrow against My enemies. To arm you for the battle ahead, I give you the weapons of My Passion, that is My Cross, which these enemies dread, and also the other instruments of My tortures. Go forward to meet these foes with the artlessness of a child and the bravery of a courageous soldier. Receive for this mission the benediction of the Father, of the Son and of the Holy

Ghost."

And again, "Think now, My daughter, of the outrages inflicted by this Society of Communists. . . These Communists have also dared to lay their hands on the priests of the Lord, but all their plotting is in vain, because their schemes will not succeed. Have they not committed the crime of Judas? They have sold Me for money! This information must not remain fruitless in you, because I am giving you these facts in order to fire you with new enthusiasm to carry on the fight. Act in a spirit of simplicity, because if you indulge in too much human reasoning, you will not be an adequate tool in My hands. Think rather of the glory that will be offered Me by the whole heavenly court for having conquered such formidable enemies with such a puny instrument!"

This mission Sr. St. Pierre was destined to pass on to each of us who would accept it. She met with incredible opposition from the French hierarchy, but after her death the work was continued by a saintly retired lawyer of Tours, Leo Dupont, and in 1885 Reparation through the Holy Face devotion was established canonically as an Archconfraternity by Pope Leo XIII. What merely natural means could avail against such a spiritual plague as Communism, brought upon the world precisely as a punishment for its sins? Political remedies alone could never destroy its roots, drawing their sustenance as they do from hell itself. Here in the U.S., expecting to defeat Communism by appeals to the American Constitution is like trying to fight heresy with the Book of Mormon, all part and parcel of the same Revolution. Such efforts draw tears of pity.

That so few Catholics today have even heard of Sr. St. Pierre's apostolate shows how successful the enemy has been in obliterating it, for it flourished for many years before being swallowed up in World War I. Shortly before her death Sr. St. Pierre wrote her Prioress, "Our Lord made known to me that terrible woes were impending, and He said, 'Pray, pray, for the Church is threatened by a fearful tempest!' The Savior made me understand that His justice was greatly irritated against mankind for its sins, but particularly for those that directly outrage the Majesty of God: that is, Communism, Atheism, cursing and the desecration of Sundays."

PART III: *Rome be-Spangled*

Nowhere is liberalism so firmly entrenched in Catholics as in the United States. Not only is it imbibed with mother's milk and breathed in daily at home and school, but it has been actively promoted from the nation's beginnings by Catholic officialdom carrying out the policy set by Lord Baltimore and Archbishop Carroll. Not to be a liberal is to be un-American. Even a "conservative" is a liberal in America, for what he seeks to conserve is merely the liberalism of the past. America's brief counter-revolution smashed with Lee's surrender at Appomattox, even her Catholics fell easy prey to the Marxist dialogue which began accelerating immediately thereafter and which provided the enemy ready entry into large segments of the Church Universal here, and as we shall see, abroad.

Engels, who outlived his friend Marx by some 12 years, remained in close contact with his American cadres, one of them his assiduous young correspondent Florence Kelley Wischnewetsky, translator of his *The Condition of the Working Classes in England in 1844* into English. Still living in 1932, she spans the whole interim between the "constitutional" and the full "revolutionary" phases Marx discerned. Her exchanges with Engels reveal much of the methods employed to hasten the red dawn in America. During the great strike movement for the eight hour day which swept the U.S. in 1886, Engels wrote her from London:

"The American working class is moving, and no mistake. And after a few false starts they will get into the right track soon enough. This appearance of the Americans upon the scene I consider one of the greatest events of the year. What the downbreak of Russian Czarism would be for the military monarchies of Europe — the snapping of their mainstay — that is for the bourgeois of the whole world the breaking out of class war in America. For America after all was the ideal of all bourgeois; a country rich, vast, expanding, with purely bourgeois institutions unleavened by feudal remnants or monarchical traditions and without a permanent hereditary proletariat. Here everyone could become, if not a capitalist, at all events an independent man, producing or trading, with his own means, for his own account. And because there were not, *as yet*, classes with opposing interests, our — and your — bourgeois thought that America stood above class antagonisms and struggles. That delusion has now broken down, the last Bourgeois Paradise on earth is fast changing into a Purgatorio. . . I only wish Marx could have lived to see it!"

This didn't happen without help. To the first wave of veteran agitators from the Europe of 1848 had succeeded fresh recruits, the majority of whom were, like their predecessors, unbelieving Jews. Among the new blood was Siegfried Meyer, a German-American

Socialist, member of the First International, who helped organize German workers in New York. There was Theodore Cuno, a German Social-Democrat expelled from his country, who helped form the International in Milan and later came to America to collaborate in the New York People's Paper. Wilhelm Hasselmann, a former member of the German Reichstag active as a Communist journalist, became an anarchist, was expelled from the Party and also emigrated to America. Another anarchist, Johann Most, worked for years in England before coming to America in 1882, where he continued to publish *Freiheit*, a paper he had launched in England. He had been expelled from the Party along with Hasselmann.

In a letter to Sorge, Marx had condemned *Freiheit* for having "no revolutionary content. . . only revolutionary phraseology." An important distinction. Marx understood, on the other hand, how some of the most revolutionary literature uses no revolutionary phraseology at all, and in many cases only Christian terminology. A case in point would be certain "conservative" publications and groups in the Catholic Church today who spread the Revolution very effectively in the name of tradition. This is classical Marxist logistics at its best, using what it finds, and battling even from positions contrary to itself, if this will exacerbate dissension.

Engels explained this carefully to Florence as regards America: "It is far more important that the movement should spread, proceed harmoniously, take root and embrace as much as possible the whole American proletariat, than that it should start and proceed from the beginning on theoretically perfectly correct lines. . . Our theory is not a dogma, but the exposition of a process of evolution, and that process involves successive phases. To expect that the Americans will start with the full consciousness of the theory worked out in older industrial countries is to expect the impossible. . . They ought, in the words of *The Communist Manifesto*, to represent the movement of the future in the movement of the present.

"But above all give the movement time to consolidate," by not "forcing down people's throats things which at present they cannot properly understand but which they soon will learn. A million or two of workingmen's votes next November for a bona fide workingmen's party is worth infinitely more at present than a hundred thousand votes for a doctrinally perfect platform. The very first attempt — soon to be made if the movement progresses — to consolidate the moving masses on a national basis will bring them all face to face. . . and if our German friends by that time have learnt enough of the language of the country to go in for a discussion, then will be the time for them to criticize the views of others. . . to bring them gradually to understand. . . "

To one of these "German friends" and co-religionists, Engels was not so tactful as to Florence. He writes Sorge that American Anglo-Saxons "are not to be converted by lecturing. This pig-headed and conceited lot have got to experience it in their own bodies. . . Hence, the trade unions, etc., are the thing to begin with if there is to be a mass movement, and every further step must be forced on them by a defeat. But once the first step beyond the bourgeois point of view has been taken, things will move quickly, like everything in America," where, he tells him in another letter, "politics are only a business deal, like any other." Thus infiltration is best gradual, imperceptible, but persistent, and appealing to men's cupidity and self-interest.

With the agricultural South and its way of life prostrate, the development of large scale industry will coincide, says he, with the rise of the Socialist movement: "It is the revolutionizing of all traditional relations through industry *as it develops* which also revolutionizes people's minds." These words were penned on New Year's Eve, 1892. Years before he had written Florence, "The less it is drilled into the Americans from the outside and the more they test it with their own experience — with the help of the Germans" — (i.e., German Communists) — "the deeper it will pass into their flesh and blood. When we returned to Germany, in spring 1848, we joined the Democratic Party as the only possible means of getting the ear of the working class; we were the most advanced wing of that party, but still a wing of it. . . Had we from 1864 to 1873 insisted on working together only with those who openly adopted our platform, where should we be today?"

• • •

This is the perspective in which the words of Pius XI forbidding Catholics to cooperate with Communists "in any way whatsoever" must be read. After all, cooperation is all they require in order to gain their ends. Like their father the devil, who perforce tempts the good only with what looks good, they set before the eyes of their dupes common goals which any conscientious citizen would normally desire to see realized. Back in 1886 Engels had written Sorge, "The movement in America is in the same position as it was with us before 1848. . . Except that in America now things will go infinitely more quickly. . . And what is still lacking will be set going by the bourgeoisie."

It's helpful to remember what Fr. Faber predicted would be characteristic of the latter times: good men being on the wrong side. It's these, and only these, who could really have succeeded in putting the Revolution not only into the whole world, but into the Church. Like the lance into the Sacred Heart of the Savior on the Cross at the culmination of the Passion, Marxist ideology has now been thrust into the very heart of His Spouse.

To ascertain the degree of penetration, one need only run at random through the Decrees of the Second Vatican Council, where Communism is nowhere mentioned by name, let alone condemned. The closest reference to it seems to be the "systematic atheism" described in the first chapter of the Pastoral Constitution on the Church in the Modern World. This Constitution, *Gaudium et Spes*, nevertheless abounds in terminology congenial to Marxists. The key is set in the Introduction:

"Today's spiritual agitation and the changing conditions of life are part of a broader and deeper revolution. As a result of the latter, intellectual formation is ever increasingly based on the mathematical and natural sciences and on those dealing with man himself, while in the practical order the technology which stems from these sciences takes on mounting importance. . . Technology is now transforming the face of the earth. . . . At the same time, the human race is giving ever-increasing thought to forecasting and regulating its own population growth. . . The destiny of the human community has become all of a piece, where once the various groups of men had a kind of private history of their own. Thus, the human race has passed from a rather static concept of reality to a more dynamic, evolutionary one." Needless to say, many critics voiced their objections to this passage, reflecting so blatantly the influence of the heresy of Teilhard de Chardin.

The document continues, "This kind of evolution can be seen more clearly in those nations which already enjoy the conveniences of economic and technological progress, though it is also astir among peoples still striving for such progress and eager to secure for themselves the advantages of an industrialized and urbanized society." This is coupled with no exhortation to resist in any way the new Atlantean civilization engulfing the world.

On the contrary, in Chapter III we read, "Thanks primarily to increased opportunities for many kinds of interchange among nations, the human family is gradually recognizing that it comprises a single world community and is making itself so. Hence many benefits once looked for, especially from heavenly powers, man has now enterprisingly procured for himself." Indeed? And furthermore, "Just as human activity proceeds from man, so it is ordered toward man. For when a man works he not only alters things and society, he develops himself as well." This is dangerously close to the purest Marxist dogma on the all-important function of work in man's self-creation.

In the Decree on the Laity laymen are told, "As citizens they must cooperate with other citizens, using their own particular skills and acting on their own responsibility." Urged to engage in welfare work, they are assured, "In so doing, they should cooperate with all men of good will." There is apparently no need to differentiate between what might be the true goals of these "other citizens" or "men of good will," for, "Among the signs of our times, the irresistibly increasing sense of solidarity among all peoples is especially noteworthy." Is it "irresistible" because evolution is automatic, as its proponents aver? The document doesn't say, but, "It is a function of the lay apostolate to promote this awareness zealously and to transform it into a sincere and genuine sense of brotherhood." In the face of this kind of togetherness, one wonders what exactly the Psalmist meant when he cried out in the ancient Mass, "*Discerne causam meam de gente non sancta!*" now that all people are good. His was, of course, the "static" approach.

Pages of such quotations could be cited, interspersed with impeccably orthodox passages, for there is fare for every taste and interpretation in the new Church whose windows have been opened wide on the world. It is only people like the prophet Jeremias who warn, "For death is come up through our windows, it is entered into our houses to destroy the children from without" (9:21).

• • •

But we are getting ahead of our story. How, exactly, was all this accomplished?

In the letter previously quoted, Engels had noted with satisfaction that "the American masses had to seek out their won way and seem to have found it for the time being in the K[nights] of L[abor], whose confused principles and ludicrous organization appear to correspond to their own confusion. But according to all I hear the K of L are a real power, especially in New England and the West, and are becoming more so every day owing to the brutal opposition of the capitalists. I think it is necessary to work inside them, to form within this still quite plastic mass a core of people who understand the movement and its aims and will therefore take over the leadership. . . The first step of importance for every country newly entering into the movement is always the organization of the workers as an independent political party, no matter how, *so long as it is a distinct workers' party.*"

Here Engels preaches a serious error specifically condemned by Leo XIII in his epochal Encyclical *Rerum Novarum* in 1891. The Catholic Church has ever upheld the workingman's natural right to form associations to protect himself and his property and to better his condition, but these may not be formed along class lines, pitting labor against capital, employed against employer. Class warfare is contrary to God's law.

The Pope called it "a great mistake. . . to possess oneself of the idea that class is naturally hostile to class; that rich and poor are intended by nature to live at war with one another. So irrational and so false is this view, that the exact contrary is the truth. . . it is ordained by nature that these two classes should exist in harmony and agreement, and should, as it were, fit into one another, so as to maintain the equilibrium of the body politic. Each requires the other . . . " Elsewhere in the same Encyclical he pointed out the great benefits to society given by the Artificers' Guilds of the past, whose membership comprised both employers and employees within one given trade working together, and where, most important, all the members were Catholic. The Pope stipulated that labor unions should be "laid in religion," and one of their specific goals the sanctification of Sundays and holydays.

But class warfare had already been unleashed. "As to those Americans who think their country exempt from the consequences of fully expanded Capitalist production," Engels wrote Florence, "they seem to live in blissful ignorance of the fact that sundry states, Massachusetts, New Jersey, Pennsylvania, Ohio, etc., have such an institution as a Labor Bureau from the reports of which they might learn something to the contrary." These Yankee states, hardened in the Union mold, had by now a relatively high Catholic population, swelled after the Civil War by thousands of immigrants seeking jobs in American factories, mines and railroads. Rootless, torn from their native cultures, often bereft of priests and many not speaking English, they were ripe for organizing into the artificial labor system. America not only caught up with Europe in this regard, she was soon taking the lead.

The K of L proved to be the fateful instrument whereby

Catholic workingmen, potentially the best source of concerted resistance to Communism here after the Civil War, were diverted into the ranks of the enemy. Organized in 1869 by by one Uriah Stephens, a Mason, Odd Fellow and Knight of Pythias, with rituals similar to these groups', the labor Knights grew with the rise of industry, and under occult direction were soon winning Victories for the enemy at the polls.

From then on Catholics were not only drawn *en bloc* into politics to safeguard their livelihood, but into revolutionary politics, and that under the prompting of their own Americanist hierarchy. In 1879 Terence V. Powderly, a Catholic who later fell away from the Church, was elected Grand Master Workman of the K of L, holding this position until 1893. During his incumbency Cardinal Taschereau of Quebec, who was well aware of the forces at work within the organization, petitioned Rome to condemn it, if only on the grounds of its being a secret society.

In the face of Pius IX's *Quanta cura* and the *Syllabus of Errors*, issued in 1864, the Second Plenary Council of Baltimore had already officially approved America's new labor unions in principle by 1866, despite the fact that many churchmen saw their dangers as constituted. Even Bishop James Roosevelt Bayley was moved to say soon after, "No Catholic with any idea of the spirit of his religion will encourage them!" Not only did the K of L's platform advocate open social and economic heresies, but its membership (700,000 by 1886, and open to all persuasions) was required to take a pledge of secrecy incompatible with the Sacrament of Penance. Public ownership of property was advocated, with the proposals of Henry George especially in favor.

It's hardly surprising that Rome condemned the organization in 1884, so patently did it violate the rules soon to be laid down by Leo XIII. With characteristic evasiveness, Cardinal Gibbons and his Americanist clergy contended that the condemnation, initially requested by the See of Quebec, applied only to Canada. "The Catholic World," by that time the recognized organ of the Paulist Fr. Hecker and the other Americanists, boldly counseled Catholics, "Be Knights!" Bishop Corrigan of New York thought otherwise, as did others in the episcopacy, holding that Catholics who persisted as Knights of Labor should be deprived of the Sacraments. He and the German bishops led so determined an opposition, a decision could not be reached by the committee meeting in Baltimore to consider the matter. It was referred to Rome.

This elicited a spirited written defense of the K of L, drafted by

Cardinal Gibbons with the able help of Bishop Keane and "the Socialist Bishop" John Ireland and submitted to Propaganda. With the hindsight we now enjoy, a faithful Catholic reading this document today can only weep. Appealing to the "spirit" of the Leonine Encyclicals concerning "the dangers of our time and their remedies," it assures the Roman authorities that the Knights mean no harm, dismissing as groundless the charges of secrecy and blind obedience required. (As sole proof, the Cardinal advances Powderly's word for this!) As for Catholics being mixed with heretics, this is inevitable, says he, in the U.S. where Catholic workingmen's confraternities under Church direction are not "possible or necessary." Catholic members are thus exposed "to the evil influences of the most dangerous associates, even of atheists, communists and anarchists, that is true; but it is one of the trials of faith which our brave American Catholics are accustomed to meet almost daily." And which accounts for the thousands lost to the Church by the back door even as a wave of conversions was greeted at the front.

Outbursts of violence are likewise simply "inevitable." Furthermore, says the Cardinal, "It is vain... to dream that this struggle can be prevented or that we can deter the multitudes from organizing," when a major instrument of Providence in modern times is "the power of the people." Continuing to plead the wisdom of cooperating with the enemy, he warns of " the evident danger of the Church's losing in popular estimation her right to be considered the friend of the people... of rendering hostile to the Church the political power of our country... of being *un-American*. " This last, according to this Americanist prelate, was apparently the worst evil which could befall a Catholic here.

He informs Rome that the faithful in this country will join the union anyway despite any formal prohibition — to be expected, certainly, considering the well-publicized views of their liberal clerical leaders. It's revealing that the Cardinal finds nothing incongruous in pointing out elsewhere in the same letter the American faithful's unquestioning obedience to Rome's strictures against the Masons, a measure which happened to receive the hierarchy's unanimous public support. As for banning the Knights in Canada, well, circumstances there were "very different."

The conformity to the world which this letter exudes, explodes with full force at Point #7 of its closing summation: "The Holy See should not entertain the idea of condemning" the Knights of Labor, for "it would be almost ruinous for the *financial maintenance of the Church* in our country, and *for Peter's Pence*." This sordid threat of withdrawing financial support from Rome was entirely omitted from the official English translation published initially in the *Moniteur de Rome* in 1887. This version, generally reproduced in other works, omitted or softened several other passages as well. There was no need for the public at large to know. And alas, the financial condition of the Holy See at the time was such that Rome succumbed to the threat. With a little help from the English Cardinal Manning, the K of L were never proscribed in the U.S.

• • •

No one would seriously accuse the American Cardinal of being a Communist. The tragedy is that he and his associates give every evidence of honest sincerity in their belief that identification with progressive Democracy was the best, indeed the only way of furthering the interests of the Church in America. But what of the Faith? After a visit from Powderly, Bishop Keane told the Cardinal regarding the K of L, "While there seems to be a rather general fear of some elements of their make-up, the impression, I think, is quite as general that we had better let such things correct themselves, as, in matters of mere pecuniary balance of interests, and in such a country as ours, is sure to take place." If this is incredible ingenuousness, it inevitably calls Fr. Faber's dictum to mind.

America by this time was faced with the real and flagrant evils inevitably spawned by rampant greed fed by usury. Such evils had to be fought, if only because Communism battened on them as Democracy once fed on corrupted monarchies. The problem lay in the choice of means. Questionable methods easily look good in comparison with the evils they pretend to remedy. To desperate men thinking with hearts instead of heads apart from faith and reason, the new ideology began to look like Providence's chosen instrument.

Suckled on the American principle of "if it works, it's right," the liberal Bishops unfortunately shared the native pragmatic disregard for intellectualizing problems, for thinking action through to its final consequences. Where progress is automatic, "things correct themselves." They in fact gloried in their contempt for "theory." Not so the enemy, who had studied American failings carefully before laying his plans.

Almost at that very moment, Engels was writing Sorge, "The Americans are worlds behind in all theoretical things," and to Florence, "There is no better road to theoretical clearness of comprehension than *durch Schaden klug werden* (to learn by one's mistakes). And for a whole large class, there is no other road, especially for a nation so eminently practical as the Americans. The great thing is to get the working class working *as a class*; that once obtained, they will soon find the right direction, and all who resist, H[enry] G[eorge] or Powderly, will be left out in the cold with small sects of their own. Therefore I think also the K of L a most important factor in the movement which ought not to be pooh-poohed from without, but to be revolutionized from within. And later to Sorge: "When the moment comes in which events themselves drive the American proletariat forward there will be enough fitted by their superior theoretical insight and experience to take the part of leaders, and then you will find that your years of work have not been wasted . . . Without noticing it themselves, they are coming on to the right theoretical track, *they drift into it.* . . "

To such diabolical astuteness Bishop Keane would oppose only optimism and blessing, thereby paralyzing the only supernatural opponent Marxism had in America. Expecting soon to address the Knights in convention, he had prepared the following words: "As an American citizen, I rejoice at every advance towards the perfect realization of that truest and noblest ideal of social organization and government; and therefore do I rejoice to behold you and the vast body of workingmen at your backs banded together, not for violence or injustice, but for the calm, orderly, dignified assertion and vindication of your God-given rights. The Catholic Church is the old Church of 'the gospel preached to the poor', etc."

More than aware of this fact, the Communist Manifesto itself states, "Nothing is easier than to give Christian asceticism a Socialist tinge. Has not Christianity declaimed against private property, against marriage, against the State?" it asks, with the guile of the serpent. "Has it not preached in the place of these, charity and poverty, celibacy and mortification of the flesh, monastic life and Mother Church?" The social gospel now being substituted for that of the Apostles was developed in detail long ago by Marx and Engels.

In his exegesis of the Apocalypse written for "Progress" in 1883, Engels would have us believe that the early Christian communities were not like modern parish congregations, but rather "like local sections of the International Workingmen's Association. . . Christianity got hold of the masses, exactly as modern socialism does, under the shape of a variety of sects. . . but all opposed to the ruling system, to 'the powers that be'. . . Christianity, like every great revolutionary movement, was made by the masses, etc." Reading this, it is not hard to see where the current blasphemy of "Christ the Revolutionary" came from, who took it up, and who is carrying it forward today. Liberation theology wasn't born yesterday.

• • •

With the condemnation of the K of L blocked in Rome, marxism was free to proselytize the Catholic working classes of the U.S. In 1891, when Leo XIII approved workingmen's "associations" in *Rerum Novarum*, the Americanist prelates chose to consider their position on labor entirely vindicated, despite the fact that three years later the same Pope was constrained to warn Bishop Keane against identifying the Church with socialism in America. This went little heeded, so imbued was our hierarchy with the heady spirit of '76.

An unflattering vignette illustrating the American Catholic mentality of the time was penned by Bishop Baunard, who had brought both Bishop Dubourg and St. Philippine Duchesne to make foundations in America. In his biography of St. Madeleine Sophie Barat, foundress of the Mothers of the Sacred Heart, the Bishop quotes these two missionaries, who had soberly concluded that Americans *per se* were "little suited to religious life because of their independence and their love of equality, comfort and ease. It's necessary to spin, card, work in the fields. But we need only set our orphans to doing a few of these things to alienate the people, who want equality. . . . The children's ignorance is equaled only by their prideful arrogance. When we set before them the example of students in France in order to shake them from their sloth, they would reply disdainfully, 'But we aren't French!' And if one of their number happened to submit with docility, her conceited school-mates would throw at her contemptuously, 'You're obeying like a nigger! '"

Bishop Dubourg reluctantly concluded, "The greatest prejudice against religious life has its source in the American character, whose spirit of independence would hear nothing of the vow of obedience, whose spirit of equality rendered impractical the necessary distinctions which the Institute established between lay-sisters and choir nuns. Madame Duchesne admitted it would be hard to set up two ranks. Here everything must be equal. Telling a postulant she is being admitted to *serve* is a thing no one will accept here."

In this inebriating climate, which affected every echelon of the native American clergy, Rome's remonstrances were either ignored or met with some official variation of the schoolgirls' "But we aren't French!" reading, "The situation here in America is totally unlike that in Europe, and ultramontanes cannot understand our special problems. Roman policies simply do not apply in our case." All the while, at the enemy's nerve center, Engels was quietly briefing Sorge and Florence: "It will be the same with you in America too."

All this while American Catholics were encouraged to believe they were fast becoming a real power for Christ in politics, an illusion the American Protective Association and the Know-Nothings only reinforced. Enjoying peace with plurality, the faithful were told all America would in due time be won to the Faith, if only they would use to advantage the good democratic tools heaven was now placing in their hands. Disastrous as this delusion was to prove for the integrity of the Faith in the U.S., where it survives in its entirety today mostly in "ethnic" pockets which have somehow escaped major contamination, the worst is that the nineteenth century Americanists had not been content to keep their heresy to themselves. Theirs was a mission, a divine mandate to share their riches with the backward nations of the world, the old civilizations of Europe and especially the Vatican!

In an address to the New York Commandery of the Loyal Legion on April 4, 1894, Archbishop Ireland displayed these sentiments in their full glory: "America," he exclaimed, "born into the family of nations in these latter times is the highest billow in humanity's evolution [sic], the crowning effort of ages in the aggrandizement of man. . . When the fathers of the republic declared, 'that all men are created equal; that they are endowed by their Creator with certain inalienable rights; that among these are life, liberty and the pursuit of happiness,' a cardinal principle was enunciated which in its truth was as old as the race, but in practical realization almost unknown.

"Slowly, amid sufferings and revolutions, humanity had been reaching out toward " — not the reign of Christ the King, apparently — but " toward a reign of the rights of man... The Christian Church was all this time leavening human society and patiently awaiting the promised fermentation. This came at last, and it came in America. It came in a first manifestation through the Declaration of Independence; it came in a second and final manifestation through President Lincoln's Proclamation of Emancipation."

In the face of the teachings of the Popes and our Lord himself, he proclaims, "Ours is the government of the people by the people for the people. The government is our own organized will... Rights begin with and go upward from the people. . . The God-given mission of the republic of America is not only to its own people: it is to all the peoples of the earth." One would have to be told this is a Catholic speaking, let alone an Archbishop. He is voicing, of course, Orestes Brownson mysticism of the purest water, as propounded indefatigably by that difficult democratic editor and prophet in his *Boston Quarterly Review* and some 20 volumes.

Active in the radical Workingmen's Party, a founder of the Brook Farm Experiment, Transcendentalist and one-time Unitarian minister turned Catholic, Brownson was a first light of what later came to be known as the "Feeney heresy." First and foremost, however, all the while defending the temporal power of the Pope, he preached an alleged common goal of America and the Church, as set forth in the opening pages of *The American Republic:*

"Every living nation has an idea given it by Providence to realize, and whose realization is its special work, mission or destiny." This is novel teaching indeed, but to continue: "Every nation is in some sense, a chosen People of God. . . The United States, or the American Republic, has a mission, and is chosen of God for the realization of a great idea. It has been chosen not only to continue the work assigned to Greece and Rome, but to accomplish a greater work than was assigned to either," and so on. Apparently this was the mission of the U.S. to the Church, which would consecrate the whole project, with grateful thanks. For a nation which at no time formed even an infinitesimal part of Christendom, this is an exalted vocation indeed.

With true missionary zeal its apostles took it to Europe. After his dismissal as Rector of the suspect Catholic University in Washington, D.C., Bishop Keane was a foremost propagator of the Great Idea in the eternal city itself, ably assisted by Bishop Denis O'Connell, dismissed likewise for cause as Rector of the American College there. These two prelates, who, incidentally, often dined with the American ambassador in Rome, were further supported by Bishops Ireland, Spalding and the former Paulist O'Gorman. Behind them were a large number of European liberals of similar persuasion, all disciples of Fr. Isaac Hecker of the Paulists, whom Orestes Brownson had brought into the Church.

Hecker's tenets and biography had been disseminated through France by Abbé Felix Klein, who hoped to found an order of Paulists in Europe to preach Americanism to the benighted old world. Although in 1897 the Paulists numbered only 32 in the U.S., where they met with much opposition, through the zeal of Hecker's admirers the Order came to be far better known abroad than at home. A dreamer who coined the phrase "baptism of the Spirit," all the while decrying the passive virtues in favor of the active, Hecker announced at the time of the First Vatican Council the end of all religious orders, together with the Latin races, and heralded the coming Anglo-Saxon leadership of the Church. He was made to order for the Americanists, who needed a "saint", and deferred to him as one uncanonized. He became the epitome of "the American experiment", watched with fascination by Europe since 1776, and exemplified the American way of life in religious garb on the international stage.

In a private audience Pius IX tactfully suggested to him, "The Americans are so engrossed in worldly pursuits and in getting money, and these things are not favorable to religion. It's not I who say this, but our Lord in the Gospel. In the United States there exists a liberty too unrestrained; all the refugees and revolutionaries gather there." Hecker persisted nonetheless in tailoring the Gospel to American vices in order to spread the Faith, while Keane lectured at the Brussels Congress on "the ultimate religion of the future," speaking to all who would listen (and some who would not) of "letting down the bars" and "development of dogma" following on a grand "opening of windows" such as we now have. A great admirer of Bismarck, he had the effrontery to toast this enemy of Christianity along with Leo XIII and Gladstone at a banquet in Washington.

• • •

In the Encyclical *Longinqua oceani* in 1895, Leo XIII congratulated the American hierarchy on the favorable conditions then pertaining in the U.S., where the liberty of the Church remained untrammeled. "Yet," he wrote, "though all this is true, it would be very erroneous to draw the conclusion that in America is to be sought the type of the most desirable status of the Church, or that it would be universally lawful or expedient for State and Church to be, as in America, dissevered and divorced." This remark, according to Fr. John Tracy Ellis in his biography of Cardinal Gibbons, caused some uneasiness among American bishops who were fearful of its effects on non-Catholics!

"The fact that Catholicity with you is in good condition," continued the Pontiff, "nay, is even enjoying a prosperous growth, is by all means to be attributed to the fecundity with which God has endowed His Church, in virtue of which, unless men or circumstances interfere, she spontaneously expands and propagates herself; but she would bring forth more abundant fruits if, in addition to liberty, she enjoyed the favor of the laws and the patronage of the public authority." (A large factor in the Church's expansion here, we might note, was simply the horde of Catholic immigrants from elsewhere.)

Despite papal disapproval, "A considerable number of French and Italian writers agreed that the modern Church should adapt itself everywhere to the Anglo-Saxon pattern," writes Robert Cross in *The Emergence of Liberal American Catholicism in America.* "Edward Demolins argued that liberty, energy, openness to new experience made Americans the archetypes not only of secular civilization, but of modern religious life. He was sure that the Church in America had greater moral and religious energy than in Europe. Many of the French clergy wished to emulate the American liberals' program. Some praised the campaign to save the Knights of Labor, and regarded Ireland and Gibbons as true prophets of social Catholicism. . . This group wanted the Church to copy American methods of spreading the Gospel. . .

"A group of French 'neo-Christians' shared the Paulists' conviction that in an era of liberty, equality and individuality, the Church should stress the internal direction of the Holy Spirit. Some Italian churchman, convinced that the separation of Church and State was as desirable in Italy as America, recommended that the Pope abandon claims to the temporal power. At various times in the 1890's all these groups called themselves or were called *américanistes.*"" In England Cardinal Manning summed it all up by proclaiming, "The future of Catholicism is in America!"

• • •

We have said that it was not so much the Rhine as the Potomac flowing into the Tiber that caused the crisis the Church suffers today. Although theoretical democracy germinated in Europe and was transplanted into Catholic America in early colonial times, it was in America that democracy in its modern viral form first established itself in a body politic so as to produce a working model. The American Revolution had come to a successful close before the French had even begun. We need not therefore be surprised to find the so-called "pastoral" social precepts of the Second Vatican Council worked out many years beforehand in the U.S., traditional proving ground of democracy's most radical experiments.

There had been violent reactions to Americanism on the part of orthodox Catholics on both sides of the Atlantic as soon as it appeared. Fr. Charles Maignen, a French Vincentian theologian, published some admirable, scholarly refutations of the major errors which were collected into a volume entitled *Le Père Hecker Est-Il un Saint?* It was heavily endorsed by the Roman authorities, including Cardinal Satolli, the Apostolic Delegate to the U.S., who had been sympathetic to Americanism at first, but changed his opinion radically after viewing it on its home ground. Among other services, Fr. Maignen showed how Americanist errors consisted essentially of the last four condemned propositions of the Syllabus. As proof that the movement was "one of the greatest dangers threatening the Church," he quoted from "Romanus," a pseudonym used by Rome-based clergy writing for London's *Contemporary Review:*

"Liberal Catholics are not so foolish as to expect authority to retract any of its past decrees; the dexterity of theologians will always be amply sufficient to prove for convincing reasons that a given embarrassing decision is entirely contrary to what was previously supposed or accepted, or even contrary to what appears to be its true meaning." Romanus concludes that there are probably few ex cathedra decrees which cannot be disposed of by one or the other of such procedures. It was not hard for Fr. Maignen to predict, "The authority of the Holy See will be hard pressed in the face of a party like the one now rising. . . against the most solemn acts of the Church's magisterium." His words have been sadly borne out by hosts of theologians who have literally dissolved dogmatic definition by free interpretations "in the spirit of Vatican II."

Other defenders of the Faith had little difficulty linking Americanism to Communism, not to mention Semitism, Protestantism, Masonry and outright Satanism. A Catholic paper in Paris accused Cardinal Gibbons of partiality to Masonry on the basis of his persistent defense of such organizations as the Odd Fellows, Knights of Pythias and the Temperance societies, all condemned by Rome, and of secret societies generally in the States. The French Canadian Jules Tardivel dubbed America "the eldest daughter of the sect," and Leo XIII's Belgian biographer stated its true center was located here.

In 1899 Leo XIII was finally forced to write *Testem benevolentiae* condemning Americanism specifically as a heresy. In the face of the threatened Peter's Pence, however, none of the heretics was designated by name, although everyone knew who they were and had expected them to be formally excommunicated. Robert Cross relates that one Roman periodical, referring to the "Satanic spirit" of America, exclaimed, "Put the mask aside, O Monsignor Ireland; bow down before the Vicar of Jesus Christ and deny the blasphemous theories of the heretical sect which are embodied in you!" *Civiltà Cattolica* dubbed the heresy "purely American. . . employed at first to indicate in general the 'new idea' which was to rejuvenate the Church, and in particular the 'new crusade' against the uncompromising position of Catholics of the old creed."

All the heresiarchs loudly disclaimed being tainted by what they termed a "phantom heresy" existing largely in the minds of the Curia or at best in a few French dioceses, and they continued as before. The American flag was displayed ever more prominently at altar-side, despite the frowns from Rome, which steadfastly refused approval of the tricolor within the sanctuary. Episcopal progress in socialism was steady. At the close of the First World War the American bishops under the leadership of Msgr. John Ryan became so convinced that "so-called 'socialistic' measures were practically synonymous with Catholic moral principles" — to quote a popular Catholic history textbook — that they boldly embarked on their own social program. Advocated were minimum wage legislation, unemployment and old age insurance, prohibition of child labor, legal protection of unions, national employment service, public housing for workers, control of monopolies, curtailment of excess profits, participation of labor in management and wider distribution of stock ownership. Christ was now harnessed to the Revolution as to His Cross.

"Judge by the results!" critics were challenged. And sure enough, in 1928 indulgent America permitted a Catholic, Al Smith, to run for the Presidency for the first time in the nation's history. Ten years later in Madrid the anti-Catholic writer George Seldes was able to say in *The Catholic Crisis*, "The future of Catholicism may lie in America because of the growing Catholic population, the large increase of bishoprics, the financial support of the Church which is said to be larger than that contributed by the rest of the world. But it may lie in America because America is the stronghold of democracy. American Catholicism is the Catholicism of the famous credo of Al Smith. . . which states that the *Syllabus* of Pius IX which is anti-liberal, anti-democratic, and in a way anti-American, has 'no dogmatic force' as Cardinal Newman said long ago. . .

"By the Smithian system of dialectics no Catholic need fight Socialism or Communism, or pay any attention to *Rerum Novarum*,

Quadragesimo Anno, Casti Connubii, Lux Veritatis, or the late Pope's utterances in favor of Franco Spain, if he individually disagrees. The American Catholic, according to its most important spokesman, can take it or leave it. However, *no Catholic outside the United States has ever expressed the same views and remained in the Church."*

They have now. Apparently. As Bishop O'Gorman once wrote his friends from Rome, "Americanism, which was supposed to be our defeat, has been turned into a glorious victory. We are surely on top." The lucrative waters of the Potomac were now flowing freely into the Tiber. Only a faithful few in the U.S. today recall that their Lord "suffered under Pontius Pilate" after Pilate and the "religious" Herod became friends. "If they have persecuted Me, they will also persecute you. . . The servant is not greater than his master" And "no man can serve two masters" (John 16:20; Mat. 6:24).

Mindful of this difficulty, Hilaire Belloc predicted the "necessary" conflict between the civil state and the Catholic Church in America. He said in so many words, of course, "the Catholic Church in America." He was not referring to the star-spangled "American Catholic Church" which is after all only a Modernist sect of long standing, with a large growing membership. No conflict with Pilate should arise there.

THE STRANGE SPIRIT OF '76

PART I: *Whence It Comes*

True devotion to the Sacred Heart of Jesus has rarely, if ever, been preached in the United States. It is too embarrassingly *political*.

For two hundred years the false principles that Church and state must be separate, that all men are created equal, and that authority comes from below have been imposed as a matter of public policy. It is therefore understandable that Catholics not prepared to "suffer under Pontius Pilate" have kept this flammable devotion to the Heart of God within the jug of personal piety, with little social extension beyond the family. Lest our Lord be deported as a subversive, He has been portrayed only as a yearning, all-forgiving — if not simpering — Savior desiring to clasp indiscriminately to His blazing breast any and every individual without the slightest concern for his politics.

The Lord who appeared to St. Margaret Mary and declared that He wished to be honored in the house of the King of France is dwelt upon mostly by specialists in mysticism. Few Americans have even heard of the vision subsequently accorded to St. Catherine Labouré, of Christ the King in anguish, despoiled of His royal insignia; nor do they know that she was told concerning the destruction of the French monarchy, "Little do you know what you have lost!" Yet the consequences of the French Revolution are clear in the world today. The divine predilection for kings and hierarchical government remains a forbidden subject in a country where monarchy is denied not merely in practice, as for instance in England, but in principle, where every schoolchild must absorb the idea that kings are *per se* the villains of history and the insurgent mob its heroes.

Our Lord did not stand before Pilate and declare, "I am a President." Nor your Big Brother. He said simply, "I am a King." During His public ministry He had furthermore specifically characterized His enemies as men who "will not have this man to rule over us" (Luke 19:14). Countless times in the Gospels He spoke of a Kingdom which is to come, one He taught us to ask for daily in the Lord's Prayer. Is it possible He was ignorant of the *progressio populorum* bound to take place?

His apparently archaic politics have, alas, been treated as just that. We are led to believe that He really doesn't care about politics, yet the implication is that if He were on earth today He would favor democracy or communism as more highly evolved forms of Christianity. As those bent on His destruction ever maintain, "Whosoever maketh himself a king, speaketh against Caesar" (John 19:12). This explains why even the Infant of Prague, clad in royal robes and diadem, with the world in His hand, has been largely reserved to the piety of little old ladies with financial problems. It would hardly do to publicize the fact that this miraculous image was originally granted as a focus for the prayer of royalists pitted against ravaging democracy, and known as "le petit Roi de Gloire."

To keep our Lord out of trouble with secular authority it is essential to relegate His kingship to the purely spiritual — whatever that is. But then, why did God become man? Wouldn't His divinity have sufficed for purely spiritual ends? If the Gospels are to be believed, our Lord had something more in mind. Faith without works denies the Incarnation. As Pius XI laid down in *Quas Primas*, ". . . the title and power of King belongs to Christ as man in the strict and proper sense," not just "figuratively and spiritually."

He told Pilate His Kingdom is "not from hence" (John 18:36.) This formally excludes modern democracy, whose sole *raison d'être* is derivation of authority "from hence," that is, from here below; but this doesn't mean that Christ's kingdom isn't here, in the world, embedded in time and space, producing visible effects in society. He assured the venal bureaucrat Pilate that even he would have no power over Him if it hadn't been conferred from above. Our Lord reigns as absolute monarch in this world: "All power is given to me in heaven and in earth" (Matt. 28:18.) Evil exists here only by His express permission, for our perfection or chastisement. If His Kingdom appears to be waning, it does so only in men's wills, for His rule continues intact.

In the very heart of the Passion He was pleased to show us "democracy" in action, manipulated by the instruments of Satan.

Pilate, turning to the people in hopes of saving the Prisoner he knew to be innocent, asks, "What, then, am I to do with Jesus who is called Christ?"

And they answered, prompted by their leaders, "Let him be crucified!" (Matt. 27:22-23) and elected Barabbas.

Thus was our Lord's death demanded and ratified by Jews who had espoused the democratic process, preferring human rule to God's. Let there be no mistake. The real objective of the liberty, equality and fraternity touted by the forces of humanism is always the death of God.

Our Lord nevertheless directed each instant of His Passion, then as now in His Mystical Body, using the forces of evil to accomplish the decrees of His Father. He tells Pilate that if His Kingdom were of this world, that is, "from hence," His servants would have fought to deliver Him; but they did not, explains St. John Chrysostom, because He didn't want them to. It was as simple as that. His enemies, on the other hand, had not only been powerless to apprehend Him until the moment He willed, but even to change the inscription on the Cross which proclaimed Him "King of the Jews." He is so because He is accepted by all the children of the promise of Abraham, all true Jews being Christians. Others, He told St. John on Patmos "say they are Jews and are not, but are the synagogue of Satan" (Apo. 2:9.)

The battle joined in Pilate's hall has continued through the centuries and is now rising to fever pitch. No one saw the opponents more clearly than St. Ignatius Loyola, when in the mortal throes of the Reformation he laid out the points for his famous meditation on the two standards: one army fighting under the flag of Satan, and the other under Christ's. Unfortunately this is not just a battle to the death, for it extends beyond. We tend to forget that Satan's kingdom, which he seeks to establish over the whole world, is just as eternal as Christ's.

The damned will be resurrected with the elect. Although Satan allows us to think his rule is merely "from hence" and limited to the joys of this life, those who cleave to him will be his subjects not only now, but forever. Far from believing in democracy, equality or any separation of church and state, what Satan has in mind is actually an anti-theocracy of worshiping slaves, beginning like Christ's on earth, but continuing in hell. That's politics.

By St. Ignatius' time the temporal rule fostered by Christian principles which we call Christendom was already challenged by sub-states won to Satan's cause. Everywhere the hierarchical structures patterned on the divine government in the heavens — literally the "Kingdom coming on earth as it is in heaven" — were crumbling under rebellious demands for "freedom of conscience" and "equality." As once on Calvary, the satanic commanders sought to divest Christ of His earthly, natural Body, so that His spiritual empire might be left unprotected.

In a position paper from the English Counter-Reformation League, Mr. David Boyce puts it thus: "The essential Kingdom is not of this world, but the Church has given rise to Christendom — the Christian political, social order with authority from God, not from the people, and the proper Christian expression of this temporal authority is kingship, the logical and natural consequence of Catholic belief. Now the modern anti-Christian 'machine' knows this, and so it is an essential part of the programme in preparing for the reign of Antichrist that Christian kings should first disappear. Hence 1789 and 1914-18, when three great Christian monarchies, two Catholic and one schismatic, were removed, namely France, Austro-Hungary and Russia. The Church engendered Christendom, and Antichrist will first demolish Christendom before attempting the final assault on the Church."

Any blow against a legitimate monarch being actually directed at Christ, anointed kings had to be murdered or shorn of power, with mob rule setting up dictators or "constitutions" in their place. Inexorably confining Christ to the "purely spiritual," in due time these succeeded in denying Christ's own Vicar his official rights over temporal rulers, eventually depriving him of even his temporal estates. At this stage, it's convenient to forget that St. Pius V, as spiritual head of Christendom, once found it his simple duty not only to excommunicate the heretic Elizabeth of England, but formally to *depose* her as unfit to rule Christ's sheep!

The beautiful international union of the Church and her Holy Roman Empire — joined as it were "hypostatically" for the temporal and eternal happiness of mankind — has been long ruptured. At the behest of the two-horned beast looking "like a lamb," but who "speaks as a dragon" (Apo. 13:11), the partisans of Barabbas are now closing in for the kill by democratizing the Church herself. As Mr. Boyce warns, "Christians are unknowingly apostates in wanting to come to terms with the new anti-Christian social order. If they now try to come to terms with the new anti-Christian religious order, they will become knowingly apostate."

• • •

To explain how the Sacred Heart was denied rule in the United

States, it is necessary to go back several centuries and uncover some truths not generally admitted about the French, for it was against them the satanic one-world utopia first mounted its latter-day artillery. By that lightning flash St. Joan of Arc were its machinations first exposed to the naked eye.

To be sure, she is a "difficult" saint. Like devotion to the Sacred Heart and the Kingship of Christ to which she is organically related, devotion to her must be considerably diluted before it can be ingested by Catholics weaned on revolutionary pap. As often as not she is represented as a medieval feminist, a prefiguration of the happy day of sexual equality when at last women can wear pants, cut their hair and do everything men do, only better. That she did all this no one can deny, but to dwell on these details is to overlook their causes: her virginity, her nationality and her mission.

St. Joan was French. As the very personification of her *patrie* and its territorial integrity, she has to be a woman and virginal. A village girl, of the people, she was commanded by her "voices" — St. Michael's, the primitive St. Margaret's and St. Catherine's — to save the French monarchy in the face of English occupation, and that by force of arms. There is no explaining away St. Joan. She is living proof of God's interest in politics, not to mention His approval of just warfare.

She furthermore reasserted the ancient tradition that God himself had constituted the King of France, under the Pope, temporal regent for Christ over all the other kings of Christendom. Why God so decreed is His secret, but Joan understood her orders, for on driving the English from Rheims she insisted on the immediate consecration of the dauphin Charles VII before continuing the campaign further. Historians missing this point cannot properly assess the French Revolution of 1789, let alone what followed. Neither will they understand why the Sacred Heart appeared in France rather than in some other nation, to entreat its king at a most crucial point in history to re-consecrate the wayward French royal house to Him.

At St. Joan's beatification in 1908 Pope St. Pius X took care to quote from the famous letter written to King St. Louis of France by Pope Gregory IX some 200 years before Joan's birth: "God... having established various kingdoms here below in accordance with diversities of language and climate, has conferred special missions on a large number of governments in order to accomplish His designs. And as once He preferred the tribe of Judah over those of other sons of Jacob, favoring it with special blessings, thus He chose France in preference to all the other nations of the earth for the protection of the

Catholic faith and for the defense of religious liberty. For this reason France is God's own kingdom, the enemies of France are the enemies of Christ. For this reason, God loves France because He loves the Church which crosses the centuries recruiting legions for eternity."

And St. Pius concludes by instructing the French cardinals to tell their compatriots to "treasure the testimony of St. Remi, of Charlemagne and St. Louis, testimony summed up in the words so often repeated by the heroine of Orléans: Long live Christ, King of the Franks!" He was attesting to an unbroken tradition dating from the miraculous baptism of Clovis in Rheims Cathedral on Christmas 438, as described by the saintly priest Hincmar:

"Suddenly a light more brilliant than the sun floods the church. The face of the Bishop glows with it. At the same time a voice resounds: 'Peace be with you! It is I! Fear not! Persevere in my favor!'" This was accompanied, we are told, by a heavenly perfume, whereupon the king and queen threw themselves at the feet of the Bishop, St. Remi, who addressed Clovis thus:

"Know, my son, that the kingdom of France is predestined by God for the defense of the Roman Church, which is the only true Church of Christ. This kingdom will one day be great beyond all other kingdoms... It will be victorious and prosperous as long as it remains faithful to the Roman faith, but it will be severely punished whenever it is unfaithful to its vocation" (J. Gonthier, *Malédictions et Bénédictions*, Editions du Carmel, pp. 66-67).

This predestination, also confirmed by Pope Anastasius, explains why French kings have been consecrated by a special ceremony never used by other monarchs. "Above all the nations under heaven," Pope Stephen II told the French, "has been set the Frankish nation, which is favorable to me, Peter, apostle of God. This is why... I have confided to you the Church I have received from God, to free her from the hands of her enemies."

And so through the centuries. Even Leo XIII, generally credited with having "baptized" democracy for motives of expediency, asserted in the encyclical *Nobilissima Gallorum Gens:* "At all times has Providence been pleased to confide the defense of the Church to the valiant arms of France." In 1933 Pius XI asserted that when St. Remi baptized King Clovis, he "baptized the French nation itself," making of it the political center of the Catholic faith, the foundation stone of temporal Christendom.

Thus can be seen that the very unity of a nation resides in the person of its king. Within natural law it is as impossible to conceive of a nation without its king as the king without the nation. Far from being a tyrant, a true monarch is the very principle of political unity. Nor is his power absolute, for he too is subject to his nation's laws. The concept of the divine right of kings is a perversion which actually ushered in the downfall of Christian monarchy. As early as the eighth century Pope Zachary told the French, "The Prince is responsible to the people, whose favor he enjoys. Whatever he has — power, honor, riches, glory, dignity — he has received from the people." He does not, however, receive his essential authority from them.

Cardinal Bellarmine says, "It is false that political princes have their power from God only : for they have it from God only so far as He planted a natural instinct in the minds of men, that they should wish to be governed by some one" (See Archbishop Hughes, *The Civil and Ecclesiastical Power in the Governments of the Middle Ages*, Catholic Cabinet, 1843, pp. 660-1). Before this St. Thomas had laid down that civil governments are not by divine right, but by human right, under God, and "When anything is to be enacted for the common good, it ought to be done either by the whole multitude of the people or by their representative."

Here is no authorization, however, for the oppression of a minority by a majority as interpreted by modern democracy. Ideally the "representative" of a nation is its king, under God. How well St. Louis understood this is clear in the words he addressed to his barons: "I am not the king of France, I am not the Church; *you* are, insofar as you are all the King, who are the Church." This is Christian politics in its deepest dimension.

With such texts before us we can understand better why France, of all nations, is in so pitiable a condition. She has been Satan's special target. Nevertheless, St. Pius X prophesied back in 1911, "The people who made a covenant with God at the baptismal font of Rheims will repent and return to her first vocation." Countless saints and mystics have persistently foretold a "great monarch" of French royal blood who would arise near the end of time to restore Christendom, no less an authority than St. Thomas promising, "A king will reign who will be wise. . . From him flows the royal priesthood" (See Pierre Virion, *Le Mystère de Jeanne d'Arc et la Politique des Nations*).

St. Joan is therefore not just a French patriot, a national saint, but a saint for the Universal Church. Popular painters who depict her at the head of her army carrying a banner sporting the lilies of France are falsifying history. Documents of the period tell us she carried no such thing, but a banner bearing *the figure of Christ the King reigning in glory*. She furthermore testified at her trial that the standard had been designed by our Lord himself, as relayed to her by her Voices. Joan's mission was not just to save France from the English, but to save Christendom, at a particularly poignant moment in history. As she declared at Rheims, "Those who war against the Holy Kingdom of France war against Jesus the King." She could not save Christendom without first saving France, the apex of the political order whose authority comes from above.

The occult forces plotting this destruction were already well organized before Joan's birth, working through the human ambitions of the English king, Henry V of Lancaster. In league with France's internal enemies, he was already laying out the one-world superstate built on rational power principles independent of religion when he declared himself "King of France and of England." His strategy for the domination of Europe is known to historians: By mercantile and marital alliances he sought unified control of the three great old world capitals: London, Paris and Jerusalem. It was into the teeth of this that Joan came to cast her battle cry, "Our Lord served first!" Sent by heaven at an eleventh hour, she was empowered to thwart the enemy — for a time.

• • •

The plot continued to thicken. Two centuries later, in 1618, there appeared in Frankfurt the *Themis Aurea*, the "Golden Law", by Michael Mayer, an organizer of the Rose-Croix, in which he states that this secret confraternity must remain so for a century. It's hardly coincidence that precisely one hundred years later, in 1717, Freemasonry emerged from its wraps — in England — and organized its first Grand Lodge.

The *Themis* had also stated that at the time the author wrote, the "Law" had already been in existence since 1413, which would have placed its birth at the rise of the Hussite rebellion in Bohemia, the heresy derived from the Englishman John Wyclif, who had himself adapted it from the Albigensians. The staggering import of the Hussite affair, notes Pierre Virion, lies in its "union of a political upheaval with a religious revolt which presumed to remain within the Church but against Rome, transforming the Mass, opting for the vernacular... for Communion under both species, denying five of the Sacraments, removing their sacramental character, especially with regard to Orders, thereby suppressing the ministerial priesthood, arrogating to the laity the right to preach and interpret Scripture."Thus Joan — who incidentally invited the English to join the French against the Hussites — was confronting exactly the same forces so potently at work today.

And we might note that it was the Hussites who later founded the communities in Moravia which so resembled soviet communism. Certainly the basic principles and even the vocabulary of the judeo-masonic revolution were well developed by St. Joan's time. Liberty, equality, fraternity — the sovereignty of the people, the rights of man, separation of religion from politics — were not only known, but openly preached in the universities, which spread the virus throughout the Mystical Body. A hundred years before Joan, a lawyer named Pierre Dubois had actually laid out a plan for a court of international arbitration staffed by laymen from all nations, from which the Pope was to be specifically excluded, in all essential respects like the United Nations.

By the eighteenth century these ideas only needed systematizing, and no one ever did that more brilliantly than their latter-day prophet Jean-Jacques Rousseau, who is often erroneously credited with inspiring the French, (and the American) Revolution. Of all democratic balderdash his still reads the best. For instance, in his *Discourse on Political Economy*, written in 1755, wherein he lays down the "general will" as the most important rule of government:

"The body politic is also therefore a moral being possessed of a general will; and this general will, which tends always to the preservation and welfare of the whole and of every part, and is the source of the laws, constitutes for all the members of the state, in their relations to one another and to it, the rule of what is just or unjust : a truth which shows, by the way, how idly some writers treated as theft the subtlety prescribed to children at Sparta for obtaining their frugal repasts, *as if everything ordained by the law were not lawful.* . . It is to the law alone that men owe justice and liberty," and it is "the first duty of the legislator to make the laws conformable to the general will."

More coldblooded rejection of the rule of the Sacred Heart over mankind could hardly be formulated. Totally perverting the principles laid down by St. Thomas, its horror lies not so much in its implicit denial of original sin by postulating that the general will automatically tends to good of itself, but in the complete dethronement of God through the enthronement of man — and collective man at that. Rousseau was not just a political reformer. He created a mystique, making of politics a branch of metaphysics.

A better description of the welfare state could hardly be found than the following: "It is one of the most important functions of government to prevent extreme inequality of fortunes; not by taking away wealth from its possessors, but by depriving all men of means to accumulate it; not by building hospitals for the poor, but by securing the citizens from becoming poor." There is the Antichrist's "war on poverty," in open contradiction of the Lord who promised the poor would always be with us and that poverty should be a virtue towards which all strive.

After declaring that the second duty of government is making all particular wills conform to the general will — the essence of "democracy" — Rousseau then lays down provision for public wants as the third duty. Needless to say, these wants are not individual, but collective. Although he maintains that "the foundation of the Social Contract is property," he envisioned a huge public domain for the support of bureaucracy. He also laid down the principle of no taxation without consent, but for him the consent of the people was always the "general will". He in fact proposed an income tax.

These ideas sound very familiar to Americans born and reared in the miasma of revolution. That their palpable immorality raises no eyebrows is testimony to the thoroughness of the indoctrination.

Christian historians being for the most part European, it's only natural that they should have focussed attention on the French Revolution to the exclusion of ours, which was regarded as little more than a minor side-show. Certainly the French one was bloodier and more spectacular, being fiercely resisted by fervent segments of a Catholic population — as ours was not — but in some respects ours may be the more interesting, with effects reaching farther in some sinister directions. Not to be overlooked is that the French revolt was largely inspired by English Freemasonry transplanted into French soil, whose members used the colonies for leverage not readily available elsewhere.

The American Revolution, engineered with relative ease on ground where there was no Catholic political structure to oppose it, was in many ways a dress rehearsal for the French, a kind of trial balloon launched thirteen years before for the admiration and study of the French Jacobins. It cannot be denied that it was the English colonial Benjamin Franklin who sponsored Voltaire into the Lodge of the Nine Sisters in Paris, and not the other way round, as one would expect.

The role played by Masonry in detaching the colonies from their sovereign has yet to be compiled fully, but the vocabulary alone of the Declaration of Independence has a sufficiently suspicious ring, not to mention the gradualism and subterfuge employed in drawing the people to outright rebellion. Reputable historians now agree that agitation for independence had not been at any time a popular movement, but the work of an active, well organized and obscurely motivated minority. Certainly the average colonist was too busy with his own survival problems to foment trouble with the home government. The demonstration known as the Boston Tea Party was staged for propaganda purposes by a handful and ignored by most.

The people had to be led cautiously. Although mostly a long diatribe against George III, the initial Declaration of Independence stressed if anything the independence of the states from one another as much as from the mother country. Once this fateful step was taken, however, the Articles of Confederation could be proposed as a logical defensive measure in accordance with Franklin's famous "If we don't hang together, we'll all hang separately." Only years after the fighting ceased was the Constitution finally accepted, at which point thousands of colonists fled the country rather than submit. Descendants of many of them live in Canada today.

With the fabrication we call the United States of America the first viable plan for an artificial government of unlimited extension finally left the drawing-board. It prefigured and encouraged not only the French Revolution, but every "democratic" revolt then in the making. Who were its engineers? Its financiers? And who were merely its figureheads?

Realizing back in 1798 that more had been afoot than met the eye, the canny Scot professor John Robison wrote the long and well-documented *Proofs of a Conspiracy against All the Religions and Governments of Europe,* which has never been refuted. This was followed a year later by Abbé Barruel's *History of Jacobinism,* in which the roots of revolution were ruthlessly traced to their Masonic sources. The modern Masonic author Jean Bon does not scruple to state, "The Jacobin Society, which was the great author of the French Revolution, was you might say merely the exterior aspect of the Masonic Lodge." This quotation is drawn from one of the best contemporary authors on this voluminous subject, Vicomte Léon de Poncins.

• • •

It's hard to ascertain how early Freemasonry was at work in the colonies, but we know the first Grand Lodge was formally established in Boston in 1733, a mere sixteen years after its emergence in Britain. Countless subsidiaries followed, the most important in Philadelphia and Charleston. Much recruiting of new members was done by military lodges traveling in the ranks of British regulars, as well as in the American forces. Blacks and Indians were also admitted. This is an enormous subject beyond the limits of this paper, but from the fact that out of the fifty-five delegates signing the Constitution twenty-three were avowed Masons, it's clear that Freemasonry's influence in American politics must have been enormous.

The following excerpt from the *Masonic Messenger* concerning Washington's inauguration can give us an inkling:

"The population of the City of New York was 33,000 when on April 30, 1789, this eventful ceremony took place. Yet, with all the growth and prosperity of America's largest city, it cannot today point to any occasion which transcends in importance this single event. For a Mason it has a very special meaning.

"Robert Livingston, Chancellor of New York, who administered the oath of office, was Grand Master of New York from 1784 through 1800. The Bible used in the ceremony was brought there by General Morton, Marshal of the day from St. John's Lodge, of which he was Worshipful Master. . . Thus was laid the cornerstone of our country and forever Washington — the Mason who exemplified in his every act and deed the principles of Masonry — will stand as the strong foundation of our Government.

"The selection of Washington's Cabinet would make up another thrilling Masonic story. It is especially noteworthy that Edmund Randolph, the first Attorney General, was serving as Grand Master of Virginia when he issued the charter to Alexandria Lodge with Washington as its first Master. Masons had lighted the fires of liberty for all mankind. In the inauguration of Washington there was the fulfillment of man's dream to walk unafraid in the sunlight of Freedom" (Quoted in *The New Age*, Washington, D.C., Sept. 1961).

After the Revolution lodges proliferated throughout the states and territories, meeting the hardest opposition in Texas, where for some time Spanish priests remained among the people. According to material published by the Masonic Service Association, Masons who succeeded Washington in the Presidency were Jefferson, Madison, Monroe, Jackson, Polk, Buchanan, Johnson, Garfield, McKinley, Theodore Roosevelt, Taft, Harding, Franklin D. Roosevelt and Truman, to which list we must add Dwight Eisenhower and Gerald Ford. An impressive roster.

Lest we think Masonry's Franco-American ties have slackened with time, let us listen to the following, from a eulogy given at Franklin Delano Roosevelt Lodge in Paris in 1947 by Brother J. Regenstreif: "In December 1776 Brother Benjamin Franklin was sent to Paris by the U.S. to ask France to support their cause. Without waiting for an understanding to be reached, the Marquis de la Fayette left for the American war on a ship outfitted at his expense which he called the Victory. Just like Roosevelt, La Fayette was what he had always been: an American hero and a Freemason. . . America is Franklin Delano Roosevelt, apostle of peace. To him our eternal gratitude is due. Today Roosevelt Lodge pays homage to the ardent champion of the Liberty and Justice which are the foundation of Universal Brotherhood.

". . . Let's hope that one day. . . the whole earth will be civilized and every part of humanity's home enlightened; then by the light of the flaming Star, we shall see reason's most beautiful, magnificent dream accomplished, having the whole World for its fatherland and all Humanity for its Nation" (Quoted by de Poncins in *Christianisme et Franc-Maçonnerie,* 1969, pp. 218-9).

U.S. history shows how all Catholic government, whether English, French or Spanish, was gradually crowded out to make way for this dream, on a continent liberally watered by the blood of martyrs from all parts of Europe who first planted the Cross of Christ there and who sought no other end than consolidating His peaceful possession. In 1531, hardly forty years after Columbus' arrival, long before there were any "United States" in America, Our Lady of Guadalupe had appeared in glory with the apocalyptic signs at the geographical center of her Son's new world to ratify His claim.

She told the Indian Juan Diego she was "The Entirely Perfect Virgin", in other words, the Immaculate Conception, (to whom the Catholic bishops would one day consecrate the United States). She also declared herself "Holy Mary, who would crush the stone serpent." This serpent, Quetzalcoatl, who was worshiped by the Mexicans as the Morning Star, was therefore no other person than Lucifer, her primordial enemy. Asking that a sanctuary be erected on the spot of her apparition, the Queen of heaven promised Juan:

"Here I will demonstrate, I will exhibit, I will give all my love, my compassion, my help and protection to the people. I am your Merciful Mother, the merciful Mother of all of you who live united in this land, and of all mankind, of all those who love me, of those who cry to me, of those who seek me, of those who have confidence in me. Here I will hear their weeping, their sorrow, and I will remedy all their multiple sufferings, necessities and misfortunes."

It was clear Our Lady knew what was in store for the Christians of the New World. Four hundred years later Pope Pius XII declared Our Lady of Guadalupe Empress of all the Americas. May she intercede for us!

PART II: *Whither It Goes*

The Cross had been well planted in America, for the battle brought there from Europe continued to rage. Hardly fifty years had elapsed since the Revolution when the Frankenstein's monster put together in the new world by the enemies of Christendom began showing serious rifts in its body politic. By 1832 an anti-Masonic political party had actually been formed. It was fervent, but could not survive the election of the powerful Masonic candidate Andrew Jackson.

The artificial republic proceeded to fall apart, however, on another issue. This was not slavery, as myth would have it, but on the rights of the States which the Declaration of Independence had proclaimed sovereign and independent. As we know, a bloody Civil War ensued, again engineered by an unseen minority, for Abraham Lincoln's greatest obstacle in preserving the Union was anti-war sentiment, not so much in the South, but in the North! Many Americans saw no reason why states couldn't withdraw peacefully if they wanted to, from a political union freely entered into. The slavery issue had to be raised to whip up the proper belligerency — although it is of public record in the Douglas debates that Lincoln was what we would call today a "racist".

What some Catholics thought of all this is illustrated by the fact that the priests of Baltimore Cathedral refused to read the prayer for civil authorities composed by Archbishop Carroll back in 1791, because it begged for preservation of the Union. When it was read by Bishop Kenrick, people walked out of the Cathedral in protest.

Everything was at stake for the forces of the Revolution, for its showcase experiment must under no circumstances be allowed to fail before the world. The melting pot must be made to melt, regardless of how much heat must be applied. The U.S. was a model not only for nations who wished to do without the inconvenience of kings. Far more than that, it provided visible proof of the feasibility of man-made political organization on an international scale: The U.S. was the forerunner not just of united states, but of united nations, as witness the old League of Nations hatched by the First World War and the United Nations hatched by the Second.

By their artificial union of diverse nationalities, the master-minds of American democracy were out to prove that any number of people could be fused into one without regard to creed, color, race, culture, heredity, language — or God. *E pluribus unum.* The Union had to be saved. It was. At the expense of both North and South, resistance was ruthlessly crushed, to prove that "any nation so conceived and so dedicated *can* long endure."

In the aftermath of that conflict there occurred a happening which may seem of small significance to those not reading the signs of the times: A copper-sheathed women's libber known as the Statue of Liberty was dedicated on old Bedloe's Island in New York harbor on October 28, 1886 by President Grover Cleveland. Originally called "Liberty Enlightening the World", she was a gift from the French Masonic government commemorating the fateful alliance made between France and the rebellious colonies in 1778. As it turned out, she caused considerable diplomatic embarrassment, for Americans had so little enthusiasm for her it was impossible to appropriate the money for the necessary pedestal. Eventually Joseph Pulitzer had to mount a massive newspaper campaign to extract it from the public at large.

It's interesting to note that the cornerstone of this pedestal was laid two years before the dedication, with Masonic rites by the Grand Lodge of New York. The Lady herself, whose iron entrails were put together by no less a person than the Gustave Eiffel who later perpetrated the famous Tower in Paris, was the work of Frédéric Auguste Bertholdi, a Mason from Alsace. In 1903 the sonnet "The New Colossus" by the Jewess Emma Lazarus was inscribed in bronze and affixed to the base. Therein is hailed this

"... mighty woman with a torch, whose flame
Is the imprisoned lightning, and her name
Mother of Exiles,"

whose "silent lips" cry to anything entering New York harbor,

"... Give me your tired, your poor
Your huddled masses yearning to breathe free,
The wretched refuse of your teeming shore.
Send these, the homeless, tempest-tossed to me,
I lift my lamp beside the golden door!"

The Masonic Madonna, at the very doors of the United Nations, flanked by the World Trade Building, has brazenly supplanted our Lady of Guadalupe as America's Queen and official hostess. Broken shackles at her feet, she sports a fearsome seven-spiked diadem and bears in her left hand the book of the New Law, dated July 4, 1776. Facing eastward to greet all visitors from that mystical direction, she keeps her back turned at all times to that other, the Merciful Mother of Guadalupe, who on the opposite side of the continent continues to reassure her children as she had Juan Diego,

"Let nothing discourage you, nothing depress you. . .
Are you not under my shadow and protection?
. . . Are you not in the crossing of my arms?"

At the National Shrine of the Immaculate Conception in the Nation's Capital at Washington, D.C. the iron "Mother of Exiles" shares with the Merciful Mother of Perpetual Help a large mosaic on the right hand wall of the Byzantine Chapel. The iron maiden, torch aloft, dominates the whole foreground, and as always has her back turned to the other, refusing the confrontation seen so clearly with the eyes of faith. Hardly any symbol of U.S. officialdom is more ominous than Ms. Liberty, although there are many such. She is the very goddess of the new religion of Man.

• • •

And religion, of course, is what the Revolution is all about, for no one believes less in separation of Church and state than Satan. What he seems to destroy he merely intends to replace with something of his own. Hear Rousseau on this, who discerned clearly the logical consequences of democracy: "There is therefore a purely civil profession of faith of which the Sovereign should fix the articles, not exactly as religious dogmas, but as social sentiments without which a man cannot be a good citizen or a faithful subject."

That democracy has evolved a civic liturgy even now in effect no one can deny. It has a "ferial" cycle disturbingly reminiscent of the Catholic one: New Year's Day in place of Christmas; Independence Day for its Easter; Thanksgiving Day for Pentecost, Memorial Day for All Souls, and even a Mother's Day to replace the Assumption. And there is a rich sanctoral cycle of "saints" like George Washington, Abraham Lincoln, or Martin Luther King to choose from, not to mention other possibilities like Earth Day or Halloween. And there are hymns, too, begging the vague but universal "god of your choice" to crown America's good with Brotherhood from sea to shining sea — all useful aids for reinforcing the civil dogmas.

"While it [the civil profession of faith] can compel no one to believe them," admits Rousseau, "it can banish him, not for impiety, but as an anti-social being, incapable of truly loving the laws and justice, and of sacrificing at need his life to his duty. If anyone, after publicly recognizing these dogmas, behaves as if he does not believe them, let him be punished by death: he has committed the worst of all crimes, that of lying before the law.

"The dogmas of civil religion ought to be few, simple, and exactly worded, without explanation or commentary. . . Its negative dogmas I confine to one, intolerance, which is a part of the cults we have rejected. . . Now that there can be no longer an exclusive national religion, tolerance should be given to all religions that tolerate others, so long as their dogmas contain nothing contrary to the duties of citizenship. But whoever dares to say: 'Outside the Church there is no salvation,' ought to be driven from the State, unless the State is the Church, and the prince the pontiff" (See *The Social Contract*).

So much for the "tolerance" of the new religion. Let no one think to be joined with Christ who is not prepared to be crucified under Pontius Pilate, for the godless state is ever Satan's arm.

That the authors of the Revolution were against the Faith has been amply documented. We have the word of that high priest of Masonry Albert Pike to the effect that "Masonry, in 1717, and afterwards to 1745, had for one of its purposes at least, if not the chief one, to sustain the Act of Parliament settling the succession and excluding the Stuarts and all Papists" (Quoted by Joseph Fort Newton in his foreward to *The Old Constitutions of Masonry*).

Thomas Paine's famous *The Age of Reason*, written in Paris in 1794, is one long blasphemous dissertation against revealed religion, in which the author's familiarity with Scripture is little short of astounding. Of note is the fact that the work ends with a section entitled "Origin of Freemasonry," in which he attempts to prove that both Masonry and Christianity are derived from sun worship.

It is morally impossible to separate religion from politics. As St. Thomas showed, politics deals specifically with the choice of means whereby man, in consideration of his nature, can reach God most easily and properly. He viewed politics in architectural terms, in that it related the human practical and speculative sciences much as architecture relates arts and techniques into one harmonious building. In this sense politics is the first of the practical sciences, whose specific virtue is prudence. Its intrinsic end is the virtue of the individual; its extrinsic end, God.

In other words, politics which help us get to heaven are good; those which do not, and especially those which of their nature ignore God, are bad. St. Thomas gave every sanction to democracy as an institution operating within the context of hierarchical government, as for instance workingmen's guilds or religious communities which freely elect officers or superiors — or even a king duly crowned by popular acclamation — as also he sanctioned the "communism" of religious orders holding property in common by free mutual consent; but democracy which arrogates to itself the summit of authority, or communism which denies private property rights on principle, are quite simply satanic.

"It is necessary in every practical science," says he, "to proceed synthetically, that is to say, to apply universal principles to the particular beings in whom action takes place" (In Ethic., Bk. I, Ch. 3,35). It follows therefore that where the principles applied are false, only tyranny or chaos can result. The Declaration of Independence states:

"We hold these truths to be self-evident: That all men are created equal; that they are endowed by their Creator with certain inalienable rights; that among these are life, liberty and the pursuit of happiness. That, to secure these rights, governments are instituted among men, deriving their just powers from the consent of the governed; that whenever any form of government becomes destructive of these ends, it is the right of the people to alter or abolish it, and to institute a new government. . . "

Here is formal canonization of revolution. In the face of it, to insist that Church and state must — or can — remain separate is to make every citizen a moral schizophrenic. To tell him it's "self-evident" that all men are created equal leads him to deny the evidence of his senses; to tell him that authority comes only from the people, is to make of him a formal revolutionary with a mandate to turn against any authority that doesn't suit him. This is why "democracy," doomed from the beginning, is even now disintegrating beyond repair.

Our Lord defined true democracy very simply: "For where there are two or three gathered together in my name, there am I in the midst of them " (Matt. 18:20). In His name we are all kings and priests, for as Head and source of all hierarchical authority, He entrusts to one — as He did to St. Peter — what is to be communicated to all. Modern democracy entrusts to all, thereby communicating to none. As St. Leo the Great put it:

"For all who are born again in Christ, the Sign of the Cross makes kings, and the anointing of the Holy Ghost makes priests; so that apart from the special service of our ministry, let all spiritual reasoning Christians know that they are of royal birth, and sharers of the priestly office. For what is so kingly as the soul that is subject to God and the ruler of its own body ? And what is so priestly as to dedicate to the Lord a pure conscience, and to offer Him on the altar of our hearts the unstained gift of love?"

Can democracy offer this?

In Old Testament times only kings and priests were anointed, a practice faithfully followed in Christendom. Each in his own sphere is *alter Christus,* one as King, the other as Priest. No President has ever been accorded this dignity from on high. The contrivers of Revolution, knowing their program does not truly conform to natural law, are aware it is deeply repugnant to human nature. What to do? Rousseau, again, gave the bald answer in *La Nouvelle Heloise:*

"He who dares to undertake the making of a people's institutions ought to feel himself capable, so to speak, of *changing human nature,* of transforming each individual, who is by himself a complete and solitary whole, into part of a greater whole. . . of altering man's constitution for the purpose of strengthening it and of substituting a partial and moral existence for the physical and independent existence nature has conferred on us all. He must, in a word, take away from man his own resources and give him new ones alien to him."

So runs the utopian dream of all revolutionaries from the devil on down, for without such a program no artificial government could subsist long. It explains brain-washing, social engineering, transactional analysis, cursillo, compulsory education, much of psychiatric practice and all the other tools of the superstate for the moral and spiritual butchery by which natural man is put into unnatural shape. The State no longer conforms to human nature as God created it, but human nature to the state as man created it.

• • •

The most efficient tool of all is probably the decompression chamber we call "atmosphere". And that brings us to the sad plight of America's Catholics, who literally by the millions have been enlisted into the ranks of the continuing Revolution without even knowing it.

Near the head of the list surely stand Charles Carroll, the only Catholic to sign the Declaration of Independence, and his cousin Daniel Carroll, who not only signed the Articles of Confederation and the Constitution, but who received the degree of Master Mason in 1781 and ten years later officiated as Commissioner at the Masonic ceremony laying the cornerstone of the new Capitol. It might be argued that Irishmen like these and Daniel's brother, Archbishop John Carroll, should be forgiven a natural odium for England and its inhuman penal laws, and that their desire for the religious freedom offered as bait by the new republic was easily played upon, were it not that many other Catholics refused allegiance, some even fleeing the country. Nor could they have been unaware of the pronouncements already fulminated against Masonry and its dark work by Clement XII in 1738 and Benedict XIV in 1751.

Under the circumstances such men chose to be "ecumenical," as had the Catholics of Maryland in Lord Baltimore's ill-fated colony, and democracy was soon worming its way into the colonial Church. So accepted were democratic principles that Rome deemed it expedient at first to allow the American clergy to choose their own Bishops, a privilege later revoked, but exercised in the election of the first three, of whom Carroll was the first. At the same time, the people were quite understandably agitating to elect their own pastors! Archbishop Hughes tells us that Carroll, "who himself took part in the Revolution by which American independence was won, wished to assimilate as far as possible the outward administration of Catholic church property in a way that would harmonize with the democratic principles on which the new government was founded" (Theodore Maynard, *The Story of American Catholicism*).

This means he approved lay trusteeship as practiced by the Protestants. As Fr. Andrew Greeley notes in *The Catholic Experience*, "The native American Church which John Carroll had founded, organized and shaped for three decades had been, despite all the obstacles, shaped pretty much in his image and likeness. . . fiercely and independently American, and its institutions. . . as American as Carroll could possibly make them."

As early as 1787 he opted for the vernacular, ascribing "chimerical fears of innovation" to its opponents. "In the U.S. our religious system has undergone a revolution, if possible, more extraordinary than our political one." To a Roman friend he wrote, "Toleration is a blessing and advantage which it is our duty to preserve and improve with the utmost prudence, by demeaning ourselves on all occasions as subjects zealously attached to our government and avoiding to give any jealousies on account of any dependence on foreign jurisdiction more than that which is essential to our religion, an acknowledgement of the Pope's spiritual supremacy over the whole Christian world."

So wholeheartedly did he believe this, he had actually tried to persuade the French Canadians to join the revolutionary cause. But this need surprise no one. As Fr. Greeley notes, "Just as historians in the United States point out that the liberal tradition in this country is the older tradition and the authentic conservatism consists essentially of conserving this liberal tradition, so the Americanizing tradition within the Church has on its side both seniority and the approbation of being the 'official' position." There lie the John Birch Society and others of like ilk, whose "conservatism" is essentially the old-fashioned liberalism of '76.

Although often bitterly resented, liberalism gained a stranglehold on the Church in the U.S. with the elevation of the witty and popular James Gibbons to the Cardinalate in 1886. This churchman's biographer Allen Sinclair Will tells us that when visiting his Carolina flocks, "The Bishop, standing in a Methodist pulpit, read from a Protestant Bible, and the only part of the service which was distinctively of his own faith was the sermon." Of his own work, *Faith of Our Fathers*, the Cardinal himself boasted, "Of all things about the book, the point that gratified me most is that, although it is an explanation of the Catholic religion, there is not one word in it that can give offense to our Protestant brethren. There was originally a reference that seemed to displease Episcopalians, but when my attention was called to it I promptly ordered it to be expunged."

A sentence from his Pastoral Letter of 1884, printed in Fr. Isaac Hecker's old "Catholic World", need therefore not surprise us: "The hierarchy of the Catholic Church in the U.S. share the conviction that American political institutions are in advance of those of Europe in helping a man save his soul, and that they promise a triumph for Catholicity more perfect than its victory in medieval times." Not all the Bishops really shared that conviction, but Cardinal Gibbons continued to support separation of Church and state, and in 1893 he didn't hesitate to appear at the World Congress of Religions with Bishop Ireland, even addressing the gatherings.

Long before, Rome had had to remind the Second Plenary Council of Baltimore that the Church in the U.S. was Catholic as well as American, so enthusiastic had its Fathers become about revolutionary liberties. The Third Council nevertheless exhorted the faithful to "teach your children to take a special interest in the history of their country. We regard the establishment of our national independence, the definition of its liberties, and the acts of its legislators as the special work of Providence."

• • •

In view of such ecclesiastical policy, we may suspect that many Catholics in our brave new world may never have been Catholics at all, but rather members of an Americanist sect. Are they actually heretical? Perhaps, for Americanism as such is an aberration of the Faith defined by Pope Leo XIII in the famous letter Testem *Benevolentiae* addressed to Cardinal Gibbons on January 22, 1889 — by which time the evil was well-nigh out of control. In fact the Pope acted at the insistence of Bishop Corrigan of New York and various ethnic groups, particularly the Germans of the midwest, who could see the ruin being perpetrated by the blind imposition of revolutionary principles in what was left of the organic body of the Church.

American bishops were sharply, if unevenly divided between those who considered American life basically Protestant or worse and not to be compromised with, and those who like Gibbons thought their flocks should immerse themselves in the social scene. Archbishop Ireland openly deplored parochial schools and praised the public system, being much in favor of state aid. Bishop Spalding, who also sponsored women's rights, publicly declared at the Gésù in Rome, "We find it necessary to abandon positions which are no longer defensible, to assume new attitudes in the face of new conditions. We must remember that though the Church is a divine institution it is nonetheless subject to the law which makes human things mutable, that though truth must remain the same, it is capable of receiving fresh illustration, and that if it is to be lifegiving, it must be wrought anew into the construction of each individual and each age" (Andrew M. Greeley, *The Catholic Experience,* Doubleday and Co., Garden City, N.Y. 1967, p. 173).

It's worth noting that the Knights of Columbus were organized at the height of this kind of Americanist fervor. Without vouching for its veracity, here is an interesting passage from the Masonic author William Adrian Brown: "We who are Masons should understand that this secret society of Knights of Columbus should have our blessing as it was established by Catholics who were seeking to overthrow the bulls against all secret societies. Ever since Pope Clement's first bull edict, a few Catholics have been trying to overrule the Church. As we know from history, in the period before and during the Middle Ages the Masonic orders were filled with Catholic Brethren. During and after the Civil War there was a fraternity called the Red Knights which was composed of Roman Catholics. In 1882 a Catholic by the name of [Fr.] McGivney wrote three degrees of ritual and had the society incorporated on March 29, 1882. . .

"It is surprising to note how much of our early historical Masonry is inculcated in the Knights of Columbus and how closely they have tried to follow the teachings in the Order of the Knights Templar. There are many secrets which are withheld on both sides, but in the written work we find a similarity of Christian ideas.

"The Catholic Church at the Vatican level does not relish the idea of the secret society of the Knights of Columbus for in it they see the danger of men seeking light or knowledge. However, they are reluctant to break the order, as it might create a greater break within the Church of Rome" (*Facts, Fables and Fantasies of Freemasonry*, 1968, p. 158).

Be that as it may, for reasons of expediency Leo XIII stopped short of denouncing in his Letter the particular individuals, religious communities and organizations promoting Americanism, although these were known and continued to operate freely. There was a move in Rome to put Fr. Walter Elliott's biography of Fr. Hecker, founder of the Paulists and a leading Americanist, on the Index. Nothing came of it, although the book was removed from sale. Already three years before, Archbishop Keane had lost the Rectorship of the newly launched Catholic University of America, noted from the outset as a center of liberalism.

Otherwise the Letter had little effect. As a matter of fact, Archbishop Ireland wrote from Rome in May, 1900, "The Pope told me to forget the letter on Americanism, which has no application except in a few dioceses in France" (Maynard, *Op. cit.*).

Alas, His Holiness may have been poorly informed. Today, in the light of Vatican II, the five specific errors cited by the Letter are more than ever pertinent to America: The first is a rejection of the necessity for external spiritual direction in favor of individual guidance by the Holy Ghost, in essence a kind of pentecostalism; second, an extolling of the natural virtues above the supernatural; and third, of the active virtues over the passive. The fourth error is rejection of religious vows as incompatible with Christian liberty. And finally, the new method of apologetics which watered down Catholic doctrine in order to attract converts more easily, the whole wrapped up in a kind of suspension of authority, so that the individual might develop his own initiatives in the apostolate.

Perhaps the best characterization of Americanism was given by

Leo XIII's biographer Msgr. T'Serclaes: "A spirit of independence which passed too easily from the political to the religious sphere." It extends to the supernatural order premises which are purely natural, if not outright false. Certainly Americanists don't think of liberty as St. Paul did, which even a slave could enjoy, but as a constitutional right of man, guaranteed not by God, but by other men. In other words, they brought the whole paraphernalia of the Revolution into the Church, in full anticipation of the Second Vatican Council. As Fr. Greeley put it, "It can be argued that the Americanists were ahead of their time, that they would have been giants of the Second Vatican Council if they had lived to attend it."

Actually the apogee of Americanism was probably reached by the U.S.'s only professing Catholic President. In an interview for Look magazine in 1959, John F. Kennedy said, "Whatever one's religion in his private life may be, to the officeholder nothing takes precedence over his oath to uphold the Constitution and all its parts." *Ave, Caesar.*

• • •

Reporting the aforementioned Council's debate on the schema on the Church, the notorious "Xavier Rynne" dismissed as of no moment what he called "a rambling, semi-hysterical discourse by Bishop Reyes of the Philippines, who insisted on the royal character of the Church's rights, due to the Kingship of Christ." Such is the pass to which the holy international order established by Christ had come, with the revolutionaries in command not only of the temporal structures, but the spiritual as well. As once in His Temple in Jerusalem, our Lord is now treated as a stranger in His Church. If He is to be tolerated, He must submit to the plebiscite and mouth the jargon of the Revolution like everyone else.

Pope Paul VI, on arriving at Kennedy Airport in 1965, greeted "the America of the states, where we have so very many brothers, sons and friends in the faith, and where a populous nation founds its very modern civilization upon" — not God's law, but "the brotherhood of its citizens." Let him who reads understand.

Later, addressing the United Nations General Assembly, His Holiness declared himself convinced "that this organization represents the obligatory path of modern civilization and of world peace. The peoples of the earth turn to the United Nations as the last hope of concord and peace. The edifice which you have constructed must never fall. . . You mark a stage in the development of mankind from which retreat must never be admitted. . . Your vocation is to make brothers not only of some, but of all peoples... Study the right method of uniting to your pact of brotherhood, honor and loyalty, those who do not share it... Let unanimous trust in this institution grow... We feel that you thus interpret the highest sphere of human wisdom and, we might add, its sacred character... We must get used to thinking of man in a new way... "

This should cause us to "look up and lift up our heads" (Luke 21:28), for according to the Fathers of the Church such a state of affairs is one of the major signs of our Lord's second coming. In a famous reply to Bishop Hesychius, St. Augustine wrote that inasmuch as the world has always suffered periodic earthquakes, astral disturbances, wars, famines and other calamities, these are in themselves no sign of the last days. The end can be expected however, "when tribulations shall be so spread throughout the whole world that *it will affect the Church.* "

Then will she be persecuted in every place, says he, precisely by those who will say "peace and security", as St. Paul predicted to the Thessalonians. "I consider that these things should be better understood *in the Church,* lest the Lord Jesus may appear to be foretelling as extraordinary events which shall foretell His coming, things which have happened in the world even before His first coming... for *the Church* is the sun and the moon and the stars... and she shall not be seen, as her persecutors rage against her without measure."

In the very midst of this great evil, luxurious feasts and pleasure will be engaged in, much as in the days of the Flood eating and drinking, buying, selling and marrying went on until the last moment. St. Augustine's teacher St. Ambrose says, "Many apostatizing from Christianity, the brightness of the Faith will be dimmed by this cloud of apostasy, since the heavenly Sun grows dim or shines according to my faith. And as in its monthly eclipse the moon, by reason of the earth coming between it and the sun, disappears from view, so likewise the holy Church, when the vices of the flesh stand in the way of the celestial light, can no longer borrow the splendor of His divine light from the Sun of Christ... Also, the stars, that is, men surrounded by the praise of their fellow Christians, *shall fall* as the bitterness of the persecution mounts up... for so the good are proved and the weak made known."

Origen interprets the moon which does not give her light as "the whole church of the wicked, which frequently professes both to have and to give light," but which "shall then, together with its rejected teachings, lose its light." Obviously the true Church always gives light, although men are not always capable of receiving it. St. Gregory says that it is only to the elect that our Lord is speaking when He says, "When these things come to pass, look up and lift up your heads; " whereas at the same time, "all the tribes of the earth shall mourn" at these troubles, for these earthly tribes are reprobates, so carnal-minded they cannot see to rejoice at what is happening.

Our Lord's second coming will not be unannounced any more than His first, which was preceded by much prophecy and expectation and the preaching of John the Baptist. Like the fig tree which our Lord tells us to consider, first little shoots will appear before the full foliage. "By this He foretells," says St. Chrysostom, "the spiritual summer, the calm the just shall possess after their present winter; while for sinners, winter shall follow the summer." St. Hilary says the fig tree is a mystical figure of the synagogue, "its branch Antichrist, the son of the devil, the portion of sin; who when he begins to show life and to put forth leaves, with a sort of triumphant flowering of sin, then the summer, that is, the day of judgment, is seen to be nigh."

However, "We shall know that it is nigh," warns St. Augustine, "when we see, not *some* of the promised signs, but *all* of them, including this: that *the son of Man shall be seen coming.* " Yet not actually "seen", but "seen coming".

Before the end there will be apparently a period of great apostolic activity, during which our Lord's kingdom will make visible strides on earth once more, corresponding with the period after our Lord's Resurrection and perhaps with the period of peace our Lady promised at Fatima, when the apostles of the latter times predicted by St. Louis de Montfort and at La Salette would re-evangelize the earth after a great disaster.

It's precisely in the darkening of the world's lights that the Savior will be seen gradually approaching. "The kingdom of God is at hand," said Titus, Bishop of Bostra, because when these things come to pass, the end of things has not yet come, but they now move toward their end; for the actual coming of the Lord, putting an end to the power of all other rulers, prepares the way for the kingdom of God." In this light, the modern breakdown of political authority which began with the overthrow of the monarchies is a sure portent. The reprobate will see the Son of Man coming, but will not know it, being unable to read the signs correctly. They will continue as before, while the Ark is a-building and the clouds gathering.

• • •

Unless pursued in this context, devotion to the Sacred Heart of

Jesus is little more than a sentimental pastime. In the very beginnings of modern democracy He promised the French nun St. Margaret Mary, "I shall reign despite Satan and all opposition." Through her He came to recall the erring French monarchy to its duty to defend His rule over Christendom. Referring to Louis XIV, the king then occupying the consecrated throne of Clovis, Charlemagne, St. Louis and Charles VII, He said, "Tell the eldest son of my Sacred Heart that, as his natural birth was secured by devotion to the merits of My holy Childhood, in like manner may he obtain the birth of grace and eternal glory by consecrating himself to my adorable Heart, which desires to triumph over his, and through his agency over that of the great ones of this earth."

At that very moment an organized ring of occultists were at work among persons highly placed at court endeavoring to compass the king's destruction. The "outrages" the Sacred Heart spoke of to the saint were not figurative, but actually being perpetrated by priests become satanists like the infamous Fr. Gibourg, and by witches like La Voisin. Despite the monarch's lack of response, the Sacred Heart assured the saint categorically, "Even by means of a small number, I shall draw the weak and wavering, and I shall be victorious, for the hour is now at hand when I shall reign despite Satan. The whole world shall see that I am not only the mystical spouse of pure, fervent souls, their consoler and confidant, but that I am also their God, KING OF THE CHURCH AND OF THE WORLD, and that victory does not depend on armed force, nor on numbers, but on My will."

Continuing His appeals as French politics progressively degenerated, He appeared again during the French Empire to another mystic, Madame Royer. She was granted a series of prophetic visions, one of which she described thus: "I seemed to be in a great temple, the ruin of which was being prepared by a sort of infernal machine: I could take this temple for the universal Church, which seemed to me indestructible, miraculously preserved despite the explosives piled up to destroy her... If the Sacred Heart calls France to penance before all others, it's the way He called Mary Magdalene, because France has much to atone for, and should love much in return!"

Madame Royer was shown that the Sacred Heart intended to work through France as He had once before, to bring about the conversion of the other nations of the world. "At Montmartre in 1877, I believe I saw the Sacred Heart preparing himself a throne there, radiant with light and glory, from whence His love, His mercy, enkindled the entire world with fiery splendor."

Later, in the dark days of 1915, Madame Royer wrote, "The

Sacred Heart will save us, but when? How?" The answer wasn't long coming, and it was always the same. As our Lord had appealed to the monarchy, and then to the Empire, He now offered His mercy to the Republic: During the first World War yet another French mystic, the nun Claire Ferchaud, received one more startling visit from the Sacred Heart.

Even now hardly known outside France (except to chosen apostles of the Sacred Heart like the late Fr. Mateo,) our Lord's message was: "Go tell the head of the government of France to go to the Basilica of the Sacred Heart of Montmartre together with the kings of the Allies. There the flags of each nation shall be solemnly blessed; then the President must pin the image of My Heart to each of the banners present. Afterwards Monsieur Poincaré [the French President] and all the allied kings at the head of their countries shall officially order the Sacred Heart painted on all the flags of each French and Allied regiment. Every soldier must wear this insignia of salvation."

In return our Lord promised total victory to the Allies, after which He asked that France and the other nations be consecrated to His Sacred Heart and to the Immaculate Heart of Mary at Montmartre. (Before concluding this tale, be it noted that our Lord at no time sanctioned revolt or reprisals against the Empire or the republican government, which would be to sanction the methods of the Revolution under cover of religion. He showed how to start from where we stood, resisting evil by overcoming it with good. Once any government would officially acknowledge its allegiance to Him, it's clear He would do the rest and help them against their enemies.)

Claire Ferchaud obtained an interview with Raymond Poincaré, a believing Catholic. Under pressure from her he promised to lay the matter before the Chamber of Deputies, but alas, did not keep his word. Later, when the Armistice was signed without any change having been made in the flags, Claire was generally discredited, but until her death in 1972 she never changed her story. "I have never considered the peace of 1918 as the end of the war," she insisted, "but only a truce granted by God." This was accorded, she maintained, as a reward to certain victim souls who offered themselves as living flags to the imprint of the lacerated Sacred Heart, and to the many heroic soldiers and civilians who wore the insignia privately.

Claire Ferchaud never saw World War II or any subsequent hostilities as anything but the continuation of one great war, raging ever more fiercely in new guises. As Lucy of Fatima said to Fr. Fuentes, postulator of the causes of Francisco and Jacinta in her interview in

1957: "The devil is waging his decisive battle, in other words, his last one, from which one or the other will emerge victor or vanquished. Either we are with God, or we are with the devil."

It is in this satanic activity that our Lord can be seen, not yet come, but " coming." As once it prepared His Resurrection, so will the Revolution prepare that of His Church. St. Augustine reminds us, "He shall send His angels from the four parts of the world, that is, He will gather together His elect from the whole earth. All this He does at that last hour, coming in His members as in the clouds, or in the whole Church as in a great cloud: as He now comes without ceasing. But then He shall come with great power and majesty; because greater power and majesty shall be seen by the saints, to whom He shall give great virtue, that they may not be overcome by such persecution."

This will be His great Advent, of which His first will by comparison seem the merest prefiguration. In the light of current events, the beautiful texts of the ancient Advent liturgy take on added prophetical luster. In the words of St. John the Baptist, the ax is indeed being laid not just to the trunk, but to the very root. "All that seems to you enduring and unchangeable, is not enduring and without change in eternity. And everything of Mine that seems to pass away, is enduring and without change," says St. Gregory, speaking for our Lord, "because My Speech, that passes away, utters thoughts which endure forever." On Gaudete Sunday the Holy Ghost cries through Isaias, "Say to the faint-hearted, Take courage and fear not; behold, our God will come and save us!"

So may Sacred Heartless America beg in this same Holy Ghost, "COME, LORD JESUS!"